Lecture Notes in Computer Science   11498

Commenced Publication in 1973
Founding and Former Series Editors:
Gerhard Goos, Juris Hartmanis, and Jan van Leeuwen

More information about this series at http://www.springer.com/series/7410

Maurizio Naldi · Giuseppe F. Italiano ·
Kai Rannenberg · Manel Medina ·
Athena Bourka (Eds.)

Privacy Technologies and Policy

7th Annual Privacy Forum, APF 2019
Rome, Italy, June 13–14, 2019
Proceedings

 Springer

Editors
Maurizio Naldi (iD)
Università di Roma - Tor Vergata
Rome, Italy

Giuseppe F. Italiano (iD)
LUISS Guido Carli University
Rome, Italy

Kai Rannenberg
Goethe University Frankfurt
Frankfurt, Germany

Manel Medina (iD)
Universitat Politècnica de Catalunya
Barcelona, Spain

Athena Bourka
ENISA
Heraklion, Greece

ISSN 0302-9743   ISSN 1611-3349   (electronic)
Lecture Notes in Computer Science
ISBN 978-3-030-21751-8   ISBN 978-3-030-21752-5   (eBook)
https://doi.org/10.1007/978-3-030-21752-5

LNCS Sublibrary: SL4 – Security and Cryptology

This Springer imprint is published by the registered company Springer Nature Switzerland AG
The registered company address is: Gewerbestrasse 11, 6330 Cham, Switzerland

Preface

With this volume we introduce the proceedings of the 2019 edition of the Annual Privacy Forum (APF), that took place in Rome, Italy, during June 13–14, 2019. APF 2019 was organized by the European Union Agency for Network and Information Security (ENISA), the Directorate General for Communications Networks, Content and Technology (DG CONNECT), and jointly hosted by the University of Rome Tor Vergata and LUISS University Guido Carli.

This conference, already in its seventh edition, is currently firmly established as an opportunity for convergence among the various actors playing a role in the privacy debate: industry, universities and research institutes, regulatory bodies, professionals and legal firms. This edition coincided with the first year of applying the General Data Protection Regulation (GDPR) and the coming into force of the Cybersecurity Act, both of which mark discreet courses of action to implement far-reaching legal stipulations.

There were 50 submissions in response to the APF call for papers. Each paper was peer-reviewed by at least three members of the international Program Committee (PC). On the basis of significance, novelty, and scientific quality, only 12 papers were selected (a 24% acceptance rate) and are compiled in this volume. The papers are organized across four broader thematic area, namely:

- Transparency ("Towards Real-Time Web Tracking Detection With T.EX – The Transparency Extension," "Towards Transparency in Email Tracking," "Sharing Cyber Threat Intelligence Under the General Data Protection Regulation")
- Users' rights ("Fight to Be Forgotten: Exploring the Efficacy of Data Erasure in Popular Operating Systems," "Privacy Beyond Confidentiality, Data Science Beyond Spying: From Movement Data and Data Privacy Towards a Wider Fundamental Rights Discourse," "Making Machine Learning Forget")
- Risk assessment ("A Multilateral Privacy Impact Analysis Method for Android Apps," "Re-using Personal Data for Statistical and Research Purposes in the Context of Big Data and Artificial Intelligence," "IoT Security and Privacy Fact Labels")
- Applications ("Digital Forensics and Privacy-By-Design: Example in a Blockchain-Based Dynamic Navigation System," "A Data Protection by Design Model for Privacy Management in Electronic Health Records," "Security Analysis of Subject Access Request Procedures").

The conference program also included the following three panel sessions:

- Privacy by Design: Defaults, Information, and Users' Rights
- Security, State of the Art, and Certification
- Artificial Intelligence and Inferred Identities

The conference was opened by the Executive Director of ENISA, Prof. Udo Helmbrecht, the European Data Protection Supervisor, Giovanni Buttarelli, and the Deputy-Chair of the European Data Protection Board, Ventsislav Karadjov. In addition, we had the pleasure of hosting an opening speech by Prof. Paola Severino (Italy's former Minister of Justice and currently Vice President of Luiss University) on "Data Protection Compliance and Criminal Law" and two keynote speeches by renowned experts Prof. Ross Anderson (University of Cambridge) and Prof. Joe Cannataci (UN Special Rapporteur on the right to privacy).

Any conference is the fruit of the work of many people, and APF is no exception. We wish to thank Springer, which continues an established tradition of publishing APF proceedings in its LNCS series, and all the good people who contributed to the successful organization of APF 2019. In particular, we wish to thank the members of the PC, who devoted their time to review the papers on a tight time schedule, the authors, whose papers make up the bulk of the content of this conference, and the attendees, whose interest in the conference is the main driver for its organization. Finally, we also wish to thank the event sponsors whose financial support is hereby acknowledged.

May 2019

Maurizio Naldi
Giuseppe F. Italiano
Kai Rannenberg
Manel Medina
Athena Bourka

Organization

Program Committee

Alessandro Mantelero	Politecnico di Torino, Italy
Andreas Mitrakas	ENISA, Greece
Bettina Berendt	Katholieke Universiteit Leuven, Belgium
Carlo Colapietro	Università degli Studi Roma Tre, Italy
Christos Kalloniatis	University of the Aegean, Greece
Claude Castelluccia	Inria, France
Corradino Corradi	Vodafone, Italy
Daniel Le Métayer	Inria, France
David Martin	BEUC, Belgium
Diana Dimitrova	FIZ Karlsruhe, Germany
Elise Lassus	EU Agency for Fundamental Rights, Austria
Erich Schweighofer	University of Vienna, Austria
Fabrizio Gagliardi	ACM, Spain
Fernando Silva	CNPD, Portugal
François Pellegrini	Inria, France
Gabriela Zanfir-Fortuna	Future of Privacy Forum, USA
Georgios Yannopoulos	National and Kapodistrian University of Athens, Greece
Giuseppe D'Acquisto	Garante per la protezione dei dati personali, Italy
Haralambos Mouratidis	University of Brighton, UK
Herbert Leitold	A-SIT, Austria
Irene Kamara	VUB/TILT, Belgium
José M. Del Álamo	Universidad Politécnica de Madrid, Spain
Konstantinos Limniotis	Hellenic Data Protection Authority, Greece
Laura Liguori	Portolano Cavallo, Italy
Lukasz Olejnik	Independent security and privacy researcher, Belgium
Marco Orofino	University of Milan, Italy
Maria Grazia Porcedda	University of Leeds, UK
Marit Hansen	Unabhängiges Landeszentrum für Datenschutz Schleswig-Holstein, Germany
Marko Hölbl	University of Maribor, Slovenia
Markus Tschersich	Continental, Germany
Meiko Jensen	Kiel University of Applied Sciences, Germany
Nikolaos Tantouris	University of Vienna, Austria
Nikolaos Tsouroulas	11Paths Telefonica Cybersecurity Unit
Nineta Polemi	University of Piraeus, Greece
Prokopios Drogkaris	ENISA, Greece
Robin Pierce	TILT Tilburg Law School, The Netherlands

Sebastian Pape   Goethe University Frankfurt, Germany
Sokratis Katsikas   Center for Cyber and Information Security, Greece
Stefan Schiffner   Uni.lu, Luxembourg
Zoe Kardasiadou   European Data Protection Board, Belgium

General Co-chairs

Giuseppe F. Italiano   LUISS University, Rome, Italy
Maurizio Naldi   University of Rome Tor Vergata, Italy

Program Co-chairs

Athena Bourka   ENISA, Greece
Kai Rannenberg   Goethe University Frankfurt, Germany
Manel Medina   Universitat Politècnica de Catalunya, Spain

Additional Reviewers

Argyri Pattakou   University of the Aegean, Greece
David Harborth   Goethe University Frankfurt, Germany
Katerina Mavroeidi   University of the Aegean, Greece
Majid Hatamian   Goethe University Frankfurt, Germany
Stavros Simou   University of the Aegean, Greece
Wladimir De la Cadena   University of Luxembourg, Luxembourg

Authors

Adham Albakri
Andreas Gutmann
Axel Küpper
Bettina Berendt
Cédric Lauradoux
Coline Boniface
Cristiana Santos
David Billard Baptiste
  Bartolomei
Eerke Boiten Rogério de
  Lemos

Giorgia Bincoletto
Imane Fouad
Jacob Leon Kröger
Jasjeet Dhaliwal
Kai Rannenberg
Kevin Roundy
Lothar Fritsch
Majid Hatamian
Mark Warner
Matteo Dell'Amico
Matthias Hollick

Max Maass
Nataliia Bielova
Nurul Momen
Philip Raschke
Pierre-Antoine Vervier
Saurabh Shintre
Sebastian Zickau
Stephan Schwär
Urbano Reviglio
Yordanka Ivanova
Yun Shen

Organizers

Contents

Applications

Transparency

Towards Real-Time Web Tracking Detection with T.EX - The Transparency EXtension

Philip Raschke[(✉)], Sebastian Zickau, Jacob Leon Kröger, and Axel Küpper

Service-centric Networking, Weizenbaum-Institut, Telekom Innovation Laboratories,
Technische Universität Berlin, Berlin, Germany
{philip.raschke,sebastian.zickau,kroeger,axel.kuepper}@tu-berlin.de

Abstract. Targeted advertising is an inherent part of the modern Web as we know it. For this purpose, personal data is collected at large scale to optimize and personalize displayed advertisements to increase the probability that we click them. Anonymity and privacy are also important aspects of the World Wide Web since its beginning. Activists and developers relentlessly release tools that promise to protect us from Web tracking. Besides extensive blacklists to block Web trackers, researchers used machine learning techniques in the past years to automatically detect Web trackers. However, for this purpose often artificial data is used, which lacks in quality.

Due to its sensitivity and the manual effort to collect it, real user data is avoided. Therefore, we present T.EX - The Transparency EXtension, which aims to record a browsing session in a secure and privacy-preserving manner. We define requirements and objectives, which are used for the design of the tool. An implementation is presented, which is evaluated for its performance. The evaluation shows that our implementation can be used for the collection of data to feed machine learning algorithms.

Keywords: Web tracking · Browsing behavior · Data privacy ·
Browser extension · Data quality · Machine-learning ·
Classification algorithm

1 Introduction

There is no doubt that our Web browsing behavior is very sensitive. The websites we visit and the content we consume reveal information about our personality, our preferences, orientations, and habits. We give away our physical addresses, our phone numbers, and bank account information to use services or order goods. Simultaneously, the majority of websites nowadays integrates content from multiple external sources or third parties. Consequently, when visiting a website (also referred as first party) these third parties are given notice about our visit the moment our browser requests the external content. While our

© Springer Nature Switzerland AG 2019
M. Naldi et al. (Eds.): APF 2019, LNCS 11498, pp. 3–17, 2019.
https://doi.org/10.1007/978-3-030-21752-5_1

physical address, phone number, or bank account information is not disclosed to these third parties, a link to the website we visited is.

The reasons for websites to integrate external content are manifold. Services embed images, audio, or videos without having to host or being allowed to host the content on an own server. But also many third-party scripts are integrated for various reasons. They are in particular critical, since their integration enables the execution of third-party code on the user's machine. There, they can access and gather information of the device and send it to a server where it is aggregated and analyzed. This way, a malicious third party can track every mouse movement, every key stroke, and every change of the scroll position of a user on a *different* website even without his or her awareness.

While on paper this sounds like a severe data security and privacy threat, this technique is widely used in the field of targeted advertising and Web analytics to track user behavior across multiple websites. In fact, Web trackers are an inherent part of the modern Web, because of their economic value for content providers and publishers. Websites display advertisements provided by ad exchanges or advertising networks in exchange for a payment per view or click. This way, each user of a website generates revenue.

While there is a variety of browser extensions that promise to tackle the issue, they are mostly blacklist-based, i.e. manual effort is required to identify trackers, which are then blocked (often by the domain name). This has four major disadvantages: (i) trackers can easily change their domain name, (ii) websites may offer relevant content or services, while also tracking user behavior (Amazon, Google, etc.), (iii) blacklists can be wrong, not complete, or outdated, and (iv) blocking requests to domains might create errors that prevent access to the desired content of the first party. The latter also occurs in the opposite causal direction, i.e. first parties block users from their content, if they block requests to third parties. Another conceptual flaw of blacklists is that they are not transparent themselves by providing little to no information on the third party in question and why it is blocked or not.

Consequently, an automated approach to detect Web trackers is desirable. This is a classification problem, which can be solved with machine learning techniques. However, machine learning approaches require rather large amounts of training data, which ideally is real data. However, researchers in this field often use bots to generate this data by crawling the Alexa.com top K websites. While this method produces large amounts of data rather quickly, it has a major drawback: it is not *real* data. These bots open the website, wait until it is finished loading, and then open the next in the list. These bots cannot log into websites like Facebook or Twitter, which even have implemented countermeasures for artificial users of their services. Even worse, the front page of these services are very limited and only offer a login form. It can be safely assumed that most of the third-party communication takes place after the login. By using bots, tracking of user interactions like moving the mouse, pressing a key, or scrolling is completely neglected.

For this reason, we present *T.EX: Transparency EXtension (T.EX)*, a secure browser extension to enable client-side recording, storage, and analysis of individual browsing behavior. With this tool researchers can generate data sets with real users in a secure, privacy-preserving, and user-friendly way. In this paper, we define requirements concerning security, privacy, and usability and explain how they were met. In addition, the extension provides data visualization capabilities allowing (experienced) users to assess their browsing behavior and the third-party communication involved in it.

The remainder of this paper is structured as follows: Sect. 2 defines the objectives and requirements of the tool. Section 3 elaborates on the limitations and the derived design decisions. Section 4 gives an overview of related work and assesses whether suitable solutions already exist. Section 5 presents the implementation of the tool. In Sect. 6, we evaluate the tool with regard to the specified objectives. Finally, a conclusion is given including an outlook.

2   Objectives and Requirements

As stated above, the main objective of the tool is to enable the generation of *real* user data in a secure, privacy-preserving, and user-friendly manner by allowing users to record browsing sessions. On this basis, we derive the following objectives:

Obj1 The tool needs to be able to monitor Hypertext Transfer Protocol (HTTP) and Hypertext Transfer Protocol Secure (HTTPS) traffic, including header information, parameters, and the body.

Obj2 An accurate differentiation between first and third party must be realized. The first party should not be identified only by its host name but rather by the actual page (HTTP path) the user visited.

Obj3 The network traffic must be persistently stored for a certain amount of time. This data must be securely (i.e. encrypted) stored on the user's device, so no other (malicious) software on the user's machine can access it.

Obj4 The extraction of data must be in a privacy-preserving manner, i.e. only relevant data should be collected. Furthermore, no external servers must be involved.

Obj5 The user must be able to completely delete the data at any time. There should be a means to prove the erasure of the data.

Obj6 Furthermore, the user must be able to export the data in a machine-readable format.

Obj7 The user must be able to disable the recording of network traffic at any time. Ideally, the user can be given a guarantee or proof that the recording is stopped.

Obj8 Usage of the tool should be user-friendly to the extent that the perceived Quality of Experience (QoE) is not impacted by it.

Obj9 The tool must offer data visualization capabilities so that users can review the recorded data before they export it. A search function enables users to check if any sensitive information are contained within the data set.

3 Limitations

Unfortunately, the above defined objectives cannot be realized without constraints. In this section, we infer limitations from these objectives and elaborate on consequent design decisions for the tool.

In order to realize Obj1, HTTP and HTTPS traffic needs to be intercepted. Obviously, this is a severe data security risk and infringement of the user's privacy. For this reason, the collected and recorded data must remain on the user's device (see Obj4). However, intercepting HTTPS traffic on the network layer is not possible without aggressive intervention. A *man-in-the-middle* attack could be used in order to intercept the encrypted traffic, but this would put the user's overall data security at risk.

Fortunately, we can rely on capabilities offered by browser vendors. Experienced users or system administrators have the expertise to obtain the data using the browser's developer tools like Google Chrome's *DevTools* or the *Inspector* of Firefox. However, the data, that is logged there, is separated from other browser sessions (tabs). Consequently, for a holistic view, an aggregation of the data is required. The user would need to open the corresponding tool before the begin of each browsing session in each tab. The log is cleared with every new page the user visits, so a checkbox needs to be ticked to persist the log (in each tab). To export the recorded data, only Firefox' *Inspector* offers a complete export of the data, while Chrome's *DevTools* only offer an option to export one request at a time. Collecting data using this method is cumbersome and error-prone, which violates Obj8. Further inspection of this method also revealed that Obj2 is violated, since the exported data either does not contain the first party (Chrome) or only gives the host name of it (Firefox).

Clearly, a more sophisticated method is required. Luckily, HTTP and HTTPS traffic can be logged using Chrome's or Firefox' extension Application Programming Interface (API). So, Obj1 can be best implemented in a browser extension. In fact, we found no alternative approach to realize Obj1 without aggressively interfering with the user's device. Using the extension API also allows us to identify the first party including the HTTP path (see Obj2). Besides an *initiator* field in the traffic log, it is possible to map a request to a certain open and active tab of which the URL can be used.

To persistently store the data like stated in Obj3, a sophisticated database like *MySQL* or *MongoDB* would be ideal, however this would require users to install additional software on their device (violation of Obj8) or to transmit the data to an external server (violation of Obj2). Browser extensions are able to store data in the so-called *local storage*, which offers limited storage capabilities. The local storage is a key-value store, thus complex queries cannot be easily expressed. Furthermore, the local storage is not encrypted, thus malicious software on the user's device could easily gain access to it. Therefore, encryption must be implemented within the browser extension. However, inconvenient key-pair generation and management must be avoided in order to not violate Obj8.

In order to realize a collection of data in a privacy-preserving manner (Obj4), only the outgoing traffic is recorded. This way, we follow a data minimization approach. The HTTP response, besides the actual content the user consumes, contains cookies and identifiers that are assigned to the user and which are used for subsequent requests. By neglecting the HTTP response, we miss these assignments. However, we assume the preserved privacy is of higher value than the benefit gained from the HTTP responses. Moreover, it is not sure whether the accuracy of a classification algorithm to detect Web trackers would be increased if the HTTP response is taken into consideration. It would be interesting to investigate this in a separate study.

Since the HTTP body is used to transmit sensitive data like passwords, messages, photos or videos, recording it can be highly sensitive. Therefore, it is not recorded by default but the user is able to enable this feature at own risk. The reason why we do not completely exclude it, like we do with the HTTP response, is that we could observe Web trackers using it for passing identifiers to their servers.

The local storage can be cleared at any time; therefore, the user is given a button to trigger the erasure of all data (Obj5). Moreover, the local storage is file-based, i.e. its content can be found in plain text in files on the user's machine. Thus, to ensure the erasure of all personal data, the user can additionally delete the corresponding files. The path to these files is static, it can be given to the user so he or she can find it.

To export the data in a machine-readable format (Obj6) the whole local storage must be queried, requests must be decrypted, and saved to a dedicated file. Since data in the local storage is in JSON format, it is reasonable to export it as such. Due to the diverse structure of the recorded data, an export in CSV is rather unhandy.

Disabling the recording (Obj7) can be realized with a set of means: by implementing blacklists (or whitelists), by offering a button to start and stop recording at any time, or by disabling the extension completely. The latter is undoubtedly the safest and easiest way to guarantee that the recording is disabled. Blacklists or whitelists determine on which websites recording should be disabled or enabled respectively. This approach, however, requires users to invest some effort for pre-configuration, which might violate Obj8. A button to start and stop recording is rather easy to implement, but offers no advantage compared to enabling or disabling the extension, since this can be triggered with one click as well.

To achieve Obj8, all other objectives must be realized by involving as less user effort as possible. This means that the usage of the extension itself is realized in a user-friendly manner. But furthermore, the usage of the extension should not impact the perceived QoE while browsing the Web, i.e. websites should not take longer to load or that CPU and memory consumption drastically increase so that other applications are affected.

The visualization of the data (Obj9) can be done in the browser using Hypertext Markup Language (HTML), Cascading Style Sheets (CSS), JavaScript, and Scalable Vector Graphics (SVG). To highlight the communication flows, we chose a graph representation of the data. A search function is provided to users allowing them to query the data for personal information they do not want to be included in a resulting data set, which is further processed.

4   Related Work

Trackers enjoy a long presence in the history of the Web. In fact, they exist almost as long as the Web itself. Lerner et al. [11] proved the presence of Web trackers in 1996 by examining and analyzing the Web Archive. The Internet, as a distributed system, is built upon interconnections of nodes, thus, third parties are conceptually nothing to despise. However, for the precise personalization of displayed advertisements, personal data is required, which is often collected without a user's awareness using Web tracking techniques. One could argue that the most severe issue with third-party content is not its presence but users' unawareness of it. A study by Thode et al. [14] shows that users' expectations regarding third-party tracking heavily differ from reality. With the General Data Protection Regulation (GDPR) [7] coming into effect in May 2018, this circumstance becomes problematic, since it requires the processing of personal data to be transparent.

Bujlow et al. [2] published a sophisticated survey on all known Web tracking techniques to date. Most modern and often more accurate methods mostly rely on third-party scripts that are executed on the user's device to obtain a set of data items to generate a so-called *browser fingerprint*, which is sufficient to uniquely identify the user among other users.

Today Web trackers are subject to extensive studies due to the threat they impose on our data privacy. A very sophisticated study was conducted by Englehardt et al. [6] in 2016, who aimed to measure and analyze the extent of third-party presence on one million websites. Therefore, they designed and developed the tool OpenWPM to measure and record HTTP traffic. Yet, OpenWPM uses Selenium to crawl the top one million websites, which is a framework to simulate and automate user interactions. Thus, their measured data is not real user data. Regardless of the data quality, they found third-party scripts present on nearly all considered websites. Their results further show that only few third parties are present on a high number of first parties. This is clear evidence for data monopolies of the most prominent Web trackers. However, this circumstance is also an advantage: one has to identify and block the few most prominent third parties only to effectively protect oneself from Web tracking on the most popular websites at least. This is one of the reasons why the blacklist-based approach is so popular: it is very effective.

There are many browser extensions for all major browsers that follow this approach. Their promise is to protect users from unintended and unauthorized third-party information disclosure. Browser extensions like Ghostery [10], Ultra-Block - Privacy Protection & Adblocker [16], Crumble [4], or Privacy Badger [13] are very popular tools with millions of users. However, only Privacy Badger tries to identify Web trackers based on their prominence in addition to blacklists. Privacy Badger blocks a third party if its presence is observed on three distinct first parties. An additional challenge of these browser extensions is to maintain the same level of user-perceived QoE after the extension has been installed. From a user's perspective, blocking third-party requests is very beneficial, since loading times are decreased and computing resources are spared, as a study of Kontaxis and Chew [8] confirms.

However, the above presented browser extensions give little to no information on the tracking third party itself nor technical details about the process of data exposure. However, there are browser extensions that give more information: uMatrix [17] and uBO-Scope [15]. The extension uMatrix provides the user with insights on the type of HTTP requests issued to the corresponding third parties. While, to our knowledge, the extension uBO-Scope is the only one that accurately gives information on the extent of presence of a specific third party during the current browsing session. A high presence of a third party is indicated with red in the extension's pop-up window.

Nonetheless, all the above presented browser extensions rather aim to identify and block tracking activities than serving as tool to assess data flows to third parties. They offer limited data visualization capabilities and no recording options, which makes it difficult to analyze or further process the measured data. The browser extension closest to the objectives of T.EX is Firefox' Lightbeam [9], which has strong visualization features (Obj9), but fails to give more insights on the communication that has taken place and the third parties itself (Obj1). Lightbeam allows to export the recorded data in machine-readable format (Obj6), yet the exported information does not include the first party with its HTTP path (Obj2).

The idea to use machine-learning techniques to identify Web trackers was proposed by Bau et al. [1] in 2013. They elaborate on useful data sources and how to obtain labeled training sets. Following the paper's position, there were several publications of researchers in the following years describing supervised or unsupervised classification of Web tracking activities. In 2014, Metwalley et al. [12] present an unsupervised approach that leads to successful results. Their algorithm is able to detect 34 Web trackers that have never been documented before. Similar results are achieved by Wu et al. [18] in 2016. They use a supervised approach and detect 35 new tracking parties. Despite their successful revelation of new Web trackers, both research groups use crawlers to generate the data with which they feed their machine-learning algorithms.

The importance of proper data quality is highlighted by the publication of Yu et al. [19], who achieve remarkable results with regard to accuracy and performance of detecting Web trackers. The authors are a research group from the Cliqz browser development team, which is a German browser vendor of the same-named browser Cliqz [3]. Through their product, they were able to use browsing

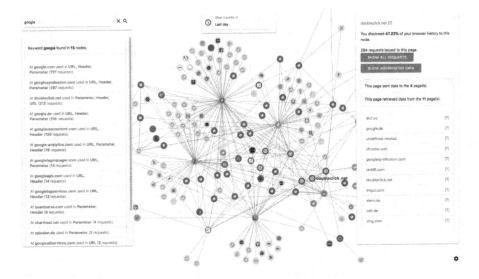

Fig. 1. The user interface of the browser extension including a graph, a search feature, and further information on the third parties. Highly connected nodes are colored red to indicate third parties with high extent of presence on other websites. (Color figure online)

data of 200.000 users for their algorithm. This way, they were able to outperform their commercial competitor Disconnect.me [5], which is also used by Firefox.

5   Implementation

This chapter presents the implementation of T.EX and explains how the individual objectives were realized. T.EX has been implemented for Google Chrome, however it is planned to port the implementation to Mozilla Firefox. Since the offered browser extension APIs of the two browser vendors are based on the WebExtension APIs, it can be expected that most of the code can be reused for the implementation of a Firefox extension.

5.1   HTTP and HTTPS Traffic Logging and Recording

To intercept and log HTTP and HTTPS traffic, the interface *webRequest* is used. Chrome and Firefox emit an event *onBeforeRequest* before a request is issued. Extensions can subscribe to the event by adding a listener to it. Both browsers provide extensions with valuable information on the issued request, including all necessary information on the target t of the request, search parameters S, request headers H, form data F and even data in the request body B. Interestingly, determining the source s of a request requires more effort in Google Chrome. While Firefox emits the initiator of a request in the *originUrl* field, Chrome only

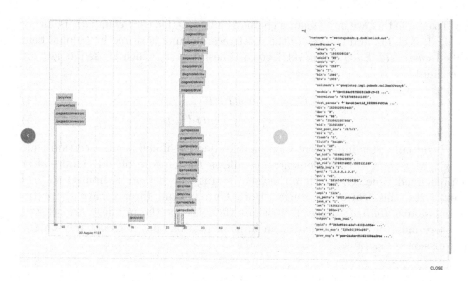

Fig. 2. Records visualized on a timeline enabling users to investigate requests initiated by a certain website to a certain third party. By selecting an event, users can see the corresponding record including all recorded data.

gives information on the source in an optional field called *initiator*. To retrieve the source even if the field is not set, a query of open tabs with the *tabId* is required. A logged event is called *record r*, which is defined as follows:

$$r \in R := (s, t, S, H, F, B) \tag{1}$$

$$kv := (key, N) \in S \cup H \cup F \cup B \tag{2}$$

$$v, kv \in N \tag{3}$$

5.2   Persistent Storage of Records

Records need to be persistently stored in order to enable an assessment of them later in time. The local storage of browsers is rather limited with regard to performance and expressiveness of queries. The local storage is a so-called key-value-store that allows to load values for certain keys or a set of keys, yet does not offer possibilities to query ranges. Each key has to be unique and queried explicitly. This means in practice that the local storage cannot be queried to return records that have been recorded in the last seven days for example. Furthermore, it is not advisable to get or set values in a high frequency, since the local storage can be easily overwhelmed, which directly leads to a bad QoE.

For this reason, two strategies are implemented: the aggregation of records into chunks and the writing of chunks into the local storage in a defined interval *i*. This way, the local storage is less demanded and the work load is evenly distributed over time. However, these strategies raise the question of appropriate keys that can be used for the chunks, so that they can be queried later in time.

To enable this, we implement a chain of chunks C, i.e. each chunk c is pointing to the last chunk and the key of the most recent chunk is stored in a global field called *currentId*. Each chunk retrieves a timestamp ts, which is used as key for the chunk.

$$c \in C := (ts, lastId, R_{[ts-i,ts]}) \tag{4}$$
$$currentId = ts \tag{5}$$

Eventually, this implementation enables queries of chunks in a certain time range. Moreover, this implementation allows the erasure of old chunks after a predefined time. Given that the local storage by default is limited to 5.24 megabytes, this feature is crucial. Both Chrome and Firefox have the extra permission *unlimitedStorage*. Extensions that ask for the privilege are allowed to store more data. Nonetheless, an implementation that does not rely on the permission is desirable.

5.3 Encryption and Decryption of Chunks

Since the local storage resides on the user's machine unencrypted, encryption needs to be implemented in order to ensure data security. Otherwise, a malicious application on the user's device could gain access to this data and gain valuable information like passwords, the browser history, email addresses, bank account information and suchlike. Without encryption, T.EX would rather constitute a severe risk than contribute to improved data security and privacy.

To implement encryption, the user is prompted to generate a key pair (*pubKey* and *privKey*) after the installation of the browser extension. This requires the user to enter a password *pwd*. The generated private key is encrypted with the entered password using the Advanced Encryption Standard (AES). The generated public key and the encrypted private key *encPrivKey* are then stored in the local storage.

To encrypt chunks, a random key *aesKey* is generated that serves as symmetric key for the encryption. This random key is used for the whole browsing session until the browser is closed. This key is encrypted with the public key so that only the private key can decrypt it. This encrypted symmetric key *encAesKey* is stored along with the encrypted chunk in the local storage. To decrypt chunks, the user is prompted to enter the password to decrypt the private key, which is then used to decrypt the symmetric key to eventually retrieve the chunks.

5.4 Data Visualization

As it can be seen in Fig. 1, data flows are represented by a graph $G := (V, E)$, which illustrates connections between visited websites (green-colored nodes) and involved third parties (beige or red-colored nodes). Red-colored nodes are highly connected nodes that retrieve data from various websites and Web applications. For the coloring, a rather simple rule-based approach was used for the beginning. However, it is planned to extend the coloring function at a later point in time.

Algorithm 1. Set-up and encryption of chunks

1: $privKey, pubKey \leftarrow generateKeyPair()$
2: $pwd \leftarrow$ user-entered password
3: $encPrivKey \leftarrow encrypt(privKey, pwd)$
4: $save(encPrivKey, pubKey)$
5: $c = (ts, lastId, R_{[ts-i,ts]})$
6: $aesKey \leftarrow generateRandomKey()$ for each session
7: $encAesKey \leftarrow encrypt(aesKey, pubKey)$
8: $c' \leftarrow (ts, lastId, encrypt(R_{[ts-i,ts]}, encAesKey), encAesKey)$
9: $save(c')$

Algorithm 2. Decryption of chunks

1: $encPrivKey \leftarrow$ load from local storage
2: $pwd \leftarrow$ password prompt
3: $privKey \leftarrow decrypt(encPrivKey, pwd)$
4: $c' \leftarrow$ load from local storage
5: $aesKey \leftarrow decrypt(c'_{encAesKey}, privKey)$
6: $c \leftarrow (ts, lastId, decrypt(R_{[ts-i,ts]}, aesKey)$

A more gradient color function is currently researched to highlight only the Web trackers in the graph.

$$G := (V, E) \tag{6}$$
$$V := \{r_s, r_t | r \in R\} \tag{7}$$
$$E := \{(r_s, r_t) | r \in R\} \tag{8}$$

Users can search for keywords that might appear in URLs, headers, or parameters. Purple-colored nodes (as seen in Fig. 1) are nodes that contain the keyword in the record. By clicking on a node the user is able to retrieve more information on the corresponding node such as to which nodes data has been sent to or from which nodes data was retrieved. For further investigation of the occurred communication, the user can investigate requests to or from one node, which are visualized on a timeline. By selecting an entry on the timeline the record is visualized (see Fig. 2).

6   Evaluation

The aim of this section is to evaluate whether the usage of T.EX implies an unneglectable impact on the user-perceived QoE while browsing the Web. Therefore, we investigate whether the loading time of a website noticeably increases, when using T.EX. We measure loading times by recording key events: *onDOM-ContentLoaded* and *onCompleted*. Both events occur strictly sequential, i.e. the *DOMContentLoaded*, which indicates that the Document Object Model (DOM) is fully built, always occurs before *DOMContentCompleted*, which indicates that also all referenced resources are fully loaded and initialized. From a user's perspective, the first event occurs close to the moment when the user is able to see the website. In contrast to the latter, which is triggered when the loading indicator of the browser disappears.

Analogously, we measure the resource consumption (i.e. CPU and memory usage) during a website request and loading in order to learn the impact of the browser extension on hardware resources. For this purpose, we request and compute CPU and memory usage in a determined interval (so-called tick each 50 ms). Besides CPU and memory usage, we further evaluate the disk space consumption of T.EX on a general level to find out how fast the extension reserves disk space for its purpose.

As stated above, we open websites with and without T.EX activated. We additionally repeat the procedure with a different, comparable browser extension activated in order to be able to assess the performance of T.EX in comparison with other extensions. For this purpose we identified Privacy Badger as good candidate, since it uses the same APIs to analyze traffic in real-time. However, we know that Privacy Badger decreases loading times of websites, while we expect T.EX to increase loading times. This is due to Privacy Badger preventing HTTP requests from occurring, thus saving time to load, while T.EX logs, processes, and stores HTTP requests. For both hardware resources are used. With this evaluation procedure we aim to put the increased hardware usage of T.EX into perspective.

As appropriate websites for the test, we use the German news site *spiegel.de* and the front page of *google.de*, which differ in the amount of third-party content they integrate. While accessing *google.de* triggers *only* 23 requests, which only request content from Google servers, requesting *spiegel.de* involves more than 400 requests to more than 50 third parties. We expect hardware usage and loading times to increase linearly with the number of involved requests, thus we selected two websites that are rather bipolar in that respect. The experiment was conducted on a machine with an Intel Core i7 (2.2 GHz quad-core) and 16 GB memory. The machine was connected to the Internet via a 1 Gbit Ethernet connection. The experiments were repeated three times each to detect anomalies.

The results of the experiment are depicted in Fig. 3. The rows represent the corresponding runs without T.EX activated (top), with T.EX activated (middle), and with Privacy Badger activated (bottom). In each run the CPU usage (left column), memory usage (middle column), and loading times (right column) were measured.

By comparing the individual results displayed in the first column, an increase of CPU usage is clearly observable. The CPU is working much closer to capacity and maintains this level during the whole time the website is loaded. The reason for the CPU demand of T.EX is found in the steady encryption of records in the background. Thus, disabling the encryption would gain performance, yet would constitute a violation of the extension's main objectives. Additional CPU capacity is used, since requests are preprocessed before they are stored in the local storage. This preprocessing could be executed at a later point in time, for

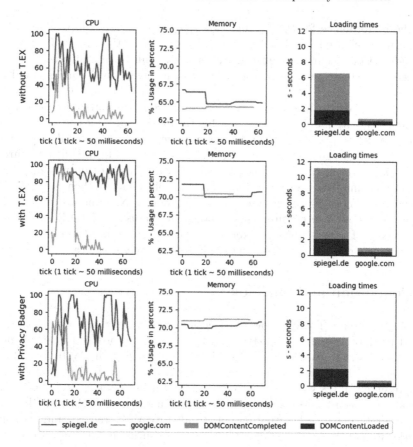

Fig. 3. The results of the evaluation: the first column shows the CPU usage, the second column the memory usage, and the third column the loading times. The first row represents the measurements without T.EX activated, the second row with enabled T.EX, and the last row with Privacy Badger activated.

example, when the browser is in the idle state for a certain amount of time, i.e. the browser is currently not used by the user.

The memory consumption is rather consistent with our expectation: the usage is increased fairly but not excessively. Comparable browser extensions like Privacy Badger that perform similar tasks show the same level of memory consumption. The perceived QoE should not be affected to much by this circumstance. In contrast to the loading times, which seem to be strongly affected by the usage of T.EX. When comparing the third column in Fig. 3, it is noticeable that the loading time is drastically increased, when T.EX was activated. This does not apply on the *DOMContentLoaded* event, but on the *DOMContentCompleted* event. Note that the page is usable much earlier, so that the user can already interact with it, before the DOM content is fully loaded. Yet the performance of T.EX with regard to loading times requires improvement. It is also noteworthy that the performance for the loading times of *google.de* are comparable to the performance achieved in the other runs. Consequently, the drastic increase of the loading time occurs on websites with massive third-party involvement. An exponential increase relative to the number of involved third parties could be ruled out.

Finally, we aim to investigate the disk space consumption. While it can be measured easily by simply checking how big the local storage files are, it is rather difficult to define a rule to estimate the storage usage. In general, it heavily depends on the usage and browsing behavior of the user. In a dedicated three-hour lasting session, we were able to collect 80 megabyte of data, while on a different machine that is exclusively used during office hours (then extensively), we collected almost 700 megabyte in a single month. Nonetheless, it must be stated that the storage requirements imposed by the usage of T.EX exceed the requirements of other browser extensions. Therefore, users of T.EX must be aware that the recording of browsing sessions is storage intensive.

7   Conclusion and Outlook

This paper presents T.EX a browser extension to provide transparency to experienced users or system administrators, who want to record and analyze communication flows to external third parties while browsing the Web. Therefore, objectives and requirements have been defined and their implementation has been presented. T.EX will serve as tool to conduct measurements and obtain real user data in a secure and privacy-preserving manner, which might contribute to more accurate machine learning models to identify Web trackers and tracking activities in real-time. We evaluated T.EX by measuring its impact on the performance to derive consequences on the user-perceived QoE. Our results show that T.EX achieves performance, which is comparable to other privacy browser extensions like Privacy Badger. However, it has an impact on the loading times of certain websites that cannot be neglected. The issue will be investigated in future works. Furthermore, we will use T.EX to collect data that will be used to identify trackers and their tracking activities.

Acknowledgments. Supported by the European Union's Horizon 2020 research and innovation programme under grant 731601.

References

1. Bau, J., Mayer, J., Paskov, H., Mitchell, J.: A promising direction for web tracking countermeasures. In: Workshop on Web 2.0 Security and Privacy (2013)
2. Bujlow, T., Carela-Espanol, V., Lee, B.R., Barlet-Ros, P.: A survey on web tracking: mechanisms, implications, and defenses. Proc. IEEE **105**(8), 1476–1510 (2017)
3. Cliqz - Der sichere Browser mit integrierter Schnell-Suche. https://cliqz.com/. Accessed 4 Feb 2019

4. Crumble - Online Privacy, Stop Tracking. https://chrome.google.com/webstore/detail/crumble-online-privacy/icpfjjckgkgkocbkkdaodapelofhgjncoh. Accessed 4 Feb 2019

5. Disconnect. https://disconnect.me/. Accessed 4 Feb 2019

6. Englehardt, S., Narayanan, A.: Online tracking. In: Proceedings of the 2016 ACM SIGSAC Conference on Computer and Communications Security - CCS 2016, no. 1, pp. 1388–1401 (2016)

7. Regulation (EU) 2016/679 of the European Parliament and of the Council of 27 April 2016 on the protection of natural persons with regard to the processing of personal data and on the free movement of such data, and repealing Directive 95/46/EC (General Data Protection Regulation), OJ L 119, pp. 1–88, 4 May 2016

8. Kontaxis, G., Chew, M.: Tracking protection in Firefox for privacy and performance. In: IEEE Web 2.0 Security & Privacy, June 2015

9. Firefox Lightbeam - Add-ons for Firefox. https://addons.mozilla.org/de/firefox/addon/lightbeam/. Accessed 4 Feb 2019

10. Ghostery Makes the Web Cleaner, Faster and Safer! https://www.ghostery.com. Accessed 4 Feb 2019

11. Lerner, A., Simpson, A. K., Kohno, T., Roesner, F.: Internet Jones and the raiders of the lost trackers: an archaeological study of web tracking from 1996 to 2016. In: Usenix Security (2016)

12. Metwalley, H., Traverso, S., Mellia, M.: Unsupervised detection of web trackers. In: IEEE Global Communications Conference (GLOBECOM), pp. 1–6 (2015)

13. Privacy Badger - Electronic Frontier Foundation. https://www.eff.org/privacybadger. Accessed 4 Feb 2019

14. Thode, W., Griesbaum, J., Mandl, T.: I would have never allowed it: user perception of third-party tracking and implications for display advertising. Re:inventing information science in the networked society. In: Proceedings of the 14th International Symposium on Information Science (ISI 2015), Zadar, Croatia, 19th–21st May 2015, vol. 66, pp. 445–456 (2015)

15. BO-Scope: a tool to measure over time your own exposure to third parties on the web. https://github.com/gorhill/uBO-Scope. Accessed 4 Feb 2019

16. UltraBlock - Block Ads, Trackers and Third Party Cookies. https://ultrablock.org/. Accessed 4 Feb 2019

17. Matrix: point and click matrix to filter net requests according to source, destination and type. https://github.com/gorhill/uMatrix. Accessed 4 Feb 2019

18. Wu, Q., Liu, Q., Zhang, Y., Liu, P., Wen, G.: A machine learning approach for detecting third-party trackers on the web. In: Askoxylakis, I., Ioannidis, S., Katsikas, S., Meadows, C. (eds.) ESORICS 2016. LNCS, vol. 9878, pp. 238–258. Springer, Cham (2016). https://doi.org/10.1007/978-3-319-45744-4_12

19. Yu, Z., Macbeth, S., Modi, K., Pujol, J. M.: Tracking the trackers. In: Proceedings of the 25th International Conference on World Wide Web - WWW 2016, pp. 121–132 (2016)

Towards Transparency in Email Tracking

Max Maass(✉)📷, Stephan Schwär, and Matthias Hollick📷

Secure Mobile Networking Lab, TU Darmstadt, Darmstadt, Germany
{mmaass,sschwaer,mhollick}@seemoo.tu-darmstadt.de

Abstract. Tracking technologies have become ubiquitous, not only on websites but also in email messages. However, while protection and transparency tools exist for the web, no such tools exist for email messages, thus obscuring privacy violations. We introduce the PrivacyMail platform to assist with the automated analysis of email messages. The platform automatically analyzes commercial mailing lists, making it easier to detect different forms of tracking. Our platform introduces transparency about the practices of companies, and serves as a tool for regulators, data protection professionals and consumers alike. Our preliminary results show widespread email tracking, where opening an email can result in information being sent to up to 13 third parties, in some cases disclosing the users' email address in the process.

Keywords: Scanner · Tracking · Compliance · Email · Privacy

1 Introduction

While discussions about tracking on websites have entered the mainstream, one issue that has received far less attention is the prevalence of tracking in email communication. Here, a large ecosystem of commercial tracking companies offers services that allow marketing professionals and private individuals alike to monitor if their emails are being viewed and which of their links are being clicked. The used techniques include *tracking pixels* and personalized links, which will in some cases leak the email addresses of the affected users to third parties [4,7]. At the same time, fewer protections for end-users exist—while web tracking can be countered to a certain degree by using ad-blockers and tracking protection systems such as PrivacyBadger [3], no such tools exist to protect against email tracking. This problem is exacerbated by the fact that emails are often being opened repeatedly on multiple devices, using different clients (Webmail, Thunderbird, Outlook, iOS Mail, ...), which allows trackers to link these devices to the same owner, and makes defense more difficult, as every client needs to be protected separately. There are few technologies providing transparency in this space, leading to a lack of awareness about the tracking practices of commercial mailing services.

Previous studies have sought to quantify the prevalence of tracking in commercial emails through a variety of methods [4,6,7], and investigated the potential privacy implications and user acceptance of these methods [12]. However,

© Springer Nature Switzerland AG 2019
M. Naldi et al. (Eds.): APF 2019, LNCS 11498, pp. 18–27, 2019.
https://doi.org/10.1007/978-3-030-21752-5_2

so far, they can only provide an aggregate analysis at a specific point in time. Their ability to provide public transparency about the practices of individual companies over time, a common approach in the area of online tracking [1,9], is thus limited.

We aim to fill this gap by designing and developing a **public email privacy benchmarking system called PrivacyMail**. The system allows anyone to register special email addresses for commercial mailing lists, and will analyze incoming emails for common tracking techniques. It will also attempt to detect the disclosure of (PII), like the email address, to third parties. This information can be used by *data protection officers (DPOs)* to check the compliance of companies with relevant regulation, by *individual users* to inform themselves about the risks of subscribing to mailings from specific companies, and by *researchers* to gain more insight into the practices of a large, crowd-sourced set of companies that send out these mailings. A beta version is available at https://PrivacyMail. info.

We will proceed by reviewing related work in Sect. 2 and providing an overview about our system in Sect. 3. In Sect. 4, we discuss preliminary results from the operation of an early version on a limited dataset to demonstrate the capabilities of the current prototype. We will close the paper by discussing future work in Sect. 5 before concluding in Sect. 6.

2   Related Work

Research on email privacy can be split into two areas (cf. Fig. 1): privacy against intermediaries (like email providers or third parties eavesdropping on communication between the (MXs)), and privacy against tracking by the sender, which is the topic of this paper. Privacy against intermediaries can be ensured through transport- and end-to-end encryption, and has been studied in some detail (cf. [2] for an overview). In contrast, privacy against the sender has not received a lot of attention so far.

Englehardt *et al.* developed the system that serves as the conceptual basis for our own. They used OpenWPM [5] to scan a dataset consisting of over 12 500 emails from 902 different senders (a mix of popular shopping and news websites) [4]. They found that 85% of emails contained at least one embedded image from a third party, and 19% of senders contained embedded external content that leaked the email address of the recipient to a third party (by encoding it in the URL, cf. Sect. 3). They also found that repeatedly opening the same email changed which third parties were embedded in 21% of the cases. Finally, they showed that existing tracker blocking lists, designed for use against website-based trackers, missed a significant portion of third parties commonly embedded in emails.

Xu *et al.* [12] analyzed a corpus of over 44 000 emails, collected over a period of 7 years, and found widespread use of tracking in a large variety of different sectors. They also investigated the potential privacy implications of email tracking, and found that sending a small number of emails is sufficient to track some users for several weeks, including their geographical location. Finally, they performed a user study and found that users are generally unaware of the privacy

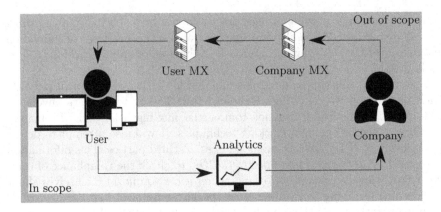

Fig. 1. Potential areas of privacy concern.

risks of email tracking, and a vast majority of users were interested in protecting themselves from it after they learned of its existence.

Hu *et al.* [7] analyzed a large corpus of emails collected from disposable email services. They crawled public mailboxes of several popular providers of anonymous, temporary email accounts and collected a corpus of 2.3 million messages from over 200 000 distinct domains. They again confirmed that email tracking is a common practice, and is disproportionately used by large companies. They also found that the market for email tracking is not yet dominated by a single company.

Haupt *et al.* [6] collected a dataset of over 60 000 emails from the newsletters of a variety of different companies. They investigated the properties of tracking images, and proposed an automated approach to detect and block them using a machine learning classifier, achieving a detection rate of 92%.

All of these studies have in common that they provide only an aggregate analysis of a snapshot of the current state of email newsletters, thus making it impossible to draw conclusions about an individual users' exposure to tracking. Such an analysis for the area of web privacy is being offered by two projects: *Webbkoll* [1] and our own prior work, *PrivacyScore.org* [9]. Both perform automated scans of websites to determine their privacy properties, and PrivacyScore also seeks to create public transparency about the practices of website operators to incentivize them to change their behavior [8]. To the best of our knowledge, aside from the platform developed in this paper, no similar system exists in the domain of email messages.

3   System Overview

In this section, we give an overview of our system, the analyses we perform, and the challenges we encountered. The platform is built using Python and the Django framework. The overall process of using PrivacyMail is shown in Fig. 2.

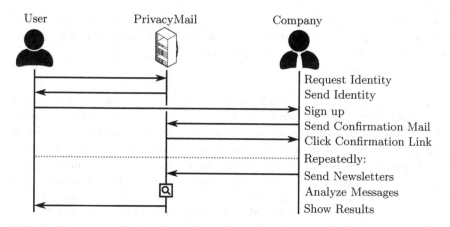

Fig. 2. Usage of the PrivacyMail platform.

3.1 Adding a Service

Any service that sends out newsletters can be registered with the system by entering its URL into the system. PrivacyMail will generate a unique identity with an email address (hosted by PrivacyMail), name, and gender (as some newsletter providers ask for this upon registration), and display it to the user performing the registration. The user will then enter that email and other required information into the newsletter sign-up form. The resulting email confirmation will be received by PrivacyMail.

The user will also be invited to add additional metadata about the service. This includes a canonical name (e.g. "Spiegel Online" for spiegel.de, or "Annual Privacy Forum" for privacyforum.eu) to facilitate a search using human-readable terms, and information about the country and industry sector of the website. This metadata can later be used for further analyses.

Each new identity must be manually confirmed by an administrator, and no automated processing takes place until then. This ensures that the email address was signed up at the correct website. If everything is in order, the administrator will confirm the registration by clicking the email confirmation link. Any future emails from the sending domain will be automatically processed without human interaction.

3.2 Analyzing Emails

When a new email from a permitted sender for a confirmed identity arrives, it is automatically processed. First, the email is saved to the database, including all relevant headers. Next, all external links (but not the embedded external resources, like images) are extracted from the email. The system attempts to deduce which of the detected links are management links (e.g., links to change subscription settings or view the email in the browser), and which are regular content links (e.g., links to news articles, products, etc.), using a mix of heuristics, including word lists and link clustering. Once all likely management links have been excluded, the system chooses one of the remaining links and marks it for later investigation.

External Resource Analysis: Email tracking is usually performed with one of two goals: The sender wants to determine if the recipient opened the email, and/or if she clicked any links embedded in the email. Depending on the goal, different techniques are used. Commonly, a small image hosted by a tracking company is embedded in the email, using a personalized URL that can be linked to the recipient. Upon opening the message, most email clients[1] will automatically load this external resource from the servers of the company, thereby notifying the company that the email was opened by this specific recipient. As this *tracking pixel* is too small to be seen, the user will not notice its presence in the email. Alternatively, the same technique can be used with visible images (e.g., product photos in an ecommerce newsletter). Such requests to tracking providers not only inform them about the fact that the email was opened, but also leak the IP address and user agent (i.e., the used browser or email client) to them. This information can be used to obtain a (coarse) geographic location of the user [12].

More than one tracker can be included using a single tracking pixel through the use of HTTP forwarding. In this case, the first tracking service will forward the user to a second one, which forwards the user even further, until all desired tracking services have been informed and the request is answered by the final destination (i.e., the 1×1 pixel image). This allows an unlimited number of trackers to be included using a single image.

To detect this tracking, we save the message to an HTML file and host it on a machine-local web server. This allows us to view it with OpenWPM, an automated Firefox browser intended for research [5]. Viewing the email like this approximates opening it in a webmail system with remote content enabled. OpenWPM will log all requests and responses generated by viewing the email, thus giving us an accurate representation of what will happen when a user views this email without clicking any links. Using this (instead of a static analysis of embedded external content) allows us to see not only the embedded external trackers, but also any additional trackers contacted through HTTP redirects. All requests and responses and the relations between them are saved in the database.

Link Analysis: If the sender wants to know if links from the email were clicked (e.g., to judge the click-through rate of advertising campaigns), they can also personalize the links. In this case, the links will point to a special URL, hosted by the tracking service, which will log the visit and forward the user to the actual target of the link (e.g., a product or news article). This tracking only becomes active when the user clicks the link, but cannot be prevented by not loading external resources. Again, more than one tracker can be informed through HTTP forwarding.

---

[1] See Table 12 of [4] for an overview of eMail client behavior.

To detect this tracking, we delete the local state (cookies, sessions, ...) of the OpenWPM browser and instruct it to visit the link we have previously selected in the email. Again, we log all requests and responses and identify the chain of HTTP redirects that takes place when visiting the link, until the final destination is reached.

Email Disclosure Analysis: Trackers use different techniques to identify email recipients in these links, however, identifiers derived from the email address are common. Previous work has shown that in many cases, hashes or encoded versions of the email address are used by tracking services [4,7], in some cases nesting different encodings or hash algorithms (e.g., `md5(sha1(email))`). This shows that the email addresses of recipients are widely shared with third parties, either intentionally by the sender of the newsletter, or implicitly by the tracking services. Previous work has shown that simple hashing of such personally-identifiable information is insufficient to guarantee privacy [10].

To detect this eMail leakage, we compute a series of hashes and encodings of the address, nested to a depth of 2, and check if any of them are found in any of the recorded request URLs for the eMail. If so, we assume that this request discloses the email address, and save this fact in the database. After this, processing of the email is finished.

Further Personalization Detection: Not all personalization uses identifier derived from the email address. Users may be identified by a different identifier that is linked to their identity on the server. To detect this type of personalization, we offer the option to register more than one identity per service. The system then uses a combination of email timestamps and subject lines to match newsletter messages between different identities. Once a pair has been found, the links are extracted from both and compared. If no personalization is used, the links in both messages should be identical when excluding subscription management links. Thus, if (partially) different links are detected, this is a strong indicator that they are personalized.

Another possibility for differing links may be the use of A/B testing, in which different versions of emails are sent out to recipients to determine which headlines are more effective at generating clicks. These practices have been observed by Englehardt *et al.* [4]. To distinguish A/B testing from other forms of personalization, we also compare the text of the messages to see how similar they are. A high similarity indicates that the same message was sent to both identities, while a low similarity indicates A/B testing.

Further Analyses: Having a large archive of emails, both for a single service over time and for a large, crowdsourced collection of different services, will also allow us to perform additional analyses. For example, does the number of trackers increase or decrease over time? What is the influence of regulatory changes like the upcoming ePrivacy directive? For services annotated with additional metadata, we can compare tracking practices between countries and industry sectors, where Haupt *et al.* found significant differences [6].

3.3 Providing Transparency

The results for all newsletters are made available using a searchable frontend on the project website (currently in development). This allows users to check if the newsletter they are interested in has already been analyzed, and if so, which trackers it uses and to which the email addresses are disclosed. We do not republish the content of newsletters, only the results of our analysis, to avoid allegations of copyright infringement.

3.4 Challenges

One concern is the handling of identities that receive emails from sources that are not affiliated with the original newsletter provider. This could be spam (e.g. due to a data breach at the newsletter provider), or due to a user registering the generated identity with more than one website. We solve part of this problem by only processing emails that come from an approved sender for the identity. emails not sent by the expected sender are held back for manual verification, at which point a decision can be made on how to handle them (e.g., set the sender as a new approved sender, mark the message as spam, or discard it).

The processing time for a single email is on the order of several seconds to half a minute. This makes the analysis a bottleneck for the performance of the system. We are already working on distributing this work to enable PrivacyMail to scale horizontally with demand.

Finally, service providers may not want their newsletters to be analyzed. As we would like to avoid unilateral action from the service providers (i.e., identifying and unsubscribing identities linked to PrivacyMail based on the used email domains), we provide them with the option to opt out of being analyzed by contacting us. To make this transparent to the users, their services will then be listed as *excluded from analysis*.

4   Preliminary Results

To demonstrate the capabilities of the current prototype, we performed a small-scale analysis on a non-representative dataset, obtained by signing up for newsletters from 20 ecommerce and news websites in Germany, the United States, France, Italy and Poland. They were chosen partially based on popularity, partially on personal familiarity, and not informed about the analysis. In total, the dataset contains approximately 2000 emails. More detailed analyses on a larger set of services will be presented at the Annual Privacy Forum.

16 of 20 companies (80%) sent emails containing at least one resource hosted by a 3rd party (i.e., a domain not directly associated with the sending company), with an average of 118.4 resources per email (median 111, min 0, max 363). These may represent tracking, but also more benign purposes, such as the use of (CDNs) to host article pictures.[2] In total, 43 distinct 3rd party domains were

---

[2] Differentiating between these cases automatically is challenging, as standard tracker blocking lists have been shown to be unreliable when applied to email tracking [4].

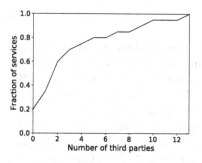
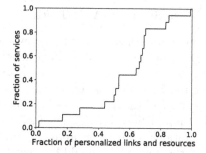

Fig. 3. CDF of third party count per service ($n = 20$).

Fig. 4. CDF of fraction of personalized links per service ($n = 18$).

contacted, with an average of 1.56 third parties per email (median 1, min 0, max 13, cf. Fig. 3 for the (CDF)).

When opening the emails, at least 4 out of 20 services (20%) leak the email address of recipient to at least one website (including their own), and 13 different websites receive them from at least one service, often hashed using the md5 algorithm. Some of the receiving websites belong to the company sending the newsletter, while at least 9 of them belong to tracking companies, many of them located in the United States.

4.1 Case Study 1: Individual Service Analysis

For our first case study, we examine the daily newsletter sent by a major French newspaper. When opening one email, mail clients that load external content will access 70 external resources, 24 of which are loaded from 3rd party domains, including a French tracking company and an advertising subsidiary of Google. Some requests are also forwarded to additional external 3rd parties, leading to the inclusion of another company. Interestingly, some requests are forwarded to the local machine of the user (`http://localhost/`), which may be either due to a misconfiguration, or used to ensure that no content is loaded.

22 of the embedded external resources contain the md5-hashed email address of the recipient, which is sent to the website of the newspaper and forwarded to a 3rd party, `ivitrack.com`.[3] The URLs also contain what is likely a message identifier, indicating that this is used to track which users have actually read the newsletter.

When clicking the link to a news article, the user is forwarded to a subdomain of the newspaper, which forwards the user via the same French tracking company that was previous included through embedded images. This is likely used to track which links are being opened by users, although it does not carry any user identities derived from the email address.

---

[3] We were unable to find details about this company, but hashed email address leaks to this company have also been observed by Englehardt *et al.* [4].

4.2   Case Study 2: A/B Testing

Our second and third case study show the added possibilities enabled by having more than one recipient for each newsletter. Comparing emails sent by the same service to different recipients allows us to detect if the service is performing A/B testing (cf. Sect. 3.2). In our dataset, we observed two services performing A/B testing, both of them German shopping companies. Each used a base email with a set of products or banners common to both emails, with one being extended with additional banners or product offers. Due to the probabilistic nature of A/B testing, these numbers should be considered a lower bound. The confidence can be increased by adding additional identities to the service under test.

4.3   Case Study 3: Link Personalization

We also compare the links sent to different identities registered for the same newsletter to detect tracking identifiers that are not derived from the email address. In our dataset, we observed different degrees of personalization. In some newsletters, almost all links and external resources were personalized, some only personalized links to their homepage, but not to individual articles from the newsletter. Only one service in the dataset used personalization only for the subscription management links. The CDF of the degree of personalization is shown in Fig. 4.

5   Future Work

Over the coming weeks we plan to include more analyses in the platform, and expose them in the frontend. We will enhance security and performance by using a distributed and containerized system for the analysis of the emails, and potentially switching from OpenWPM [5] to Privacyscanner [11]. Finally, we would like to discuss the feature wishes and requirements of practitioners in the field at the conference, and incorporate them to make the platform more useful for their purposes.

6   Conclusion

In this paper, we presented *PrivacyMail*. Similar to our PrivacyScore platform [9], we aim to shine a light on a type of privacy invasion that has traditionally been invisible. To facilitate this we designed a system that automatically analyses emails for tracking and personalization, and presented an example evaluation of a small set of services, finding evidence of email address leakage, tracking through personalized links, and A/B testing.

The platform is intended to be a public resource. Anyone can add new services to be analyzed, and the results will be made publicly available on the project homepage. The platform is available at https://PrivacyMail.info, and the source code will be released under an open license. By providing transparency, we hope to inform end users about the privacy impact of the newsletters they consume, support data protection professionals in their task of testing companies for compliance with relevant regulation, and provide interesting datasets for future research.

Acknowledgements. This work has been co-funded by the DFG as part of project C.1 within the RTG 2050 "Privacy and Trust for Mobile Users".

References

1. Andersdotter, A., Jensen-Urstad, A.: Evaluating websites and their adherence to data protection principles: tools and experiences. IFIP Adv. Inf. Commun. Technol. **498**, 39–51 (2016)
2. Clark, J., van Oorschot, P.C., Ruoti, S., Seamons, K., Zappala, D.: Securing Email. ArXiv preprint (2018). arXiv:1804.07706
3. Electronic Frontier Foundation: PrivacyBadger. https://eff.org/privacybadger. Accessed 28 Jan 2019
4. Englehardt, S., Han, J., Narayanan, A.: I never signed up for this! Privacy implications of email tracking. Proc. Priv. Enhancing Technol. **2018**(1), 109–126 (2018)
5. Englehardt, S., Narayanan, A.: Online tracking: a 1-million-site measurement and analysis. In: Proceedings of the 2016 ACM SIGSAC Conference on Computer and Communications Security - CCS 2016, no. 1, pp. 1388–1401. ACM Press, New York (2016)
6. Haupt, J., Bender, B., Fabian, B., Lessmann, S.: Robust identification of email tracking: a machine learning approach. Eur. J. Oper. Res. **271**(1), 341–356 (2018)
7. Hu, H., Peng, P., Wang, G.: Characterizing pixel tracking through the lens of disposable email services. IEEE Secur. Priv. **2019**, 545–559 (2019)
8. Maass, M., Walter, N., Herrmann, D., Hollick, M.: On the Difficulties of incentivizing online privacy through transparency: a qualitative survey of the German health insurance market. In: 14. Internationale Tagung Wirtschaftsinformatik (2019)
9. Maass, M., Wichmann, P., Pridöhl, H., Herrmann, D.: PrivacyScore: improving privacy and security via crowd-sourced benchmarks of websites. In: Schweighofer, E., Leitold, H., Mitrakas, A., Rannenberg, K. (eds.) APF 2017. LNCS, vol. 10518, pp. 178–191. Springer, Cham (2017). https://doi.org/10.1007/978-3-319-67280-9_10
10. Marx, M., Zimer, E., Mueller, T., Blochberger, M., Federrath, H.: Hashing of personally identifiable information is not sufficient. Sicherheit, pp. 55–68 (2018)
11. Pridöhl, H.: Privacyscanner. https://github.com/PrivacyScore/Privacyscanner, https://doi.org/10.5281/zenodo.2555037. Accessed 28 Jan 2019
12. Xu, H., Hao, S., Sari, A., Wang, H.: Privacy risk assessment on email tracking. In: IEEE INFOCOM, pp. 2519–2527 (2018)

Sharing Cyber Threat Intelligence Under the General Data Protection Regulation

Adham Albakri[1,2(⊠)], Eerke Boiten[2], and Rogério De Lemos[1]

[1] School of Computing, University of Kent, Canterbury, UK
{a.albakri, r.delemos}@kent.ac.uk
[2] School of Computer Science and Informatics, De Montfort University,
Leicester, UK
Eerke.Boiten@dmu.ac.uk

Abstract. Sharing Cyber Threat Intelligence (CTI) is a key strategy for improving cyber defense, but there are risks of breaching regulations and laws regarding privacy. With regulations such as the General Data Protection Regulation (GDPR) that are designed to protect citizens' data privacy, the managers of CTI datasets need clear guidance on how and when it is legal to share such information. This paper defines the impact that GDPR legal aspects may have on the sharing of CTI. In addition, we define adequate protection levels for sharing CTI to ensure compliance with the GDPR. We also present a model for evaluating the legal requirements for supporting decision making when sharing CTI, which also includes advice on the required protection level. Finally, we evaluate our model using use cases of sharing CTI datasets between entities.

Keywords: Cyber Threat Intelligence · Information sharing ·
General Data Protection Regulation GDPR · Legal evaluation

1 Introduction

Sharing Cyber Threat Intelligence (CTI) between organizations is a good strategy for building better cyber defence [1]. It assists organizations in understanding existing cyber attacks, and helps them to react against those attacks efficiently and quickly. However, CTI potentially contains sensitive and identifying information, such as IP addresses, email addresses and existing vulnerabilities [2]. Therefore, we should establish proper safeguards before sharing CTI datasets with others. When sharing CTI datasets, organizations must ensure conformance with legal and regulatory requirements, such as those required by the state and federal level in the US [3], the Japanese Personal Information Protection Act (PIPA) [4], and the General Data Protection Regulation (GDPR) [5]. In the specific context of organizations being part of critical national infrastructure, the EU NIS Directive [6] mandates some level of CTI sharing. It requires all EU member states to establish national Computer Security Incident Response Teams (CSIRT), as a single point of contact, to report cyber incidents that affect critical infrastructure and essential services. This is supported by the European Network and Information Security Agency (ENISA), which improves CSIRT capabilities by providing tools and methodologies to support network and information security [7].

© Springer Nature Switzerland AG 2019
M. Naldi et al. (Eds.): APF 2019, LNCS 11498, pp. 28–41, 2019.
https://doi.org/10.1007/978-3-030-21752-5_3

In this paper, we investigate the legal aspects for sharing CTI datasets in the context of the GDPR [2] which is the principle law in the EU for regulating the processing of personal data in the EU. Personal data is defined as "any information relating to an identified or identifiable natural person ('data subject'). An identifiable natural person is one who can be identified, directly or indirectly, in particular by reference to an identifier such as a name, an identification number, location data, an online identifier or to one or more factors specific to the physical, physiological, genetic, mental, economic, cultural or social identity of that natural person" (Art. 4 (1), GDPR).

In this paper, we will present an approach for defining the required protection level on CTI datasets, if they contain personal data, as defined by the GDPR. Based on the GDPR rules, this approach would help to make the decision of sharing and processing personal information clear. Moreover, it helps to provide some practical and clear rules to build data sharing agreements between organizations, because during the evaluation phase, we establish the purpose of the sharing, the legal basis and security measures for compliance with the law. This paper has two main contributions. First, to provide a decision process about sharing CTI datasets containing personal data in the context of the GDPR. Second, to convert existing legal grounds into rules that help organizations share such data whilst being legally compliant with the GDPR. These rules establish an association between the CTI policy space and the defined protection levels.

The remainder of this paper is organized as follows. Section 2 describes the steps of the methodology to build the approach. Section 3 gives several use cases of sharing CTI datasets to validate our approach. Section 4 discusses related work and finally Sect. 5 presents the conclusion and future research directions.

2 Methodology

This section presents the methodology we used to build an approach to evaluate the possibility of sharing personal data in the context of CTI datasets under the GDPR. The methodology consists of three main steps and is inspired by the DataTags project [8]. The first step is to define the possible levels of security requirements which agree with the principles considered by the GDPR when processing personal data in CTI datasets. The second step is to identify a *policy space*, i.e. a set of concepts, definitions, assertions and rules around the GDPR to describe the possible requirements for sharing CTI datasets. The last step is to build the decision graph, which defines the sequence of questions that should be traversed to establish and assess the legal requirements for CTI data sharing, represented with an outcome as so-called "tags". The DataTags project, developed by Latanya Sweeney's group at Harvard University, helps researchers and institutions to share their data with guarantees that releases of the data comply with the associated policy, including American health and educational legislation [9]. It consists of labelling a dataset with a specific tag based on a series of questions. Each question is created based on a set of assertions under the applicable policy.

2.1   Defining DataTags Related to Cybersecurity Information Sharing

The first step to achieving our goal is to define the tags that will be the possible decisions reached after a series of questions that interrogate CTI datasets for GDPR requirements. The legal requirements of the GDPR indicate in the first instance whether we can share or not. However, when the answer is positive, additional obligations for such sharing arise out of the principles and articles of the GDPR, in particular: the principle of data minimization; the requirement that personal data must be processed securely; and that the data must not be retained when no longer relevant. Hence, the decision process also leads to conclusions on how sharing can take place by translating these constraints into technical requirements. All of this is represented in the "data tags" of the leaves of our decision graph. The organizations that are sharing CTI datasets should ensure that the receiving organization understands the sensitivity of this information and receives clear instructions on what they are allowed to do with the information, e.g. potential on-sharing. We will follow the Traffic Light Protocol (TLP) [10] levels as a springboard, and expand them by adding security measures for each level in order to address the GDPR requirements of processing personal data when sharing CTI datasets. TLP was created to facilitate the sharing of information by tagging the information with a specific color. TLP has four colors, indicating different levels of acceptable distribution of data, namely [10]:

- WHITE - Unlimited.
- GREEN - Community Wide.
- AMBER - Limited Distribution.
- RED - Personal for Named Recipients Only.

This protocol records whether recipients may share this information with others. We have extended this protocol by adding appropriate security measures that are required for the legality of CTI sharing. To increase the trustworthiness between the entities and encourage entities to share CTI, we require the receiving organization to apply these security measures whilst keeping in mind that, in general, organizations use different approaches and levels of security practices. However, enforcing the receiver to apply these security measure is a challenge in itself and is beyond the scope of this paper. Table 2 shows the levels that we are going to use in order to label the shared datasets. Cells in columns "Type", "Description", and "Examples" are taken from the TLP description [11]. The values in columns "Security Measures" and "Transfer/Storage" are our proposals to meet the legislative requirements for securely sharing this data. We have proposed technical methods that would help organizations to achieve what the GDPR mandates as a technical requirements to ensure confidentiality and protect data subjects (Article 32). When proposing the security measures, we had to take into consideration with whom we are going to share CTI datasets and their trustworthiness because recipients who cannot be relied upon to protect the shared information need to be eliminated from further sharing.

We combine the notion of privacy preservation of the data with the trust level of the recipient organization, and because of that, we recommend the use of the Attribute-based Encryption (ABE) technique [12, 13]. For encryption, ABE can use any combination of a set of attributes as a public encryption key. Decryption privileges of the data in this type of encryption are not restricted to a particular identity but to entities with a set of attributes which may represent items such as business type and location. For example, an organization chooses to grant access to an encrypted log of its internet traffic, but restricts this to a specific range of IP addresses. Traditional encryption techniques would automatically disclose the log file in case the secret decryption key is released.

Table 1 lists example values of some attributes in the data. The first attribute is the location of the organization. Due to the different legal systems associated with international transfer information exchange, we will consider three levels: National, EU and International. The second attribute is the sector of the organization, because of the similarity of the working processes and procedures and likely similar threat models. The value might contain energy, health, education, finance and so on. Finally, the size of the organization may be relevant because the number of employees has been empirically related to the number of threats [14]. To use ABE, before sharing the data with other organizations and in case it is not shared to the public, the Setup Key Authority generates a master secret key along with a public key. It publishes the public key so everyone has access to it. The key authority uses the master secret key to generate a specific secret key for the participating organization in the sharing community. For example, there might be an organization called "Alpha" which gets a specific secret key from the key generator authority. "Alpha" is an organization operating at the national level in the telecom sector. Before sharing any dataset with "Alpha", the user will encrypt the dataset that has its own specific access policy. Hence, this user encrypts the dataset such that anyone at the national level working with the telecom business will be able to decrypt it. The organization sharing CTI datasets generates ciphertext with this policy. As a result, the organization "Alpha" will be able to decrypt the dataset.

Table 1. ABE attribute

Attribute	Value
Location	National, EU, Global
Organization sector/similarity of business	Central authority, similar business, connected groups, ...
Organization size	Small, medium, big

At all levels, Green, Amber and Red, data will be encrypted using the ABE method. In addition, we need to consider the data minimisation principle as defined in GDPR Art. 5(1)(c) "1. Personal data shall be: (c) adequate, relevant and limited to what is necessary in relation to the purposes for which they are processed (data minimisation)". Hence, sharing should be designed to provide only the required data to successfully achieve a specific goal. This implies that we should use the minimum amount of identifiable information to decrease any privacy risk on individuals whose personal data might be included. Doing so will reduce the risks of the following potential privacy attacks on the data:

Identity disclosure [15, 16]: this threat occurs when the attacker is able to connect a data subject with their record in a CTI dataset. For example, an attacker might identify a victim because the dataset contains direct identifying information such as an email address, IP address or credential information.

Membership disclosure [17]: this threat occurs when an attacker can derive that a specific data subject exists in the dataset. For example, the dataset contains information about specific malware victims. Any person established to be in the dataset reveals that this victim has been hacked by this malware.

Attribute disclosure [18]: this threat occurs when data subjects are linked with information about their sensitive attributes such as biometric data that is used to uniquely identify an individual. Some personal information is more sensitive and defined as a special category under the GDPR. The GDPR (Art. 9) defines special categories that need extra protection and prohibits processing this type of data unless certain conditions are applied.

There are methods to remove personal information from an individual's record in a way that decreases the possibility of all these attacks. Some of these methods that we can use are k-anonymity [15] which uses suppression and generalization as the main techniques, l-diversity [18, 19] which is an extension of k-anonymity to protect the shared data against background knowledge and Homogeneity Attacks, and t-closeness [20] which is another extension of l-diversity that decreases the granularity and makes the distribution of the sensitive attribute close to the distribution of the entire attribute.

Table 2. Proposed DataTags relating to four proposed classes of access

Type	Description	Examples	Security Measures	Transfer / Storage
WHITE	Information does not contain any personal data or sensitive information so it can be shared publicly.	Sharing public reports and notifications that give a better understanding of existing vulnerability.	Anonymization (Identity disclosure, Membership disclosure, Attribute disclosure).	Clear
GREEN	Information shared with community or a group of organizations but not shared publicly.	Sharing cybersecurity information within a close community. For example, sharing e-mail with malware link targeting specific sector.	Anonymization (Identity disclosure) Attribute-Based Encryption (ABE)	Encrypted
AMBER	Share information with a specific organization; sharing confined within the organization to take effective action based on it.	Sharing cybersecurity information that contains indicators of compromise, course of action to a specific community or sector e.g. financial sector.	Anonymization (Identity disclosure) Attribute-Based Encryption (ABE)	Encrypted
RED	Information exclusively and directly given to Central Authority. Sharing outside is not legitimate.	Sharing that you have been attacked or notifying central authority about an incident.	Attribute-Based Encryption (ABE). Data Minimization to share only relevant data.	Encrypted

2.2 Policy Space

We build the policy space of our model as a set of assertions using the context of the CTI dataset. The evaluation of cases will be based on the defined assertions. The assertions will contain the legal grounds under which personal data can be processed, in this case for the purpose of ensuring network and information security. For instance, assertions for sharing CTI information with other parties are based on both the purpose of sharing which is "GDPR Recital 49 - ensuring network and information security" such as the prevention of any access to the critical system after credentials leaks, and the related legal basis which is "GDPR Art 6.1 (c) - processing is necessary for the purposes of the legitimate interests pursued by the controller or by a third party". These steps offer a clear, practical framework, justifying the sharing of cyber threat Intelligence. The tagged data which meets the rules based on applicable assertions will be derived from the decision graph. In order to build the CTI policy space, we use a JSON file maintained by Computer Incident Response Center Luxembourg CIRCL [21] for the related context of use of data by CSIRTs. The goal of the file is to track processing personal information activities and support automation. Many assertions refer to the GDPR Art. 30 which prescribes all the recordable details of processing activities. The main categories of the assertions contain:

- Purpose: "The purpose of the processing. Ref GDPR Art. 30 (1) (b)"
- Legal ground: "Lawfulness/grounds for the processing activity. Ref GDPR Art. 6 & 5 (a)."
- Data subjects: "Categories of the data subjects. Reference GDPR Art. 30 (1) (c)."
- Personal data: "Personal data processed. Reference GDPR Art. 30 (1) (c)."
- Recipients: GDPR Art. 30 (1) (d).
- International transfer: "Whether any personal data in this processing activity is transferred to a third country or an international organization. Reference GDPR Art. 30 (1) (e)".
- Retention period: "Retention schedule/storage limitation. Reference GDPR Art. 30 (1) (f) and Art. 5 (e)".
- Security measures: "Security measures & Integrity & Confidentiality. Security measures can be technical and/or organizational. Reference GDPR Art. 30 (1) (e), 32 (1) and Art. 5 (f)."

Based on the previous assertion list, we need to extract the relevant assertions categories specifically related to CTI sharing. We will consider only those assertions that are directly related to CTI sharing. In the GDPR the purpose of processing personal data should be precise and for that the GDPR offers clear recognition of "ensuring network and information security" GDPR Recital 49 as the purpose of processing personal data for actors such as public authorities and CSIRTs. The legal grounds for processing personal data are provided in GDPR Art. 6 & 5 (a). CIRCL has published a discussion [22] of the legal grounds of information leak analysis and the GDPR context of collection, analysis and sharing information leaks. The legal grounds relevant in our context are "processing is necessary for the compliance with a legal obligation to which the controller is subject" where it applies to CSIRTs and data protection authorities and "processing is necessary for the purposes of the legitimate interests pursued by the controller or by a third party" otherwise. In the "legitimate interest" sharing CTI information will enable organizations to better detect and prevent attacks by, for example, identifying the IP address of a malware communications and control hub. We do not consider "consent" GDPR Art. 6 (1) (a) a credible legal basis for processing personal data in the context of sharing cyber threat Intelligence. This is because it is very hard to get consent of data subjects especially when dealing with huge amounts of data [22] (e.g. 1bn Yahoo accounts were compromised from a 2013 hack [23]) or when personal data such as IP addresses concerns the perpetrator of a cyber-attack. Also, the vital interest Art. 6 (1) (d) is not feasible to be used to justify sharing and processing CTI. The rationale is most likely there is no personal data in CTI datasets which would relate to a threat to life. However, the public interest Art. 6 (1) (e) would be the justification to process personal data in the case of acting under specific authorization from an official authority to check that the cyber incident could affect the public interest. The description of the personal data that pertains directly to the GDPR is described in Art. 30 (1) (c). The conditions under which personal data can be transferred to third countries or an international organization are described in GDPR Art. 30 (1) (e). As a result, the CTI policy space is described in Fig. 1.

2.3 Decision Graph

In this step, we propose an assessment based on the previous assertions. This assessment contains a set of questions, and the answer to each question will lead to different questions or a final decision and as a result, we will assign a specific tag to the CTI dataset or even in some cases, the decision would be to not share. This assessment is not definitive, but it gives a chance to reflect on our understanding of sharing CTI datasets under the GDPR. Figure 2 shows the decision graph for sharing CTI datasets under the GDPR. Some of the decisions in the graph still require human judgement, so we make no claims of the process being fully automatable. This judgement could be assisted by the Data Protection Officer (DPO) whose main duties are ensuring compliance with the GDPR and providing support regarding data protection (Article 37) (Recital 97). The GDPR requires the appointment of a DPO in a public authority or organisations performing specific risky types of processing actions (Article 37) (Recital 97).

The process first establishes whether the proposed data sharing falls within the scope of the GDPR. Then it establishes the legal basis for any special category data included. This is likely to be rare in CTI datasets, but we could imagine biometric data following an attack that included a physical breach. Next, it establishes the legal basis for the overall processing. Then, it checks and selects appropriate retention and security protections. We assume the "trust level" node's result has been determined based on previous knowledge of the trustworthiness of the entity that we are sharing with. The outcome matches one of the TLP tags as described in the previous section. Of course, the CTI datasets are also likely to contain "sensitive" information about the infected asset and the exploitable vulnerability that should be protected. The outcome reflects concerns for the data protection angle only; included information that is sensitive in a different dimension might require strengthening of the security measures.

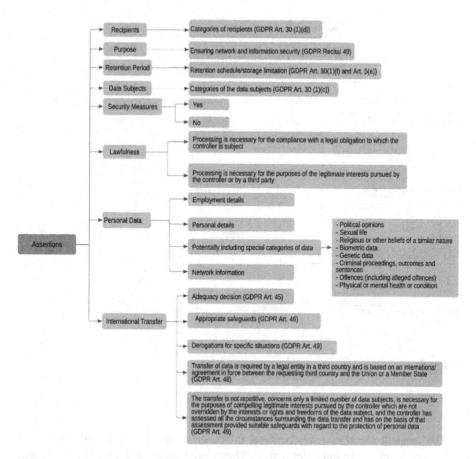

Fig. 1. CTI policy space

3 Use Cases

Sharing information regarding current or ongoing attacks including information on threat actors, attack vectors, victims and impact of the attack is an essential scenario of sharing cyber threat Intelligence. In order to see how to apply the tags on CTI datasets two different use cases were developed. In the first use case, the organization that is the victim informs a central authority about the attack. In the second use case, an organization informs another organization about a recent attack that affects the availably, confidentiality or integrity of services.

Use Case 1: Informing Central Authority

This case study consists of two organizations, A and C (Central Authority) where an organization A wants to report an incident to organization C about a remote access tool (RAT) used by different threat actors. Before sharing the information, the reporter wants to be sure that sharing it is legitimate under the GDPR.

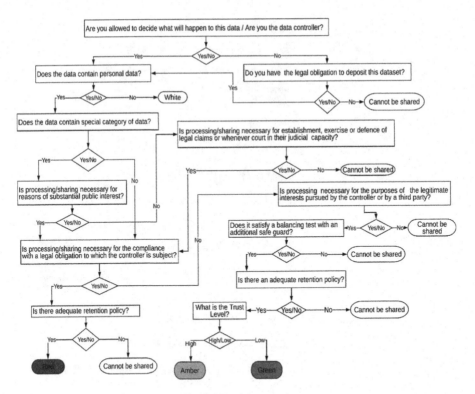

Fig. 2. Decision graph

The incident report contains personal information such as contact information of the reporter and credential information. Therefore, sharing and processing of such personal data would need to be legitimate under the GDPR. In order to decide how to share this information, the reporter needs to run an evaluation. The organization A is the owner of this dataset and has the right to process this information, hence in this scenario the organization A is considered the controller. Although the incident information contains personal data, it does not contain any special category data, such as, biometrics or political opinion, religious or philosophical beliefs, etc. In order to share this information with a Computer Security Incident Reporting Team CSIRT or the central authority, the reporter can rely on GDPR Art. 6 (1) (c) where the legal ground states "processing is necessary for the compliance with a legal obligation to which the controller is subject". Organization A has a retention policy in place. The security measures that should be applied to reduce the risk of harm to data subjects before sharing this dataset are: encrypted storage associated with a secure protocol to transmit this information. Moreover, the data will be encrypted by using ABE techniques with the properties (National, CA, Big) so as a result the final tag for this data will be RED. Figure 3 shows a sample questionnaire covering this case study.

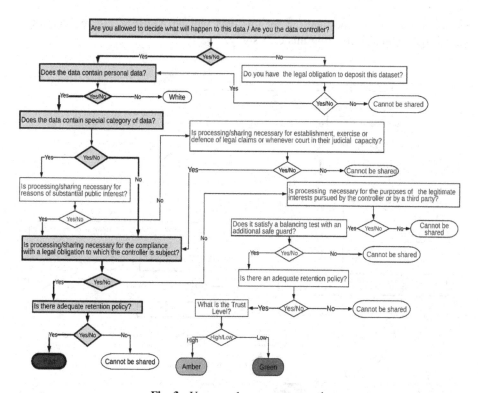

Fig. 3. Use case 1 assessment graph

Use Case 2: Sharing Information About Port Scanning For Incident Prevention

Suppose an organization O1 in the energy sector detects port scanning from a specific IP address for port range 0–1023 which is considered a potential threat. For incident prevention purposes, they may want to share information containing the source IP address, port range, the time of the incident, signs of the incident, and the course of action such as improve monitoring on these ports.

The personal information in this scenario consists of the reporter information along with that of the individual who has made the observations. Organization O1 is the controller of this data and needs to share this information with trusted company O2. Because the dataset contains personal information, sharing needs to be legitimate under the GDPR. The dataset does not contain any special category data so we can continue and check the purpose of this sharing, which is the GDPR Recital 49 – "ensuring network and information security". The reporter can rely on the GDPR Art. 6 (1) (f). The legal ground for sharing this information is "processing is necessary for the purposes of the legitimate interests pursued by the controller or by a third party". Presumably there is a retention policy in place. The security measures that will be associated before sharing this dataset are: encrypted storage associated with a secure protocol to transmit this information, Anonymization against any Identity disclosure and the data will be encrypted by using ABE techniques associated with the properties (EU, Energy sector, Medium). The trust level based on an assumed external calculation is high so as a result the final tag for this data will be AMBER. Figure 4 shows a sample questionnaire covering this case study.

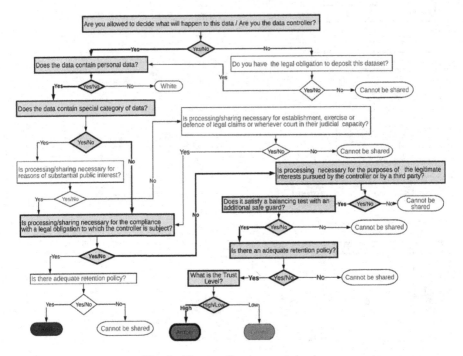

Fig. 4. Use case 2 assessment graph

As a result, we present two use cases for sharing CTI datasets between different entities. The datasets have been evaluated based on the decision graph built in Sect. 2. The decision is positive in both use cases, but it associated with different protection levels based on the flow of the assertions. Hence, our approach can give any organization intends to share CTI datasets the ability to determine that they are legally compliant with the GDPR.

4   Related Work

Many papers have addressed issues related to terms and rules extracted from regulations and policies for protecting personal data. K. Fatema, Chadwick, and Van Alsenoy [24] converted the precursor of the GDPR, the 1995 EU Data Protection Directive [25] into executable rules to support access control policies. The authors presented a system to automate legal access control policy to make automated decision concerning authorization rights and obligations based on the related legal requirements. Doorn and Thomas [26] developed a specialized tool for privacy control based on the GDPR to share sensitive research datasets. The authors defined the security measures of the data tags levels based on the DANS EASY repository [27]. The authors focused on datasets managed by researchers in a general context. Breaux and Antón [28, 29] worked to extract data access rights from a legal test of the US Health Insurance Portability and Accountability Act (HIPAA). They used ontology to classify legal rules of privacy requirements from regulations to give a decision to grant or deny the access right. In [30] Schweighofer, Kieseberg and Kieseberg, a privacy by design solution to exchanging cyber security incident information between CSIRTs is presented. This solution focused only on sharing information between closed user circles such as the CSIRTs. The authors aimed to illustrate the legal requirements about sharing CTI datasets which contain personal information between the CSIRTs without giving a systematic way to help the CTI datasets manager to check the legality of sharing such information. In our work, we aim to build a set of sharing requirements that CTI datasets managers will check to provide a decision about sharing CTI dataset(s) under the GDPR.

5 Conclusion and Future Work

In this work, we have presented an approach that can help different entities to make a decision compliant with the GDPR when sharing CTI datasets. We have suggested adequate privacy preserving methods that should be applied when sharing CTI datasets. Then we have defined the policy space that related to the CTI in the context of the GDPR and finally built the decision graph that checks the legal requirements and provides a decision on how to share this information.

There are limitations in our approach. In complex use cases, the decisions in the assessment graph may still be very demanding, such as whether the Recital 49 objective justifies any privacy impacts on the data subject. Furthermore, including additional regulations or local policies besides the way they will interact with the GDPR requirements would make the decision graph more complex. Additional legal and technical requirements might make the data tag collection harder to structure and manage, as well as complicating the decision process.

In our previous work [2], we have identified the associated threats of disclosing CTI. Here we have specifically addressed the legal risks associated with sharing CTI datasets. Our overall work aims to mitigate all threats associated with sharing CTI datasets and improve the sharing process. As future work, we will extend the current model to evaluate the trust level and the associated risks in more detail. In addition, we intend to study the tradeoff between the privacy preservation and utility of processing CTI datasets.

Acknowledgment. This work has received funding from the European Union Framework Programme for Research and Innovation Horizon 2020 under grant agreement No 675320.

References

1. Skopik, F., Settanni, G., Fiedler, R.: A problem shared is a problem halved: a survey on the dimensions of collective cyber defense through security information sharing. Comput. Secur. **60**, 154–176 (2016)
2. Albakri, A., Boiten, E., De Lemos, R.: Risks of sharing cyber incident information. In: Proceedings of International Conference on Availability, Reliability and Security, Hamburg, Germany, 10 p. (2018)
3. Sweeney, L.: Operationalizing american jurisprudence for data sharing, Technical report (2013)
4. Personal Information Protection Commission: Amended Act on the Protection of Personal Information (2016). https://www.ppc.go.jp/files/pdf/Act_on_the_Protection_of_Personal_Information.pdf. Accessed 03 Jan 2019
5. European Union: Regulation 2016/679 of the European parliament and the Council of the European Union of 27 April 2016 on the protection of natural persons with regard to the processing of personal data and on the free movement of such data, and repealing Directive 95/46/. Official J. Eur. Communities **59**, 1–88 (2016)
6. ENISA: Directive on security of network and information systems (2017). https://ec.europa.eu/digital-single-market/en/network-and-information-security-nis-directive. Accessed: 13 Dec 2018
7. ENISA: Information Security Agency, 'A step-by-step approach on how to set up a CSIRT', WP2006/5.1, 86 (2006)
8. Bar-Sinai, M., Sweeney, L., Crosas, M.: DataTags, data handling policy spaces and the tags language. In: Proceedings - 2016 IEEE Symposium on Security and Privacy Workshops, SPW 2016, pp. 1–8 (2016)
9. Sweeney, L., Crosas, M., Bar-Sinai, M.: Sharing sensitive data with confidence: the datatags system. Technol. Sci. 2015101601 (2015). https://techscience.org/a/2015101601
10. IFIRST.ORG: Traffic Light Protocol (TLP) (2001). https://www.first.org/tlp/. Accessed 14 Aug 2018
11. CIRCL: Traffic Light Protocol (TLP) - Classification and Sharing of Sensitive Information (2018). https://www.circl.lu/pub/traffic-light-protocol/. Accessed 29 Sept 2018
12. Goyal, V., Pandey, O., Sahai, A., Waters, B.: Attribute-based encryption for fine-grained access control of encrypted data. In: Proceedings of the 13th ACM Conference on Computer and Communications Security - CCS 2006, pp. 89–98 (2006)
13. Bethencourt, J., Sahai, A., Waters, B.: Ciphertext-policy attribute-based encryption. In: Proceedings - IEEE Symposium on Security and Privacy, pp. 321–334 (2007)
14. Johnson, M.E.: Information risk of inadvertent disclosure: an analysis of file-sharing risk in the financial supply chain. J. Manag. Inf. Syst. **25**(2), 97–124 (2008)
15. Sweeney, L.: k-Anonymity: a model for protecting privacy. Int. J. Uncertainty, Fuzziness Knowl.-Based Syst., **10**(05), 557–570 (2002)
16. Xiao, X., Tao, Y.: Personalized privacy preservation. In: Proceedings of the 2006 ACM SIGMOD International Conference on Management of Data - SIGMOD 2006, pp. 229–240 (2006)
17. Nergiz, M.E., Atzori, M., Clifton, C.: Hiding the presence of individuals from shared databases. In: Proceedings of the 2007 ACM SIGMOD International Conference on Management of Data - SIGMOD 2007, pp. 665–676 (2007)
18. Kifer, D.: L-diversity : privacy beyond k–Anonymity. In: Proceedings of the 22nd International Conference on Data Engineering, pp. 24–36 (2006)

19. Machanavajjhala, A., Gehrke, J., Kifer, D., Venkitasubramaniam, M.L.: L-diversity: privacy beyond k-anonymity. In: Proceedings - International Conference on Data Engineering, p. 24 (2006)
20. Ninghui, L., Tiancheng, L., Venkatasubramanian, S.: t-closeness: privacy beyond k-anonymity and l-diversity. In: Proceedings of the International Conference on Data Engineering, no. 2, pp. 106–115 (2007)
21. CIRCL: Legal compliance and CSIRT activities (2018). https://github.com/CIRCL/compliance. Accessed 29 Sept 2018
22. CIRCL: AIL information leaks analysis and the GDPR in the context of collection, analysis and sharing information leaks (2018). https://www.circl.lu/assets/files/information-leaks-analysis-and-gdpr.pdf. Accessed: 20 Dec 2018
23. Thielman, S.: Yahoo hack: 1 bn accounts compromised by biggest data breach in history, The Guardian (UK) (2016). https://www.theguardian.com/technology/2016/dec/14/yahoo-hack-security-of-one-billion-accounts-breached. Accessed 24 Oct 2018
24. Fatema, K., Chadwick, D.W., Van Alsenoy, B.: Extracting access control and conflict resolution policies from European data protection law. In: IFIP Advances in Information and Communication Technology, vol. 375, pp. 59–72. AICT (2012)
25. Directive 95/46/EC of the European Parliament and of the Council of 24 October 1995 on the protection of individuals with regard to the processing of personal data and on the free movement of such data (1995)
26. Doorn, P., Thomas, E.: Tagging privacy-sensitive data according to the new European privacy legislation: GDPR DataTags - a prototype (2017). https://dans.knaw.nl/en/current/first-gdpr-datatags-results-presented-in-workshop. Accessed 20 Dec 2018
27. Tjalsma, H.: Data Archiving and Networked Services (DANS) (2012). https://easy.dans.knaw.nl/. Accessed 24 Oct 2018
28. Breaux, T.D., Antón, A.I.: Analyzing regulatory rules for privacy and security requirements. IEEE Trans. Softw. Eng. 34(1), 5–20 (2008)
29. Breaux, T.D., Antón, A.I.: A systematic method for acquiring regulatory requirements: a frame-based approach. In: RHAS-6 (2007)
30. Schweighofer, E., Heussler, V., Kieseberg, P.: Privacy by design data exchange between CSIRTs. In: Schweighofer, E., Leitold, H., Mitrakas, A., Rannenberg, K. (eds.) APF 2017. LNCS, vol. 10518, pp. 104–119. Springer, Cham (2017). https://doi.org/10.1007/978-3-319-67280-9_6

Users' Rights

Fight to Be Forgotten: Exploring the Efficacy of Data Erasure in Popular Operating Systems

Andreas Gutmann[1,3(✉)] and Mark Warner[2,3]

[1] OneSpan Cambridge Innovation Centre, Cambridge, UK
[2] University College London Interaction Centre, London, UK
[3] University College London Information Security Group, London, UK
{a.gutmann,m.warner}@cs.ucl.ac.uk

Abstract. A long history of longitudinal and intercultural research has identified decommissioned storage devices (e.g., USB memory sticks) as a serious privacy and security threat. Sensitive data deleted by previous owners have repeatedly been found on second-hand USB sticks through forensic analysis. Such data breaches are unlikely to occur when data is securely *erased*, rather than being *deleted*. Yet, research shows people confusing these two terms. In this paper, we report on an investigation of possible causes for this confusion. We analysed the user interface of two popular operating systems and found: (1) inconsistencies in the language used around delete and erase functions, (2) insecure default options, and (3) unclear or incomprehensible information around delete and erase functions. We discuss how this could result in data controllers becoming non-compliant with a legal obligation for erasure, putting data subjects at risk of accidental data breaches from the decommissioning of storage devices. Finally, we propose improvements to the design of relevant user interface elements and the development of official guidelines for best practice on GDPR compatible data erasure procedures.

Keywords: Privacy evaluation · Data erasure · GDPR · Cognitive Walkthrough

1 Introduction

The right to erasure (or 'right to be forgotten') in Article 17 of the General Data Protection Regulation (GDPR) is considered by some to be the most difficult obligation to comply with [3, p. 64]. It states that data subjects can, with certain exceptions, have their personal data erased by the responsible data controller. Moreover, it states that personal data should also be erased without undue delay under other circumstances. For example, where the data is no longer required for the purposes it was originally collected, or when the data subject withdraws consent on which the processing was based. The UK's national data protection authority (ICO) states that data which is subject to a valid erasure request must

M. Naldi et al. (Eds.): APF 2019, LNCS 11498, pp. 45–58, 2019.
https://doi.org/10.1007/978-3-030-21752-5_4

be placed "beyond use, even if it cannot be immediately overwritten" and can, in certain circumstances, pose a significant data protection risk [5].

The terms 'delete' and 'erase' are often used interchangeably. The Merriam Webster thesaurus lists both words as related[1], whilst the Oxford and Cambridge dictionaries list them as synonyms[2]. Yet, in computer science these words have a different meaning, and the distinction between the two has consequences for compliance with data protection legislation.

From a technical perspective these terms describe different concepts. Erase typically describes purposeful overwriting of data with other data – rendering it immediately irretrievable – whilst delete typically refers to data being "forgotten" by the operating system (OS) and being marked as available for overwrite. This allows new data to be stored in its place when required, but is often retrievable until it has been overwritten.

It is perhaps unsurprising that confusion exists between these two terms due to their linguistic similarity and interchangeable use in everyday conversation. Yet, problems can emerge if a data controller is unaware of the technical differences, with significant risks developing that could lead to exposure through non-compliance with data protection legislation. For example, deleting rather than erasing data from a decommissioned storage device could result in a data breach. As most delete and erase operations are executed through a computer's OS, the user interface (UI) of these OS are well positioned to provide users with guidance on the appropriate use of delete and erase operations to limit confusion between these terms.

In this paper we report on an analytical investigation of potential conflicts between UI file removal functions in macOS 10.14 and Windows 10, and legal requirements for data erasure. We use accidental data breaches from decommissioned USB sticks as the context for a streamlined Cognitive Walkthrough to explore the gap between the legal data protection requirements for the erasure of data, and file removal functions in two popular OS. In doing so, we discover linguistic confusion within the UI of these OS, which could lead to increased uncertainty when data controllers undertake their legal obligation to erase data. As a result, our research identifies a need for guidelines and best practice on GDPR compliant erasure. We present a set of implications for practice that could be used to improve consistency between UIs and data protection legislation. Finally, our research evidences the importance of further investigations into the suitability of those tools most commonly used by non-experts to comply with regulatory requirements.

2   Background

In this section we first explore previous research into people's data hygiene, taking a particular focus on the hygiene of decommissioned storage devices. We

---

[1] https://www.merriam-webster.com/thesaurus/delete.

[2] https://en.oxforddictionaries.com/thesaurus/delete
https://dictionary.cambridge.org/dictionary/english/delete.

then explore some of the technical nuances of delete and erase operations using modern day technologies.

2.1 Personal Data Hygiene

A large number of publications dating back to 2005 provide both longitudinal and intercultural insights into people's data hygiene. Researchers typically buy second-hand storage devices on the open market and forensically analyse them, and report their findings. The first of these studies was conducted on second-hand hard-disk drives (HDD) purchased in the UK back in 2005 [17] and was repeated yearly until 2009 [7]. Similar studies have be conducted on second-hand USB storage devices (e.g., [6]), and mobile phones (e.g., [16]). Studies of this nature are also not limited to the UK market, with similar research being carried out in other parts of the world (e.g., Australia [14] and USA [1]). Consistent across these studies is the presence of sensitive personal data from a large number of decommissioned drives due to failures in the erasure process. Jones *et al.* [7], for example, forensically analysed USB sticks bought in the UK and recovered personal data which included: birth certificates, videos of children at a school, client data, and police staff records (names and date of birth).

In addition, memory chips from decommissioned devices are commonly recycled into new electronics, even though some of their old content may still be available and could be recovered [9,10]. The risk of data breaches from recycled memory chips is likely to increase due to Directive 2012/19/EU on 'waste electrical and electronic equipment'. Article 4 aims at encouraging "cooperation between producers and recyclers" to integrate more recycled material in new equipment and Article 5 gives priority to achieving high recycle rates for small IT devices such as USB sticks.

Diesburg *et al.* [1] compared people's data hygiene practices with their intentions when decommissioning USB sticks, and found people regularly confusing delete and erase functions. The authors recovered data from 83.3% of USB sticks where previous owners anticipated it being "very hard" to recover.

In summary, people often fail to appropriately erase sensitive data when decommissioning USB sticks, and these devices can cause data breaches when sold as second-hand devices or recycled into new electronics.

2.2 Delete and Erase Functions

When files are written to a storage device, the device must be running some type of file system (e.g., FAT, NTFS). The job of a file systems is to keep a record of the existence and location of all files and folders written to the storage device. When a file is deleted, the record of the file is deleted, but the file's content remains and can usually be recovered. Over time, when additional files are written to the device, the deleted files may become overwritten, at which point they are no longer recoverable [4].

To improve the security around file deletion, *DoD 5220 Block Erase* requires that a file is overwritten (erased) a minimum of three times and then verified.

An even higher level of security is obtained by erasing an entire storage device, ideally using the device's internal secure erase function. These functions can either execute a slow secure wipe operation, or in more modern drives can quickly delete cryptographic keys that were used to encrypt each file on the device, making the data permanently unintelligible [4].

3   Methodology

We investigate and compare the UI for removing files in both macOS 10.14 and Windows 10. We focus on these two OS as they account for more than 97% of the desktop/laptop OS market share [12]. We perform an exploratory data collection using a streamlined Cognitive Walkthrough (CW) method to gain insights into how users may perceive the functionality of file removal operations in macOS 10.14 and Windows 10.

CW is a commonly used method for evaluating how well a system supports users towards achieving their goals. It places a particular focus on the users cognitive activities, e.g. their goals and knowledge [8]. This method is characterised by having an evaluator work through a series of tasks from the user's perspective, and to evaluate the systems ability to provide users with cues and prompts to guide them towards task completion.

We oriented ourselves on the process described by Rieman *et al.* [13] and Spencer [15] to prepare our CW. The context is defined by the UI's of macOS 10.14 and Windows 10. The user has basic familiarity with both systems and understands that the terms 'erase' and 'delete' denote similar concepts. The two goals were to (1) erase a single file on a USB memory stick and (2) erase all files on a USB memory stick. The necessary sequence of actions consist of locating the target for erasure, the appropriate UI elements to erase the file, and lastly erasing the file.

We installed both OS on separate devices and ensured that they were fully patched. We followed the streamlined CW approach by Spencer [15], conducting a step-by-step analysis of how the UI could guide the user attempting to execute the necessary sequence of correct actions. At each step of this process, we assess the visual cues available for the next action and the feedback given to the user after each action.

3.1   Forensic Analysis

Prior to each CW we restored the test USB stick back to its "factory state" and analysed it with FTK Imager Lite 3.4.3.3[3] to confirm that no residual data was residing on the device. We then created a text file containing *lorem ipsum* placeholder text, and saved this file inside a folder on the USB stick. At the end of each CW, we forensically analysed the USB stick with FTK Imager Lite to determine whether the CW had resulted in a delete or erase operation.

---

[3] https://forensicswiki.org/wiki/FTK_Imager.

The CW were conducted by the first author and evidenced with screenshots and note taking. The second author sighted the screenshots and notes and verified that they fulfilled the necessary sequence of actions, and were consistent with a typical user being guided by UI cues and prompts.

4 Results

In this section we report on the results from our CW following the process described in Sect. 3. Although we maintained a detailed record of step-by-step user actions during each CW, we limit our reporting to UI screens presented to users that are relevant to either delete or erase functions. We present findings from a total of nine goal-oriented CW using two different OS. We then report the results from our forensic analyses which determine the effectiveness of these functions. In doing so, we can identify any inconsistencies between the UI's reported functionality and the underlying technical operation.

4.1 macOS 10.14

Goal: Erase a Single File. To remove a file from a USB stick, the user can locate the USB stick in the *Finder* application and move the file to *Trash*. As the file is still visible in the *Trash*, the user can attempt to further remove it using either of two methods. (1) The user can right mouse button click on the file to open the context menu, and select *"Delete Immediately..."*. This opens a new dialogue window, which will inform the user that this action will immediately delete the file (see Fig. 1a) and cannot be undone. The CW concludes when the user confirms the operation by selecting the *"Delete"* button. (2) The user can right mouse button click on the *Trash* symbol in the *Dock* to open the context menu, and select *"Empty Trash"*. This opens a new dialogue window, which informs the user that this action will permanently erase all files in the *Trash* and cannot be undone (see Fig. 1b). The CW concludes when the user confirms the operation by selecting the *"Empty Trash"* button. Under both conditions our forensic analysis was able to recover the test file.

(a) Dialogue when deleting a single file from the *Trash*.

(b) Dialogue when deleting all files from the *Trash*.

Fig. 1. macOS 10.14 dialogues when deleting the test file from the *Trash*.

Goal: Erase all Files on a USB Stick. To remove all files on the USB stick, the user has two options. (1) They can remove all files similar to the removal of a single file (see above). Using this method entails that the files are deleted and likely to be recoverable under a forensic examination. Alternatively, (2) the user can launch the *Disk Utility* application, and select the *"Erase"* option on the top feature bar. This opens a new dialogue window, which informs the user that this action will delete all data stored on the USB stick and cannot be undone. (see Fig. 2). The CW concludes when the user confirms the operation by selecting the *"Erase"* button. Our subsequent forensic analysis was able to recover the test file.

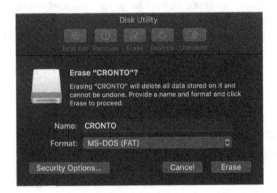

Fig. 2. macOS 10.14 dialogue when erasing the USB stick with *Disk Utility*.

In a variation to the above procedure, the user can select the *"Security Options"* prior to selecting the *"Erase"* button. This opens a new dialogue window (see Fig. 3) where the user can select a range of security options. On the default option, the dialogue window informs the user that this will not securely erase the files and disk recovery applications may recover them. For the other three options, the dialogue window informs the user that the function will erase the data. The CW concludes when the user makes a selection and confirms the operation when selecting the *"OK"* button followed by the *"Erase"* button (see Fig. 2). Our forensic analysis was able to recovery the test file when using the default security option, but unable to recover the file when using any of the other three secure erase options.

4.2   Windows 10

Goal: Erase a Single File. To remove the test file from the USB stick, the user can locate the USB stick in the *Explorer* application and physically press the keyboard delete button whilst the file is selected. This opens a new dialogue

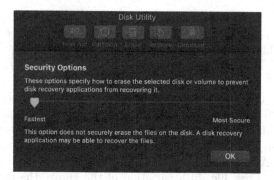

Fig. 3. macOS 10.14 dialogue to select *Security Options* when erasing the USB stick with *Disk Utility*. The lower description changes as different options are selected on the horizontal slider.

window[4], which informs the user that this action will permanently delete the file (see Fig. 4). The CW concludes when the user confirms this operation by selecting the *"Yes"* button. Our subsequent forensic analysis was able to recover the test file.

Fig. 4. Windows 10 dialogue when deleting the test file from the USB stick.

Goal: Erase all Files on a USB Stick. To remove all files on the USB stick, the user has three options: they can (1) proceed similarly to the removal of a single file[5] (see above), (2) access the *"Format"* dialogue from the *Explorer*, or (3) access the application *"Disk Management"*.

If the user chooses to access the *Format* dialogue in *Explorer*, a new dialogue window opens (see Fig. 5a), where the user can confirm the operation by selecting *"Start"*. A second dialogue window informs the user that this will erase all data (see Fig. 6). The CW concludes when the user confirms this operation by selecting *"OK"*. After performing this quick format operation, our forensic analysis was

---

[4] Windows 10 treated our USB stick as 'removable media', which is why files were not placed in the *Recycle Bin* first. This might differ under other circumstances but is unlikely to affect the overall result of this CW.

[5] This option would entail that the files are deleted and likely to be recoverable under a forensic examination.

able to recover the test file. In a variation to the above, the user deselects *"Quick Format"* (which is selected by default) before selecting *"Start"*. Our forensic analysis was unable to recover the test file after this operation.

If the user chooses to access the *Disk Management* application, they can select *"Format..."* from the context menu of the USB stick. This opens a new dialogue window (see Fig. 5b), where the user can confirm the operation by selecting the *"OK"* button. A second dialogue window informs the user that this will erase all data and suggests making a backup before formatting the USB stick (see Fig. 6b). The CW concludes when the user confirms the operation by selecting *"OK"*. After performing this quick format, our forensic analysis was able to recover the test file. In a variation of the above, the user can deselect *"Perform a quick format"* (which is selected by default) before selecting *"OK"*. Consistent with previous results our forensic analysis was unable to recover the test file.

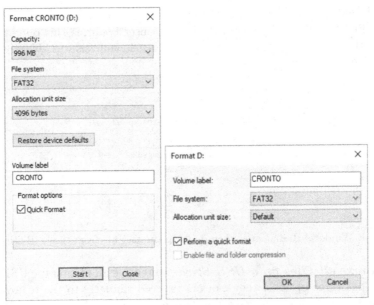

(a) Format dialogue accessed via *Explorer*.

(b) Format dialogue accessed via *Disk Management*.

Fig. 5. Windows 10 dialogues when erasing the USB stick.

Alternatively, within the *Disk Management* application, the user can select *"Delete Volume..."* from the context menu of the USB stick. This opens a new dialogue window, which informs the user that the action will erase all data and suggests making a backup before deleting the USB stick (see Fig. 6c). The CW concludes when the user confirms the action by selecting the *"OK"* button.

After performing this delete volume operation, our forensic analysis was able to recover the test file.

(a) Dialogue when selecting to start *For-matting* a USB stick in fig. 5a (*Explorer*).

(b) Dialogue when confirming the *Formatting* of a USB stick in fig. 5b (*Disk Management*).

(c) Dialogue when confirming to *Delete Volume* of USB stick. (*Disk Management*)

Fig. 6. Windows 10 confirmation dialogues for formatting and deleting a volume.

4.3 Results of Forensic Analysis

Our CW identified three methods for removing a file from a test USB stick when using macOS 10.14, and six methods when using Windows 10. However, after completing a forensic examination of our test USB stick after performing each method, the test file was fully recoverable after two of the file removal methods in macOS, and after four of the file removal methods in Windows 10. (see Table 1).

5 Discussion

Modern OS for computers commonly provide accessible data delete functionality to users. Yet, data erasure functions for entire drives are typically located at deeper levels of administrative tools, whilst functionality to erasure individual files is not provided without expert knowledge or the use of third-party software.

Restricting these functions can protect users from accidental data loss. However, omitting information, guidance, and functionality can place lay users – especially those in the role of data controller – at risk of causing accidental data breaches. This could result in data subjects having their data exposed, and organisations being non-compliant with data protection legislation.

In the following section we discuss the results from our investigation of delete and erase functions in macOS and Windows, and suggest alternative UI design

Table 1. Summary of our forensic analysis for various methods to remove data from USB sticks. Data removed with a delete function was successfully recovered, data removed with an erase function was not recoverable.

System	Function	Forensic evaluation	
		Deletion	Erasure
macOS 10.14	**Goal** Erase single file		
	➤ Finder	✓	
	Goal Erase all files		
	➤ Disk Utility (default options)	✓	
	➤ Disk Utility (changed options)		✓
Windows 10	**Goal** Erase single file		
	➤ Explorer	✓	
	Goal Erase all files		
	➤ Explorer Format (default options)	✓	
	➤ Explorer Format (changed options)		✓
	➤ Disk Management Delete Volume	✓	
	➤ Disk Management Format (default options)	✓	
	➤ Disk Management Format (changed options)		✓

approaches. We focus on default options and the terminology used to label and describe these functions in the UI; and then discuss the relevance of sufficient guidance for users. Entwined into these discussions, we argue for OS-dependent changes to the UI and highlight OS-independent implications of our findings.

5.1 Default Options

macOS 10.14 and Windows 10 provide functionality to securely erase all data from a USB stick. Yet, both OS use default options that reduce the effectiveness of these functions. We suspect that these default options are designed to increase the speed in which these operations are executed, with delete operations being much faster then erase operations to execute. Under macOS 10.14, the *Disk Utility* application contains security options (see Fig. 3) to "specify how to erase the selected disk". Its default option contains a description that the files may be recoverable using certain data recovery applications. Figure 5 shows two UI screens for formatting a drive in Windows 10, with options "Quick Format" and "Perform a quick format" preselected. These options do not provide the user with any form of description. In both OS we were able to recover the test file when these default options were set.

Defaulting an option is commonly understood by users as a recommendation, reducing the likelihood of other options being selected by the user [11]. In the context of this research, default options discourage users from securely erasing files. Yet, those users might have significant interests in a secure erasure. We recommend an active selection process which encourages users to make an informed decision. In Windows 10, for example, the single confirmation button in

Fig. 5 could be replaced with two confirmation buttons to actively select between "Quick Format" and "Full Format".

5.2 Incorrect Terminology

Inconsistent and incorrect terminology was used for delete and erase functions across both OS. For example deleting a file (or multiple files) from the *Trash* in macOS is labelled as both *delete* and *erase*, depending on whether a single file or all files are deleted (see Fig. 1). However, our forensic analysis found that both of these functions perform a delete operation, as in both cases the test file was fully recoverable.

Incorrect use of the terms delete and erase in OS UI might reinforce colloquial use and foster the misunderstanding that they denote the same technical function. This interferes with users' ability to make informed decisions. We argue the terms erase and delete should be used exclusively in relation to their technical meaning. In some cases the outcome of an operation (i.e. whether the OS will execute an erase or delete function) depends on future input from the user, e.g. in Fig. 2 the outcome of pressing the *Erase* button depends on possible changes to the default security option. Under such circumstances we recommend labelling the confirmation button with a neutral term, e.g. *'Proceed'*, and customising the description text depending on the selected security options.

5.3 Insufficient Guidance and Cues

During our CW we encountered multiple dialogue screens with insufficient or inadequate descriptions of underlying technical operation. For instance, the descriptive text in Fig. 1 provides macOS users with a warning that they "can't undo this action". Whilst it may not be possible for users to undo this action using native functions within the OS, forensic software is able to fully recover these files. This can therefore create a false sense of security that these files are no longer recoverable. In Windows 10, when a file is deleted from the system, the final description of the function (see Fig. 4) informs users that the file will be "permanently deleted" but lacks detail on what 'permanent' means and whether the file could, under certain conditions, still be recovered.

Informative and accessible descriptions are required for informed decision making. Information related to a user task should not be exclusively accessible through optional UI screens. On each screen, where a user can make a selection, the relevant consequences of this decision should be explained. We suggest adding informative text to describe the difference between delete and erase functions where it is contextually relevant within an OS UI. Furthermore, a note about the existence of file recovery applications should be added to all delete function confirmation screens.

5.4 OS-Independent Implications

Designers of UIs rely on metaphors to make complex and abstract functions more intuitive and comprehensible for users [2]. For instance, placing an unwanted *file* into the *recycle bin* uses multiple metaphors from an office environment, allowing users to relate these complex computing artifacts and processes to everyday physical items and actions. Yet, the 'delete' and 'erase' metaphors are problematic, as they denote different meaning in the UI, whilst relating back to the same constructs in the physical world. Designers should therefore consider integrating new metaphors that better distinguish between these two functions to reduce the risk of confusion for users.

As well as being well positioned to provide users with guidance on the appropriate use of delete and erase functions, OS can also provide appropriate cues and prompts towards more secure outcomes. In Sect. 2.1 we discussed past research showing how people intend to erase data from decommissioned drives but fail to do so securely, with researchers being able to recover data using digital forensic techniques. We propose OS should detect when a user deletes all (visible) files from a memory storage device, e.g. USB stick. Upon detection of this event, the OS could remind the user about the difference between delete and erase functions, nudging the user to take an informed decision before potentially decommissioning said device.

Lastly, we suggest official guidelines and best practice be developed on GDPR compliant erasure of data. This would be informative to users and provide OS a single source for developing consistent UI functionality across platforms. The European Data Protection Board[6] may be best positioned to develop these as they are already tasked with issuing guidelines, recommendations, and best practice on other GDPR-related topics (Article 70 GDPR), and consist of representatives from each national data protection authority (including EEA countries). In addition, national data protection authorities could make recommendations to carry out a data protection impact assessment (DPIA) for the process of decommissioning data storage devices, since this activity can be "likely to result in a high risk to the rights and freedoms of natural persons" (Article 35 GDPR).

6   Limitations

Cognitive walkthroughs are limited in that they do not involve (non-expert) users, the results are solely based on skills and expertise of the evaluators, and the frequency of identified problems cannot be estimated. This means that cognitive walkthroughs commonly only identify a subset of usability issues of the evaluation system. However, we do not believe this limitation reduced the validity of the issues identified in our analysis. The file system of the USB stick used in our study was set to FAT32 as it is the most commonly used file system for this type of device. We do not anticipate different file systems would have affected our findings but further work would be needed to confirm this.

7   Conclusion

We investigated possible causes for confusion around delete and erase functions, which was identified as a privacy and security threat in context of decommis-

---

[6] See https://edpb.europa.eu.

sioned USB sticks. In two of the most commonly used OS in today's market, we identified inconsistencies in the UI, insecure default options, and confusing and occasionally incorrect guidance. Finally, we propose design changes that could alleviate these issues and motivate a "call for action" for official guidelines and best practice on GDPR compliant erasure to be developed.

Acknowledgements. This work has received funding from the European Union's Horizon 2020 research and innovation programme under the Marie Skłodowska-Curie grant agreement No 675730, within the Marie Skłodowska-Curie Innovative Training Networks (ITN-ETN) framework.

References

1. Diesburg, S., Feldhaus, C., Fardan, M.A., Schlicht, J., Ploof, N.: Is your data gone?: measuring user perceptions of deletion. In: Proceedings of the 6th Workshop on Socio-Technical Aspects in Security and Trust, pp. 47–59. ACM (2016)
2. Donath, J.: The Social Machine: Designs for Living Online. MIT Press, Cambridge (2014)
3. EY: IAPP-EY Annual Privacy Governance Report 2018. Technical report, International Association of Privacy Professionals (2018). https://iapp.org/media/pdf/resource_center/IAPP-EY-Gov_Report_2018-FINAL.pdf. Accessed 21 Dec 2018
4. Hughes, G.: Tutorial on disk drive data sanitization (2006)
5. ICO: Guide to the General Data Protection Regulation (GDPR) (2018). https://ico.org.uk/for-organisations/guide-to-data-protection/guide-to-the-general-data-protection-regulation-gdpr/individual-rights/right-to-erasure/. Accessed 21 Dec 2018
6. Jones, A., Dardick, G.S., Davies, G., Sutherland, I., Valli, C.: The 2008 analysis of information remaining on disks offered for sale on the second hand market. J. Int. Commer. Law Technol. **4**(3), 162–175 (2009)
7. Jones, A., Valli, C., Dabibi, G.: The 2009 analysis of information remaining on USB storage devices offered for sale on the second hand market. In: Australian Digital Forensics Conference, p. 61 (2009)
8. Mahatody, T., Sagar, M., Kolski, C.: State of the art on the cognitive walkthrough method, its variants and evolutions. Int. J. Hum.-Comput. Interact. **26**(8), 741–785 (2010)
9. Westman, M.: eMMC Chip Off - Benefits and Risks Workshop (2017). https://www.dfrws.org/conferences/dfrws-eu-2017/sessions/emmc-chip-benefits-and-risks-workshop. Accessed 21 Dec 2018
10. Westman, M.: Where Did That Incriminating Evidence Come From? (2018). https://www.dfrws.org/conferences/dfrws-eu-2018/sessions/where-did-incriminating-evidence-come. Accessed 21 Dec 2018
11. McKenzie, C.R., Liersch, M.J., Finkelstein, S.R.: Recommendations implicit in policy defaults. Psychol. Sci. **17**(5), 414–420 (2006)
12. NetApplications.com: Operating System Market Share. https://www.netmarketshare.com/operating-system-market-share.aspx. Accessed 21 Dec 2018
13. Rieman, J., Franzke, M., Redmiles, D.: Usability evaluation with the cognitive walkthrough. In: Conference Companion on Human Factors in Computing Systems, pp. 387–388. ACM (1995)

14. Robins, N., Williams, P.A., Sansurooah, K.: An investigation into remnant data on USB storage devices sold in Australia creating alarming concerns. Int. J. Comput. Appl. **39**(2), 79–90 (2017)
15. Spencer, R.: The streamlined cognitive walkthrough method, working around social constraints encountered in a software development company. In: Proceedings of the SIGCHI Conference on Human Factors in Computing Systems, pp. 353–359. ACM (2000)
16. Storer, T., Glisson, W.B., Grispos, G.: Investigating information recovered from re-sold mobile devices. In: Privacy and Usability Methods Pow-wow (PUMP) Workshop, p. 2. ACM, University of Abertay, Dundee (2010)
17. Valli, C., Jones, A.: A UK and Australian Study of Hard Disk Disposal (2005)

Privacy Beyond Confidentiality, Data Science Beyond Spying: From Movement Data and Data Privacy Towards a Wider Fundamental Rights Discourse

Bettina Berendt[(✉)]

Department of Computer Science, KU Leuven, Leuven, Belgium
bettina.berendt@cs.kuleuven.be,
https://people.cs.kuleuven.be/~bettina.berendt/

Abstract. Although privacy and AI/data science are multi-faceted concepts, there is an increasing trend to focus on only a subset of their meaning: privacy as data privacy, with a focus on confidentiality, and AI/data science as a threat to autonomy and privacy, through data collection, unwanted inferences, and profiling. However, confidentiality and "invisibility" are not always constitutive of privacy as "the freedom from unreasonable constraints on the construction of one's own identity" – in some cases, visibility can be more important, and data collection, presentation, and inferences can help and extend a desired visibility. In this position paper, I will focus on a specific application around these phenomena: the analysis of vehicle/human trajectory data. I will discuss two recent examples of the analysis of such data: the New York City taxi rides dataset, and the use of data from the maritime Automatic Information System (AIS) for mapping refugee movements on the Mediterranean Sea. The goal is to encourage a discussion as to whether and how such wider fundamental-rights questions and their implications for privacy, data protection, and technology can and should be investigated in the scope of APF.

Keywords: Modelling of data protection and privacy requirements ·
Aspect of privacy in artificial intelligence ·
Privacy and other fundamental rights ·
Privacy of location and trajectory data

1 Introduction

"Privacy is a contested notion" used to be a stock phrase in presentations and papers throughout the nineties and noughties, and a vast number of classifications of different notions and aspects of privacy have been proposed, see [14,16,30] for just three examples. Data protection is a similarly multi-faceted concept – not only a counterpart right to the right to privacy [8], but also a means

© Springer Nature Switzerland AG 2019
M. Naldi et al. (Eds.): APF 2019, LNCS 11498, pp. 59–71, 2019.
https://doi.org/10.1007/978-3-030-21752-5_5

for protecting "fundamental rights and freedoms" in general (Article 1 GDPR).[1]
Finally, computer technology in general and Artificial Intelligence applications
in particular play many roles, ranging from the quintessential threat of profiling
(an activity that even entered the title of an article in the GDPR, Article 22)
to the mandate, in the GDPR, to use state-of-the-art (privacy-enhancing) technologies: Articles 25(1) and 32(1) require controllers and processors to give due
regard to the state of the art when choosing the technologies.

Yet, in spite of this richness of meaning in the three concepts of "privacy",
"data protection", and "AI", there is a prototype: (1) Privacy is operationalised
via data privacy and therefore obtains when information is hidden from all or
at least specific others; it is therefore centered around confidentiality. (2) Data
protection obtains when this information is removed in appropriate ways (e.g.
through anonymisation or pseudonymisation) or at least restricted to its intended
recipients (e.g. through access control), cf. for example [13] or, specifically for trajectory data, [29]. (3) AI and – particularly relevant when it comes to the processing of personal data – data science[2] are conceptualised as dangers to individuals
and their autonomy, by combining unwanted data collection with intransparent
inferences and manipulation (as exemplified in the Cambridge Analytica media
narrative).

The present paper starts from reconceptualising privacy as more than confidentiality. It goes back to the alternative of "privacy as the right to be let
alone" as formulated by Agre and Rotenberg: "the freedom from unreasonable
constraints on the construction of one's own identity" [1], also expanded on by
Hildebrand [17]. Crucially, as feminist scholars and others have pointed out,
keeping something confidential or *invisible* can serve to perpetuate oppression
and therefore counteract the very liberatory effects that a private sphere is supposed to have, cf. [27]. On the contrary, it may be necessary to make certain
information *visible* in order to fight and overcome oppression and oppressive
structures. The standard example used to be the treatment of domestic violence
as a "private matter" vs. its publication and the legal and regulatory successes
this has enabled; a current example is the #metoo movement.[3]

---

[1] Of course, the GDPR also contains and elaborates on many other principles, including requirements on data processing related to IT security (integrity and availability
in addition to confidentiality, Article 32 and Article 5(1)(f)), accountability, weighing
of interests, and others.

[2] A field situated in the intersection of machine learning (as a part of AI) and substantive expertise [7].

[3] This movement started as the encouragement of victims of sexual harassment (especially in, but not limited to, the workplace) to tweet about their experiences and
give people a sense of the magnitude of the problem. The Twitter hashtag #metoo
simplifies the retrievability of these reports, such that specific incidents as well as
patterns of sexual harassment become a public and visible phenomenon, rather than
remain "private" singular experiences. As in the case of calling out domestic violence,
the hope is that "this 'mainstreaming' of feminist activism is laying the foundation
for a collective shift towards a more just society" [24, p. 239].

This reconceptualisation will be done by contrasting two case studies that on the surface share many commonalities: human trajectories that can be derived from observed vehicle movement data and data science studies that reconstruct trajectories from these data. The case studies are (1) the New York City taxi rides dataset, and (2) the use of data from the maritime Automatic Information System (AIS) for mapping refugee movements on the Mediterranean Sea. In both cases, the data amount to "holistic trajectories", spatiotemporal data enriched with semantic information about the vehicles, the space, the voyage, and enrichable (through data-science inferences) with information about the people on that trajectory.

The first contribution of the paper is to investigate claims that have been made with regard to privacy protection in the second case study, and to argue that, unlike in the first case study, invisibility is often *not* what the affected individuals want. In their case, rather, *visibility* becomes a precondition for having rights and often life at all. Data science projects that support this goal and a counter-narrative to politically prevalent narratives, can then become tools that may further fundamental rights (rather than threaten them, as in the default narrative). Data protection law, in turn, may or may not be applicable, and in any case probably not conceptualised as in standard GDPR-related discussions. The second contribution is to highlight some possible questions that can be asked of the data and their presentation.

The paper is a position paper, a question and a proposal. It asks the question whether and how the APF community wants to engage with the highly politically charged topics around migration, data, and fundamental rights. It proposes a number of (technical and social) questions as a starting point to such an engagement. Lastly, it is (obviously) the opinion of the current author that this is a discussion worth having at APF.

2   Case Study 1: New York City Tax Rides Dataset

In 2014, the City of New York released, in response to a Freedom of Information request, data about all 173 million taxi rides in New York in 2013, with the taxi identifiers pseudonymised, and exact spatiotemporal data about start- and endpoints, as well as fares, given. This dataset provided a rich real-life dataset for a wide range of data mining studies, such as "optimization of the revenue of NYC Taxi Service using Markov Decision Processes" [21]. At the same time, the publication of the dataset was soon criticized on privacy grounds. For example, the taxi pseudonyms could easily be re-identified to their actual medallion numbers [26]. It was also argued that the data allowed inferences towards sensitive attributes of the taxi drivers, such as the patterns of breaks during the day indicating that someone is a devout Muslim [35]. Finally, with some background knowledge, inferences can be made towards the identity of taxi customers, and based on that, details about their whereabouts learned [3]. The futility even of better pseudonymisation/anonymisation approaches was demonstrated by Douriez et al. [12]. Medallion and driver license IDs were removed from NYC's taxi datasets released in subsequent years.[4]

The taxi rides represent a typical case of personal data in the sense of the GDPR. Personal data are "any information relating to an identified or identifiable natural person ('data subject')" (Article 4). Since at least some, and likely many, taxi drivers and taxi customers are easily identifiable, the dataset contains personal data. Taxi customers (and conceivably also taxi drivers) had not been asked to give their consent to these data being published online for unspecified purposes, nor are other grounds for such processing (Article 6 GDPR) present. This is textbook privacy violation by data[5] (more accurately in the EU context: a violation of data protection law). While the GDPR defines a number of exemptions for research, it does so under conditions [19,22], such that currently ethics boards in EU universities are cautious and therefore discourage the use of this dataset for any kind of data mining.[6]

This perception of a dataset assumes that the population of data subjects consists of informed individuals, who exercise their autonomy among other things by travelling in vehicle passages they pay for, and who have a reasonable expectation of privacy in doing so that requires that the data about their movements remain confidential. The main question for the responsible data scientist appears to follow from the observation that the removal of taxi identifiers "would adversely impact certain types of analysis on the data" [12, p. 148] and the need to find different analysis types.

3   Case Study 2: AIS Data for Describing Migrant Rescue Operations

The second case study is based on the Hoffmann et al. study published in a 2017 report by the IOM [18], the UN International Organization for Migration, and illustrated in an interactive and multimedia online presentation[7]. As in case

---

[4] https://data.cityofnewyork.us/browse?q=taxi.

[5] It is debatable where/when the violation occurs. Opinions differ as to whether the existence of knowledge about individuals per se represents a privacy violation, whether this only occurs when this knowledge is acted upon, or whether the publication of data as an enabler of such consequences already forms a privacy violation [4].

[6] This information was given to me under conditions of confidentiality, as was the assessment that university ethics boards tend to be conservative in their interpretation of the GDPR. The publicly available university documents that I have seen on what is and what is not allowed regarding the re-use of public datasets, do not address specific questions such as "is it allowed to re-use public datasets", rather, they refer to the general principle that GDPR compliance always also depends on the whole context of research – which is of course a correct rendering of a law that requires interpretation in context. Even if I therefore cannot provide a reference for my claim, I consider it worthwhile to mention it, for example to encourage discussion among researchers about their respective institutions' GDPR handling.

[7] http://rescuesignatures.unglobalpulse.net/mediterranean/.

study 1, the base data are in principle publicly accessible. They are data from the Automatic Information System (AIS), a maritime communications system through which vessels regularly broadcast information, including their identifier, vessel type, latitude and longitude, speed, course and destination. The information is used by maritime authorities and ships to locate nearby vessels and avoid collisions. Based on these spatiotemporal data and enriched with textual and pictorial data from other sources[8], the authors generate a type of holistic trajectories, manually label them as representing (or not) a rescue operation, and use clustering and machine learning with a view to classification and prediction. Other researchers have investigated how to model and detect such trajectories. Based on AIS data, complex events, including but not limited to SAR (search and rescue) missions, and involving one or several vessels, can be modelled and detected efficiently and in real time using combinations of exploratory, machine learning, and logics-based (event calculus) techniques [28, 36].

Hoffmann et al. mention several limitations of their method, mainly with regard to data quality, including the fact that as circumstances change, so do the data and patterns (thus, the analysis of timely data is crucial).

In a section on "privacy", the authors raise several points. The first is a reference to concerns over port security as a consequence of AIS data public availability. The second is the possibility that rescue organisations may not want the full details of their operations to be publicly known, because they are facing opposition and threats (a European far-right group threatening to attack rescue vessels is mentioned). Both concerns are not privacy concerns in the sense of European law (in particular because the agent requesting the confidentiality is not a natural person). As a third reason, the authors mention that "adversarial users could take advantage of the data to track the location of individual refugees [identified by record linkage with data such as photos or statements, or other background knowledge], attack rescue boats or guide piracy operations" (p. 40). Presumably, the attacks and piracy operations are security/safety concerns for the rescue vessels, their crews, and the rescued persons, and these concerns could arise from the public availability of the data as well as from possible predictors learned from them, i.e. the data scientists' work.

It also appears, from the sentence, that the possible tracking of individuals is considered a security/safety risk (because it could lead to attacks) rather than a typical privacy risk (by which an individual migrant would want to keep their identity or properties hidden). It is difficult to say what role such expectations of, or wishes for, privacy in our usual sense, play in this extreme situation. Also, it has been observed increasingly over the past years that rather than trying to hide their voyage, "migrants from Libya facilitated their traceability by national authorities and monitoring systems, anticipating in space and time border patrols by sending an SOS as soon as they entered the international waters"

---

[8] The authors enrich the data with broadcast warning data produced by WWNWS, a global service managed by the UN Maritime Organization IMO (data that appear to cover only a small fraction of vessels in distress, p. 37), and other data such as the tweets issued by NGO vessels.

[33, p. 576]. In other words, along their journey, migrants deal strategically with visibility and invisibility, with information disclosure and hiding/confidentiality. This is quite probably a very rational strategy given the fact that a successful and invisible journey to Europe is by now nearly impossible for many reasons, including that traffickers severely overload and under-equip their vessels, and that due to the high-resolution sensors employed in the European Border Surveillance System EUROSUR [9], even very small vessels are likely to be spotted and monitored. Strategic information disclosure (in addition to strategic information hiding) by individuals can also be observed in many other contexts that are less dramatic than the life-or-death situations faced by migrants on the Mediterranean, and it has been pointed out that strategic information disclosures too can be privacy-related behaviour [15].

A second question related to privacy is related to the referent of the data. Technically a ship's trajectory could be considered personal data in the same sense as a taxi's trajectory. (This concerns the ships provided by the traffickers as well as rescuing ships once they have been boarded by migrants.) As for taxis, the trajectory is a trajectory both of the "driver" and of the "passenger(s)".

In the NGO vessel case, the "driver" individuals are the captain and crew members. To the extent that they can be re-identified using public (or otherwise procured) records, the AIS-based trajectory data form personal data. However, their personal and professional mission is to carry out rescue tasks, and to do so in a transparent manner, and they in fact often seek visibility and publicity (for their funders as well as a political statement). It thus appears less likely that these individuals would regard the publication of the information that they were at some location at some time as a violation of their privacy (even if for security/safety reasons, they may prefer some degree of invisibility, see above). "Drivers" of non-NGO vessels such as cargo ships are likely to have other motivations, since their original task is not related to sea rescue, which may make them regard their location data differently.

As regards the "passengers", with appropriate background knowledge, similar re-identification attacks could in principle be mounted to identify individuals. These could for example be based on photos taken of individuals while on-board or disembarking, matched with named photos as background knowledge [18]. It is also conceivable that data regarding the captain or crew members and data regarding migrants are combined, and that this may result in undesired consequences. It is an open question whether such attacks are likely.[9] If such a re-identification link is not made, or is very unlikely to be made, AIS-based trajectories of rescuing ships may not count as personal data.

However, even if *individuals* may not be exposed in a traditional privacy-violation sense, there is a much more likely sense in which migrants are exposed by AIS data: as a *group*. In fact, as has been argued in this context [33] as well as in connection with other applications of big data analyses to humanitarian

---

[9] How likely they are will depend on the existence of background knowledge and the existence of and incentives for "attackers" (paparazzi, celebrity fans, law enforcement, criminals, ...).

causes [31], there is a temptation to focus on migrants as a group defined only by one feature (here: to be in need of rescue).

The fact that big data constitute new risks in the profiling of groups has been lamented often in connection with data protection laws such as the GDPR (which focus on the protection of individuals' rights and freedoms); in the humanitarian realm, it creates additional and different challenges [32].

For the data scientist, this means that also the response to these risks and threats may need to be very different, because traditional approaches to (for example) anonymisation are focussed on the protection of individuals from threats against these persons as individuals. It is an open research question what could constitute effective measures of group protection.

Data privacy, viewed technically, does not need to make a clear distinction between protecting information and control over it related to individuals (a concept rooted in human rights) and protecting information and control over it related to other entities (such as organisations, the NGOs in the current example and in the argument made by Hoffmann et al.) [11]. In data privacy, a different and independent dimension becomes relevant when one asks "whose privacy" should be protected. A useful distinction is that between data owner, data respondent (the data subject, although not always in its legal sense of an individual person), and data user; and this distinction has implications for the choice of data-privacy protection methods [11]. In the present example, one assignment of these roles that follows the argument about risks above could be: the NGO as the data owner, the migrant (or migrant group) as the data respondent, and various (potential) data users: the public, politicians, pirates, ...

Moving beyond privacy and data privacy, many other questions, technical as well as ethical, arise about information disclosure and hiding. The study and visualisation of "rescue patterns" can have different objectives. Hoffmann et al. mention operational objectives (e.g., supporting coordination of rescue operations), analytic objectives (e.g., determining conditions under which rescues are most effective), and reporting objectives. The latter are described as follows: "supplement the large amount of qualitative, descriptive coverage already produced by NGOs and the news media", "help external observers ... obtain a high-level picture of what is happening in the region over time. An overview of these patterns is critical for coordination and advocacy purposes; it enables stakeholders to see the true magnitude of rescue operations, and to quantify costs, shortcomings and future needs." [18, p. 30].

Concentrating on the reporting objective, it can be argued that rescue patterns constitute a counter-mapping practice: in the EUROSUR monitoring system, selected migratory events are produced from the sensed data and mapped in time and space [33]. The website watchthemed.net, initiated and run by a network of NGOs, activists and researchers, maps events to monitor deaths and violations of migrants' rights. In the SAR-centric applications described here, rescue events are produced and mapped. EUROSUR is run by Frontex, and its data and analytics are not available to NGOs and other external partners, whereas the rescue patterns are mined from data available publicly (AIS data) or available to partners of the research (the broadcast warnings), and enriched with further aspects from public data (such as tweets).

Mapping practices generate a narrative around their real-world phenomenon. The current data models and visualizations of rescue patterns, maybe for technical reasons (because the EUROSUR data are not available), maybe to avoid visual clutter, display these patterns in an otherwise "empty" space. Is it possible, and is it advisable, to at least represent that far more data exist (even if one does not have access to them)? In other words, should the "known unknown" data be modelled and represented too, and if so, how? These data are important for technical reasons as much as for narrative reasons – how can and should these two motivations be addressed, and how can the choices made be made in a transparent and accountable way? In the following paragraphs, I will illustrate three examples of these considerations.

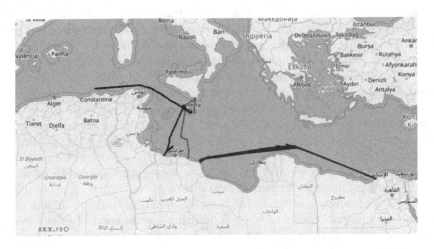

Fig. 1. The Alexander Maersk's June 2018 trajectory (in red, via Valletta). (Color figure online)

First, sometimes trajectory data illustrate very directly the influences of context and the uncertainty and the "unknowns" of vessel operators. As an example, consider the recent case of a commercial cargo ship that took on 113 people saved by an NGO rescue ship and then spent four days in a political stand-off on a zig-zag trajectory between ports before being allowed to dock in Sicily [2,5], see Fig. 1.[10] Can and should holistic trajectories measure and visualize the enormous costs caused by such decisions, as well as the incentives and influences this may have on further behaviour by vessel operators? What about similar odysseys that have since taken place in a politically more and more charged climate, such

---

[10] I thank Konstantinos Tserpes for mentioning this example and making available a visualization of the trajectory.

as those involving a coastguard and a sea-rescue NGO ship respectively [20,38]? What about, reversely, the trajectories of ships that could not and were not 'doing anything anymore' under these circumstances, with trajectories (enforced by the political context) so dis-incentivizing that it contributed to Germany's withdrawal from Sophia, the EU naval mission targeting human trafficking in the Mediterranean [10]? Could and (how) should a visualisation illustrate a progressive emptying of the knowable in the space, caused by the reduction of official and NGO sea-rescue vessels active in the area?

Second, many of the existing, but not accessible data have strong effects on the rescue events modelled. For example, the Libyan coastguard now has indirect access to EUROSUR data [25]; thus, their rescue actions, including those in cooperation or competition with European actors, may be planned based on data that are not modelled in the rescue patterns system, and which therefore can co-determine the "coordination" and "effectiveness" of a rescue. Can and should these data (or at least the fact of their existence and possible influence) be modelled?

Third, further questions concern which aspects are important to judge the legal and ethical dimensions of a rescue operation. An example is provided by [23] resp. [6]: in a case in which a commercial towboat under Italian flag rescued migrants and then handed them over to the Libyan coastguard, a key legal question revolved not around the spatiotemporal data of the rescue operation, but around whether it was instructed by the Italian or the Libyan authorities [37]. Can these aspects be modelled as part of holistic trajectories, and how could this be done if the datum itself is still being contested?

4   Towards a Comparative Analysis

The preceding sections have shown that vehicle trajectory data are often rich sources of personal data, of individuals as well as of groups. However, even if very similar in technical aspects, such data can present very different challenges in different contexts. In both examples analysed in the present paper, concerns of different stakeholders need to be weighed. Even if we only regard stakeholder groups' interests with regard to invisibility (confidentiality of the data) or visibility, further differentiation becomes apparent. For reasons of space, I cannot present a worked-out comparative analysis of the two case studies, or provide a weighing of the different interests in a GDPR sense. Instead, I will sketch some further subdivisions that arise within stakeholder groups, and argue that a weighing of these interests is a more far-reaching political decision.

As regards the stakeholder group "drivers", it appears that those in the taxi case study probably have an interest in invisibility, whereas those in the vessel case study may seek invisibility, be indifferent, have an interest in visibility, or regard being located as a security/safety risk more than as a privacy violation. Their views may also depend on whether they are in the subgroup of "NGO vessel driver" or "other vessel driver".

For the "passengers", invisibility appears a strong interest in the first case study, whereas visibility may be strongly preferred as a prerequisite for surviving by the vulnerable people in the second case study, and different protection needs of individuals and groups become apparent.

"The public" also consists of subgroups with different interests. In the taxi case study, these include citizens interested in the visibility of public city data (as the motivation of the FOI request), scientists interested in publicly available datasets, celebrity spotters interested in disclosures, and privacy activists and data scientists interested in highlighting and preventing data-privacy attacks. In the AIS data case study, different subgroups of the public are even interested in creating different overall narratives, including (a) "there is an invasion of migrants", (b) "the migration crisis is over", and (c) "people keep dying". It may be argued that these narratives [34] induce preferences for visibility (a, c) and invisibility (b), for different reasons, with different finalities, and therefore with foci on different data.

5   Conclusion

In sum, a consideration of the modelling and reporting of vehicle data and patterns, even if restricted to what data are to be included and how, what information is to be kept confidential or disclosed, can reach far beyond the traditional questions discussed under data protection and data privacy, and data science can assume the importance and responsibility normally associated with PETs. This use of modelling and AI requires a critical examination of the sociopolitical background of the mobility that these vehicles afford, support, or impede, and of the goals of the data-science project undertaken. And although "data can help citizens demand accountability", "ultimately, the inferences that can be drawn from the data are only as valuable as the actions they induce. There is a need for political momentum to address the situation in the Mediterranean, and this problem will not be solved with data alone." [18, p. 42].

Acknowledgements. I thank the members of the EU H2020 Marie-Skłodowska-Curie programme project MASTER for the inspiration to deal with the privacy aspects of AIS data and migrants, and for many valuable discussions of previous versions of this article.

References

1. Agre, P.E., Rotenberg, M.: Technology and Privacy: The New Landscape. MIT Press, Cambridge (2001)
2. Al Jazeera News: Danish cargo ship carrying refugees allowed to dock in Italy, 26 June 2018. https://www.aljazeera.com/news/2018/06/danish-cargo-ship-carrying-refugees-allowed-dock-italy-180626081632471.html
3. Atockar: Riding with the Stars: Passenger Privacy in the NYC Taxicab Dataset (2014). https://research.neustar.biz/2014/09/15/riding-with-the-stars-passenger-privacy-in-the-nyc-taxicab-dataset/
4. Berendt, B.: More than modelling and hiding: towards a comprehensive view of web mining and privacy. Data Min. Knowl. Disc. **24**(3), 697–737 (2012)

5. Borghese, L., Vandoorne, S., Vonberg, J.: Migrant rescue ship Lifeline to dock in Malta after being stranded for five days in the Mediterranean. CNN News, 26 June 2018. https://edition.cnn.com/2018/06/26/europe/migrant-ships-maersk-lifeline-intl/index.html

6. Cancellato, F.: Poche palle, i migranti della Asso 28 li abbiamo respinti noi: e la Libia è solo la foglia di fico della nostra ipocrisia. Linkiesta, 1 August 2018. https://www.linkiesta.it/it/article/2018/08/01/poche-palle-i-migranti-della-asso-28-li-abbiamo-respinti-noi-e-la-libi/39019/

7. Conway, D.: The Data Science Venn Diagram (n.d.). http://drewconway.com/zia/2013/3/26/the-data-science-venn-diagram

8. De Hert, P., Gutwirth, S.: Privacy, data protection and law enforcement. Opacity of the individual and transparency and power. In: Claes, E., Duff, A., Gutwirth, S. (eds.), Privacy and the Criminal Law, pp. 61–104. Antwerp/Oxford: Intersentia (2006)

9. Deibler, D.: EUROSUR - A Sci-fi border zone patrolled by drones? In: Camenisch, J., Fischer-Hübner, S., Hansen, M. (eds.) Privacy and Identity Management for the Future Internet in the Age of Globalisation, pp. 87–109. Springer, Berlin etc. (2015). https://doi.org/10.1007/978-3-319-18621-4

10. Welle, D.: Germany pulls out of Mediterranean migrant mission Sophia, 23 January 2019. https://www.dw.com/en/germany-pulls-out-of-mediterranean-migrant-mission-sophia/a-47189097

11. Domingo-Ferrer, J.: A three-dimensional conceptual framework for database privacy. In: Jonker, W., Petković, M. (eds.) SDM 2007. LNCS, vol. 4721, pp. 193–202. Springer, Heidelberg (2007). https://doi.org/10.1007/978-3-540-75248-6_14

12. Douriez, M., Doraiswamy, H., Freire, J., Silva, C.T.: Anonymizing NYC taxi data: does it matter? In: Proceedings of 2016 IEEE International Conference on Data Science and Advanced Analytics (DSAA), Montreal, QC, 2016, pp. 140–148 (2016)

13. Elliot, M., Mackey, E., O'Hary, K., Tudor, C.: The Anonymisation Decision-Making Framework. UKAN, Manchester (2016). http://ukanon.net/wp-content/uploads/2015/05/The-Anonymisation-Decision-making-Framework.pdf

14. Friedewald, M., Finn, R., Wright, D.: Seven types of privacy. In: Gutwirth, S., Leens, R., De Hert, P., Poullet, Y. (eds.) European Data Protection: Coming of Age, pp. 3–32. Springer, Heidelberg (2013). https://doi.org/10.1007/978-94-007-5170-5_1

15. Gürses, S.F., Berendt, B.: The social web and privacy. In: Ferrari, E., Bonchi, F. (eds.), Privacy-Aware Knowledge Discovery: Novel Applications and New Techniques. Data Mining and Knowledge Discovery Series. Chapman & Hall/CRC Press, Boca Raton (2010). https://www.esat.kuleuven.be/cosic/publications/article-1304.pdf

16. Hansen, M., Jensen, M., Rost, M.: Protection goals for privacy engineering. In: Proceedings of 2015 IEEE CS Security and Privacy Workshops (2015). https://ieeexplore.ieee.org/stamp/stamp.jsp?arnumber=7163220

17. Hildebrandt, M.: Privacy and identity. In: Claes, E., Duff, A., Gutwirth, S. (eds.) Privacy and the Criminal Law, pp. 43–58. Intersentia, Antwerp (2006)

18. Hoffmann, K., Boy, J., Leon-Dufour, J., Breen, D. Earney, C., Luengo-Oroz, M. Using big data to study rescue patterns in the Mediterranean. In: Fatal Journeys. vol. 3, Part 1: Improving Data on Missing Migrants, pp. 24–46. International Organization for Migration, Geneva (2017). https://publications.iom.int/system/files/pdf/fatal_journeys_volume_3_part_1.pdf

19. Knapton, J.: General Data Protection Regulation: academic research (n.d.). https://www.information-compliance.admin.cam.ac.uk/files/gdpr_and_academic_research_v1.pdf

20. La Repubblica: Diciotti, dopo dieci giorni i migranti sbarcano dalla nave, 26 August 2018. https://www.repubblica.it/cronaca/2018/08/26/news/migranti_diciotti_sbarco-204935293

21. Li, J.P.K., Bhulai, S., van Essen, T.: Optimization of the revenue of the New York City taxi service using Markov decision processes. In: Proceedings of DATA ANALYTICS 2017: The Sixth International Conference on Data Analytics (2017). https://www.thinkmind.org/download.php?articleid=data_analytics_2017_4_10_68005

22. Maldoff, G. How GDPR changes the rules for research. IAPP News (2016). https://iapp.org/news/a/how-gdpr-changes-the-rules-for-research/

23. Medina, J.: U.N. says migrants' return to Libya by Italian boat could be illegal. Reuters, 31 July 2018. https://www.reuters.com/article/us-europe-migrants-libya/migrants-return-to-libya-by-italian-boat-could-breach-international-law-u-n-idUSKBN1KL1K4

24. Mendes, K., Ringrose, J., Keller, J.: #MeToo and the promise and pitfalls of challenging rape culture through digital feminist activism. Eur. J. Women's Stud. **25**(2), 236–246 (2018). https://doi.org/10.1177/1350506818765318

25. Monroy, M.: Durch die Hintertür: Anschluss Libyens an europäische Überwachungssysteme. CILIP Blog, 19 January 2018. https://www.cilip.de/2018/01/19/durch-die-hintertuer-anschluss-libyens-an-europaeische-ueberwachungssysteme/

26. Pandurangan, V.: On Taxis and Rainbows: Lessons from NYC's improperly anonymized taxi logs (2014). https://tech.vijayp.ca/of-taxis-and-rainbows-f6bc289679a1

27. Phillips, D.: Privacy policy and PETs: the influence of policy regimes on the development and social implications of privacy enhancing technologies. New Media Soc. **6**(6), 691–706 (2004)

28. Patroumpas, K., Alevizos, E., Artikis, A., Vodas, M., Pelekis, N., Theodoridis, Y.: Online event recognition from moving vessel trajectories. GeoInformatica **21**(2), 389–427 (2017). https://doi.org/10.1007/s10707-016-0266-x

29. Pratesi, F., Monreale, A., Trasarti, R., Giannotti, R., Pedreschi, D., Yanagihara, T.: PRUDEnce: a system for assessing privacy risk vs utility in data sharing ecosystems. Trans. Data Priv. **11**(2), 139–167 (2018)

30. Solove, D.J.: Understanding Privacy. Harvard University Press, Cambridge (2008)

31. Taylor, L.: Safety in numbers? Group privacy and big data analytics in the developing world. In: Taylor, L., Floridi, L., van der Sloot, B. (eds.) Group Privacy. PSS, vol. 126, pp. 13–36. Springer, Cham (2017). https://doi.org/10.1007/978-3-319-46608-8_2

32. Taylor, L., Floridi, L., van der Sloot, B. (eds.): Group Privacy. PSS, vol. 126. Springer, Cham (2017). https://doi.org/10.1007/978-3-319-46608-8

33. Tazzioli, M.: Eurosur, humanitarian visibility, and (nearly) real-time mapping in the Mediterranean. ACME **15**(3), 561–579 (2016). https://acme-journal.org/index.php/acme/article/view/1223/1201

34. The Guardian: EU declares migration crisis over as it hits out at 'fake news', 6 March 2019. https://www.theguardian.com/world/2019/mar/06/eu-declares-migration-crisis-over-hits-out-fake-news-european-commission

35. uluman: Identifying Muslim cabbies from trip data and prayer times (2015). https://www.reddit.com/r/dataisbeautiful/comments/2t201h/identifying_muslim_cabbies_from_trip_data_and/

36. Varlamis, I., Tserpes, K., Sardianos, C.: Detecting search and rescue missions from AIS data. In: 2018 IEEE 34th International Conference on Data Engineering Workshops (ICDEW), Paris, 2018, pp. 60–65 (2018). http://ieeexplore.ieee.org/stamp/stamp.jsp?tp=&arnumber=8402020&isnumber=8402003

37. Ziniti, A.: Migranti, inchiesta sul comportamento del rimorchiatore italiano Asso 28. La Repubblica, 8 August 2018. http://www.repubblica.it/cronaca/2018/08/08/news/migranti_presentato_un_esposto_sul_comportamento_del_rimorchiatore_italiano_asso_28-203654671/

38. Ziniti, A.: Migranti Sea Watch anche in Italia, accordo europeo raggiunto con Malta. La Repubblica, 9 January 2019. https://www.repubblica.it/cronaca/2019/01/09/news/migranti_accordo-216163365/

Making Machine Learning Forget

Saurabh Shintre[1]([✉]), Kevin A. Roundy[1], and Jasjeet Dhaliwal[2]

[1] Symantec Research Labs, Symantec Corporation,
350 Ellis Street, Mountain View, CA 94043, USA
{Saurabh_Shintre,Kevin_Roundy}@symantec.com
[2] Center for Advanced Machine Learning, Symantec Corporation,
350 Ellis Street, Mountain View, CA 94043, USA
Jasjeet_Dhaliwal@symantec.com

Abstract. Machine learning models often overfit to the training data and do not learn general patterns like humans do. This allows an attacker to learn private membership or attributes about the training data, simply by having access to the machine learning model. We argue that this vulnerability of current machine learning models makes them indirect stores of the personal data used for training and therefore, corresponding data protection regulations must apply to machine learning models as well. In this position paper, we specifically analyze how the "right-to-be-forgotten" provided by the European Union General Data Protection Regulation can be implemented on current machine learning models and which techniques can be used to build future models that can forget. This document also serves as a call-to-action for researchers and policy-makers to identify other technologies that can be used for this purpose.

Keywords: Machine learning · GDPR · Right-to-be-forgotten · Privacy-by-design

1 Introduction

The rise of the data economy has led to the creation of a number of internet services that collect personal data of consumers and offer useful services in return. The data collected by these services is shared with other processors for further analysis or for targeted advertising. Due to this complex network of data controllers and processors, consumers often lack control of the different ways in which their personal data is stored and shared. To make matters worse, the privacy policies of the some of these services are presented to consumers in complex legal parlance that prevents them from making decisions that protect their privacy [15]. Collected data is also stored in data-centers for long periods of time which helps these services build invasive personal profiles of their users, including sensitive information like location, commercial activity, medical and personal history [24]. Large-scale collection and storage of personal information

Supported by Symantec Corporation.

leads to major security and privacy risks for consumers. The data can be hacked or leaked with malicious intent which leads to the consumer losing all control over their personal information [1]. At the same time, such information allows service providers to infer other private information that can cause personal or financial loss to the consumer [6].

To protect consumers from such risks, a number of jurisdictions have implemented regulations that control the collection, storage, and sharing of personal information. The General Data Protection Regulation (GDPR) [11] of the European Union is a comprehensive legislation that covers steps that data controllers and processors must undertake to ensure security and privacy of personal data of subjects within the EU. GDPR extends the notion of personal information from identity information, such as name and addresses, to any information that can be personally identifiable like GPS locations, IP addresses, etc. It also mandates that data controllers and processors can only collect information that is relevant to their services and require explicit user consent to do so. In addition to mandates on transparency, storage, and security, Article 17 of the GDPR also gives a consumer the right to have their personal information removed from a service provider. The "right to erasure", often referred to as the "right-to-be-forgotten", mandates that data controllers must provide a mechanism through which data subjects can request the deletion and stop further processing of all their personal information collected by the data controller [11].

While it is relatively straightforward to keep track of raw stores of private data, the implementation of "right-to-be-forgotten" is made very complex due to the use of personal information in training a variety of machine learning models [16]. Such models are used to provide insights about credit worthiness, bio-metric authentication, medical diagnosis etc [18]. Due to the popularity of machine learning as a service (MLaaS), data controllers often give data to processors that train machine learning models for the controller and delete the raw data once the training is over [21]. This allows data controllers to satisfy legislative mandates because machine learning models are not considered stores of private information under most legislation. However, it has recently been shown that machine learning models often overfit to the training data [25]; i.e., they display higher accuracy on training data than on previously unseen test data. Hence, it is possible for an attacker with access to the model to identify data used to train the model and learn private attributes [13,19,21]. Figure 1 shows the success of model inversion attacks on a facial recognition model by only using the model and the name of the subject.

In this position paper, we opine that the existence of such attacks indirectly makes machine learning models stores of personal information. Therefore, all mandates of the GDPR that apply to regular stores of personal information must be extended to machine learning models trained with such data. In this paper, we specifically look at how the "right-to-be-forgotten" can be implemented on machine learning models and introduce techniques like *influence functions* [14] and *differential privacy* [10] as potential approaches to solve this problem.

Fig. 1. Recovered training image using attribute inference attacks v/s original training image [13]

2 The "Right-to-be-Forgotten"

The GDPR framework created by the European Union provides EU residents with protection against predatory practices of data-based internet services. GDPR enforces rules about the kind of user data that can be collected, shared, stored in a persistent manner, and how it should be safe-guarded. While other regulatory frameworks, such as HIPAA and COPPA regulations in the United States, also control the collection and storage of personal information, the **"right-to-be-forgotten"** is certainly unique to the GDPR [11]. Specified in the Article 17 of the GDPR framework, the right-to-be-forgotten, also known as the right-to-erasure, states that *"the data subject shall have the right to obtain from the controller the erasure of personal data concerning him or her without undue delay and the controller shall have the obligation to erase personal data without undue delay where one of the following grounds applies:*

- *the personal data are no longer necessary in relation to the purposes for which they were collected or otherwise processed;*
- *the data subject withdraws consent on which the processing is based according to point (a) of Article 6(1), or point (a) of Article 9(2), and where there is no other legal ground for the processing;*
- *the data subject objects to the processing pursuant to Article 21(1) and there are no overriding legitimate grounds for the processing, or the data subject objects to the processing pursuant to Article 21(2);*
- *the personal data have been unlawfully processed;*
- *the personal data have to be erased for compliance with a legal obligation in Union or Member State law to which the controller is subject;*
- *the personal data have been collected in relation to the offer of information society services referred to in Article 8(1)."*

The right-to-be-forgotten also requires the data controller to take any technical steps necessary to prevent the processing of information by data processors with whom the data controller has shared this data.

3   Privacy Leakage in Machine Learning Systems

The use of collected information to train machine learning models, specifically in a Machine Learning as a Service model, makes implementation of the right-to-be-forgotten extremely complicated. Users' data is used by controllers and processors to build machine learning systems for a variety for services, ranging from facial recognition [18] to medical diagnostics as in IBM Watson. However, most of the popularly-implemented machine learning algorithms often memorize the data used to train them [25]. Therefore, even if raw copies of the training data are deleted, data can be recreated from the machine learning model [13].

Leakage of private information in machine learning models can be done via two types of attacks. In **attribute inference** attacks, an attacker can recreate sensitive features about a user by having access to the machine learning model and partial publicly-available features, such as names, gender, etc. In order to do so, the attacker simply needs access to the confidence values outputted by the model. For example, given a facial recognition model, the attacker can recreate the face of a person of his/her choice by simply identifying images that are classified as that person with high confidence [13], as can be seen in Fig. 1. Substantial evidence points to the phenomenon of *over-fitting* as a lead cause of such attacks [25]. Over-fitting occurs when a machine learning model memorizes the training data rather than learning general features about it [22]. Such a model performs extremely well on data points close to training data points while performing poorly at other data points. Thus, by identifying regions of the input space where the model predictions are confident, the attacker can recreate the training points in that region [13].

In **membership inference** attacks, the attacker wishes to learn if a certain data point was used to train a model [21]. This attack can be successful even if the attacker only has a black-box API access to the model [19]. Membership of the user's data in a specific dataset can reveal sensitive information about that user. For example, the presence of user's data in control vs experimental groups of a medical trial can reveal the user's medical condition. To implement such attacks, the attacker builds multiple shadow models for which he knows the training data. The shadow models are trained to mimic the performance of the target model and have an additional binary output deciding whether a data point is "in" or "out" of the training set. At test time, all the different shadow models are engaged and if the majority of them classify the test point as "in", then the data point is part of the original training data. The reasons behind the success of these attacks aren't fully understood due to the lack of explainability in machine learning algorithms like deep learning. Yeom *et al.* identified high influence of specific training data points on the model parameters as one of the root cause of this weakness [25].

4 Implementing "Right-to-be-Forgotten" in Machine Learning Models

Membership and attribute inference attacks described in the previous section demonstrate that machine learning models act like indirect stores of the personal information used to train them. Therefore, the right-to-be-forgotten is incomplete if it does not apply to the machine learning models trained with personal information. Apart from the reasons of privacy, the ability of machine learning models to forget certain training data points also help improve their security and usability, because the model can unlearn the effects of poisoned or erroneously created training data [7].

A straightforward way to implement the right-to-be-forgotten in machine learning models is to delete the requesting user's personal information from the training set and retrain the model entirely. This method is impractical because commercial machine learning models may have millions of parameters and are trained over large corpora of data. Retraining them requires significant cost and effort which a data processor may not be able to afford without charging a fee for entertaining such requests. Additionally, the possibility of retraining the model to comply with right-to-be-forgotten may compel data processors to persistently store personal information in its raw format, when they would not do so otherwise, which can make it susceptible to theft or leakage. Therefore, we must design solutions that allow to models to forget training data without requiring retraining. We identify three existing techniques that can potentially be used for this purpose.

4.1 Influence Functions

Influence functions are tools from robust statistics that measure the effect of a training point on the machine learning model's parameters and predictions. Specifically, they measure the change in model's accuracy at a test input when a training point is removed from the training set. Koh and Liang [14] formalized this concept for deep neural networks and provided a closed-form expression to measure the influence of a training point on the model's parameters and performance at a test input. The measurement of influence of a training point on a test input is done in two parts. First, we measure the change in the model parameters caused by the removal of a training point and then we measure the change in model loss at the test point given the change in the model parameters.

Consider a model $\mathcal{F}$, trained on the training data X_{tr}, Y_{tr} where X represents the features and Y represents the labels. Let $\mathcal{L}$ represent the loss function used to train the model. That is, the function $\mathcal{L}(\theta, \mathbf{x}, \mathbf{y})$ measures how far the prediction made by the model under parameters θ at an input $\mathbf{x}$ is from the corresponding true label, $\mathbf{y}$. For algorithms like deep learning, mean squared error or categorical cross entropy are routinely chosen as the loss function.

Given initial model parameters, model risk is measured as the average model loss over the training data,

$$\mathcal{R}(\theta) = \frac{1}{|\boldsymbol{X}_{tr}|} \sum_{\substack{\mathbf{x} \in \boldsymbol{X}_{tr} \\ \mathbf{y} \in \boldsymbol{Y}_{tr}}} \mathcal{L}(\theta, \mathbf{x}, \mathbf{y})$$

The goal of model training is to find parameters θ^* that minimize the model risk. Therefore,

$$\theta^* = \underset{\theta}{\operatorname{argmin}} \ \mathcal{R}(\theta)$$

Assuming that $\mathcal{R}(\theta)$ is convex and differentiable, we have,

$$\nabla_\theta \mathcal{R}(\theta^*) = 0$$

Increasing the weight of a specific training point $\mathbf{x}^*$ by a small amount $\epsilon \in \mathcal{R}$ leads to a new risk function

$$\mathcal{R}_{\mathbf{x}^*,\epsilon}(\theta) = \mathcal{R}(\theta) + \epsilon \mathcal{L}(\theta, \mathbf{x}^*, \mathbf{y}^*)$$

Note: setting $\epsilon = -\frac{1}{|\boldsymbol{X}_{tr}|}$ is equivalent to leaving the training point $\mathbf{x}^*$ out of the training data completely. Minimizing the new model risk leads to a different set of optimal parameters

$$\theta^*_{\mathbf{x}^*,\epsilon} = \arg \min_\theta \mathcal{R}_{\mathbf{x}^*,\epsilon}(\theta)$$

Koh and Liang were able to measure the change in optimal model parameters due to up-weighting $\mathbf{x}^*$ by an infinitesimally small ϵ as

$$\frac{\partial}{\partial \epsilon} \theta^*_{x,\epsilon} = -H_{\theta^*}^{-1} \cdot \nabla_\theta \mathcal{L}(\theta^*, \mathbf{x}^*, \mathbf{y}^*)$$

where $H_{\theta*} = \nabla_\theta^2 \mathcal{R}(\theta)|_{\theta=\theta^*}$ represents the Hessian matrix of the model risk with respect to the model parameters [14]. Koh and Liang defined the influence of a training point, $\mathbf{x}^*$, on the loss at a test input, $\mathbf{x}'$ as

$$\mathcal{I}(\mathbf{x}^*, \mathbf{x}') \stackrel{\text{def}}{=} \frac{\partial}{\partial \epsilon} \mathcal{L}(\theta^*, \mathbf{x}', \mathbf{y}') \bigg|_{\epsilon=0}$$
$$= -\nabla_\theta \mathcal{L}(\theta^*, \mathbf{x}', \mathbf{y}')^T \cdot H_{\theta*}^{-1} \cdot \nabla_\theta \mathcal{L}(\theta^*, \mathbf{x}^*, \mathbf{y}^*)$$

Thus, the quantity $Q_1 = \frac{1}{|\mathbf{X}_{tr}|} H_{\theta*}^{-1} \cdot \nabla_\theta \mathcal{L}(\theta^*, \mathbf{x}^*, \mathbf{y}^*)$ measures the change in the optimal model parameters and the quantity $Q_2 = -\frac{1}{|\boldsymbol{X}_{tr}|} \mathcal{I}(\mathbf{x}^*, \mathbf{x}')$ measures the change in model loss at a test point $\mathbf{x}'$, when the training point $\mathbf{x}^*$ has been left out from training. Koh and Liang experimentally verified that their approach is equivalent to leaving one data point out and retraining the model [14].

Our proposal: With this formulation, we propose to use influence functions to implement right-to-be-forgotten in existing models. When a user requests for his/her data to be removed, the data processor must identify all the machine learning models where the user's personal data was used for training. Having complete access to the model parameters, the processor can compute the new parameters when the user's data is removed from the training set. These new parameters can be easily computed by measuring the influence of the user's data and adding the amounts specified by Q_1 to the parameters. Influence functions also allow a neutral auditor to audit and confirm that the request to erase data was completed. To do so, the auditor must maintain the store of the current parameters used in the model. When a right-to-be-forgotten request is made, the requesting user can provide his or her data securely to the auditor and the auditor can measure the change in model parameters before and after the erasure request. If the change measures out to be the same as that specified by influence functions (Q_1), then the auditor can verify that the request was correctly processed. Even if the data processor cannot give the model parameters to the auditor, say to protect intellectual property, the auditor can maintain a standard set of test inputs and measure the change in the model's loss on these inputs. If the change is equivalent to the amount specified by influence function (Q_2), the auditor can verify that the request was properly met.

One of the advantages of using influence functions is that their use to implement right-to-be-forgotten does not require major changes to existing models or to training methods. Therefore, the use of influence functions does not adversely affect the model's performance or add substantial operating cost for the data processor. However, this approach is not a complete solution. If the model is stolen or leaked, the attacker might be able to re-create all the sensitive data. To protect user's personal information against this possibility, it is important to train models that are resilient to membership and attribute inference attacks. Differential privacy can be used for training such models [10].

4.2 Differential Privacy

Differential privacy is a framework proposed by Dwork *et al.* [10], that captures precisely how much additional information of an individual is leaked by participating in a dataset, that would not have been leaked otherwise. Responsible dataset curators can use differential privacy practices to measure the leakage of information pertaining to individuals when disclosing aggregate statistics about the data and when replying to dataset queries in general. In the context of machine learning, the differential privacy framework allows one to measure how much additional information a machine learning model leaks about an individual.

Formally, a randomized learning algorithm $\mathcal{A}$ is said to be (ϵ, δ) *differentially-private* if, for two datasets $\mathbf{X}$, $\mathbf{X}'$ differing in only data point, and a machine learning model $\mathcal{M}$,

$$Pr[\mathcal{A}(\mathbf{X}') = \mathcal{M}] \leq e^\epsilon Pr[\mathcal{A}(\mathbf{X}) = \mathcal{M}] + \delta$$

That is, the probability that the learning algorithm $\mathcal{A}$ returns a model $\mathcal{M}$ is approximately the same, whether it is trained on $\mathbf{X}$ or $\mathbf{X}'$. The lower the values of the parameters ϵ and δ are, the higher the privacy provided by the randomized learning algorithm.

Hence, differential privacy provides guarantees about how much the addition or removal of a data point from the training dataset will affect the trained machine learning model. Consequently, a learning algorithm that provides differential privacy guarantees with ϵ and δ equal to zero leaks no information about whether a single individual was part of the training dataset or not. Further, learning algorithms that provide such guarantees are immune to inference attacks by definition. Achieving this property in practice however is not trivial and the goal then becomes that of finding the lowest possible (ϵ, δ) while still maintaining utility. Despite this compromise in utility, algorithms that achieve good differential privacy guarantees are increasingly used in practice because the differential privacy metric provides one of the strongest theoretical guarantees of privacy [3].

One of the earliest works combining differential privacy and machine learning was done by Agrawal and Ramakrishnan [4] in which the authors developed a novel algorithm to learn a decision tree classifier on differentially-private data. That is, they considered the problem of building a decision tree classifier on a dataset that was differentially-private. In order to do so, they first developed a reconstruction algorithm that estimated the distribution of the original dataset and then used this estimated distribution in conjunction with the perturbed data in order to build a decision tree classifier. Chaudhari et al. [8] extended research in this direction by generalizing the approach for training differentially-private machine learning models. They did so by developing a differentially-private framework for empirical risk minimization in which they perturbed the objective function to provide privacy guarantees. Since then, other works have focused on releasing differentially-private models including logistic regression, 2nd moment matrix approximation, rule mining and more [12,20,26].

In a recent example, Abadi et al. [2] developed a method for providing differential privacy guarantees for deep learning models by adding Gaussian noise to the gradient values during model training. The amount of noise they add is carefully crafted to achieve differential privacy guarantees while still maintaining model efficacy. There has also been progress in situations when part of the dataset is sensitive and the other part is public. Papernot et al. [17] developed a framework in which first a fixed number of teacher models are trained on disjoint subsets of the sensitive data. An ensemble of these teacher models is then used to label the public data in a differentially-private manner while keeping number of labeling queries fixed in order to limit privacy cost. The public data along with differentially-private labels is then used to train a student model which provides differential privacy guarantees with respect to the sensitive data.

We note that the application of differential privacy that we have described thus far still requires individuals to place significant trust in the dataset curator. Practical implementations of solid differentially-private algorithms have been found to contain mistakes that result in significantly weaker privacy guarantees in practice than in theory [9,23]. In addition, users still have no protection against the dataset itself being breached or leaked by a malicious insider. Many of these concerns can be alleviated by the application of differential privacy mechanisms directly on individual data at the point of data collection. This practice is known as Local Differential Privacy, which systematically adds noise to the data as it is being collected. The amount of added noise depends on the desired privacy guarantees. As the collected data itself is noisy, even a breach at the data collector does not expose users' raw data. Due to such strict privacy control, local differential privacy tends to severely limit the utility provided by the dataset, and truly massive collections of data may be required to perform even simple analysis, such as frequent itemset mining [5]. In practice, local differential privacy algorithms also destroy the usefulness of the dataset for inferences other than the pre-specified ones which makes it a very attractive technique from a consumer privacy standpoint. For these reasons, it seems important for regulators to encourage the use of local differential privacy techniques when appropriate.

4.3   Machine Unlearning

Cao and Yang developed an approach of making machine learning unlearn a given data point [7]. In their approach, the machine learning model is not directly trained on the training data but on a small number of aggregates (summations) computed on the training data. Each summation is the sum of efficiently computable transformations on the training data. Once these transformations are computed, the training data is erased and only the transforms are used to train the model. To erase the effect of a specific training point, its contribution is subtracted from summed transformations. For certain machine learning algorithms like naive Bayes classifiers or support vector machines, the entire influence of training point can be removed in $\mathcal{O}(1)$ complexity. However, this approach is limited to such algorithms only and not to more advanced methods like deep learning.

   To show how machine unlearning can be implemented in practice, we will use the example of the naive Bayes classifier [7]. Given a data point with features $F_1, F_2, \cdots, F_k$, the label L selected by the classifier is the one which has the maximum probability of being observed given the feature $F_1, F_2, \cdots F_k$. The posterior probability of being observed is computed using the Bayes rules as

$$P(L|F_1, F_2, \cdots F_K) = \frac{P(L) \prod_j P(F_j|L)}{\prod_j P(F_j)}$$

Each component, such as $P(F_j|L)$ is computed from the training data by computing the number of training points that have feature F_j and the label L, i.e. $\#(F_J \text{ AND } L)$ and dividing it with the number of training points that have the label L, i.e. $\#(L)$. That is, $P(F_j|L) = \frac{\#(F_J \text{ AND } L)}{\#(L)}$. From the point of view of the classifier only these aggregates are important and once they are computed, individual data points can be discarded. To unlearn a data point, we only need the feature F and the label L of the data point and update these counts. Say we need to remove a data point that has both the feature F_j and the label L, we need to update $P(F_j|L) = \frac{\#(F_J \text{ AND } L)-1}{\#(L)-1}$. Other sophisticated algorithms like Support Vector Machines and k-mean clustering can also be represented in this form [7].

Despite its efficacy and efficiency, machine unlearning suffers from two main drawbacks. One, it still requires that the data point to be removed must be submitted in its raw format to an auditor to fulfill the removal request. This is so because the model creator may have removed all the raw data and might only be storing the summations and the features/label of the data point have to be re-submitted by the user to update the summations. Machine unlearning shares this drawback with the use of influence functions proposed in Sect. 4.1. Two, machine unlearning provides no way to tell whether a specific data point is currently being used to train the current machine learning model or not. This is in contrast to the use of influence functions where low influence of a data point may imply that either it is not part of the training set or it is not an important piece of data for training. This makes the job of an auditor difficult as model designer can claim that the user's data is not being used from training.

5   Discussion and Conclusions

In this position paper, we identify machine learning models as indirect stores of personal information. We described membership and attribute inference attacks that can be used to recover the personal information hidden in these models. Due to this fact, we suggest that the right to erasure enshrined in GDPR Article 17 must extend not only to raw storage of personal information but also to machine learning models trained with such information. We describe three methods (i) influence functions (ii) differential privacy, and (iii) machine unlearning that either allow erasure of specific data points from trained models or train models from which original data cannot be recovered. Such methods can allow services that build models on personal information to maintain users' privacy with minimal cost and service disruptions.

Each method has its own benefits and limitations. Influence functions have an advantage that they can work on existing models without requiring any fundamental change to model training and therefore, do not impact the utility of the model. However, removal of data using influence functions requires that the raw data be submitted to the auditor. Differential privacy provides the strongest guarantee of privacy among all the listed methods but it requires the development of new training methods altogether and may suffers from loss in the model's utility (some works [17] claim that differential privacy acts as a regularization technique and may actually improve model performance). Machine unlearning requires some logistical changes in training. Also, it does not work with all machine learning models, requires raw data sample to be submitted for removal, and provide no way to inferring if a data point is already being used to train the algorithm. Thus, each approach may be suitable in some context while not in others. The goal of achieving privacy in machine learning models also appears to be at odds with other desirable properties, such as explainability and transparency. Therefore, it is important to invest in lines of research that develop models that maintain privacy while providing transparency and explainability.

References

1. Equifax identifies additional 2.4 million customers hit by data breach (2018). https://www.nbcnews.com/business/business-news/equifax-identifies-additional-2-4-million-customers-hit-data-breach-n852226

2. Abadi, M., et al.: Deep learning with differential privacy. In: Proceedings of the 2016 ACM SIGSAC Conference on Computer and Communications Security, CCS 2016, pp. 308–318. ACM, New York (2016)

3. Abowd, J.M.: The US Census Bureau adopts differential privacy. In: Proceedings of the 24th ACM SIGKDD International Conference on Knowledge Discovery & Data Mining, KDD 2018, pp. 2867–2867 (2018)

4. Agrawal, R., Srikant, R.: Privacy-preserving data mining. In: ACM SIGMOD Record, vol. 29, pp. 439–450. ACM (2000)

5. Bittau, A., et al.: PROCHLO: strong privacy for analytics in the crowd. In: Proceedings of the 26th Symposium on Operating Systems Principles (SOSP), pp. 441–459. ACM (2017)

6. Cadwalladr, C., Graham-Harrison, E.: Revealed: 50 million facebook profiles harvested for cambridge analytica in major data breach (2018). https://www.theguardian.com/news/2018/mar/17/cambridge-analytica-facebook-influence-us-election

7. Cao, Y., Yang, J.: Towards making systems forget with machine unlearning. In: 2015 IEEE Symposium on Security and Privacy, pp. 463–480, May 2015. https://doi.org/10.1109/SP.2015.35

8. Chaudhuri, K., Monteleoni, C., Sarwate, A.D.: Differentially private empirical risk minimization. J. Mach. Learn. Res. **12**(Mar), 1069–1109 (2011)

9. Ding, Z., Wang, Y., Wang, G., Zhang, D., Kifer, D.: Detecting violations of differential privacy. In: Proceedings of the 2018 ACM SIGSAC Conference on Computer and Communications Security, CCS 2018, pp. 475–489. ACM, New York (2018)

10. Dwork, C., McSherry, F., Nissim, K., Smith, A.: Calibrating noise to sensitivity in private data analysis. In: Halevi, S., Rabin, T. (eds.) TCC 2006. LNCS, vol. 3876, pp. 265–284. Springer, Heidelberg (2006). https://doi.org/10.1007/11681878_14

11. Regulation (EU) 2016/679 of the European Parliament and of the Council of 27 April 2016 on the protection of natural persons with regard to the processing of personal data and on the free movement of such data, and repealing Directive 95/46/EC (General Data Protection Regulation). Official Journal of the European Union L119, pp. 1–88, May 2016. http://eur-lex.europa.eu/legal-content/EN/TXT/?uri=OJ:L:2016:119:TOC

12. Evfimievski, A., Srikant, R., Agrawal, R., Gehrke, J.: Privacy preserving mining of association rules. Inf. Syst. **29**(4), 343–364 (2004)

13. Fredrikson, M., Jha, S., Ristenpart, T.: Model inversion attacks that exploit confidence information and basic countermeasures. In: Proceedings of the 22nd ACM SIGSAC Conference on Computer and Communications Security, CCS 2015, pp. 1322–1333. ACM, New York (2015). https://doi.org/10.1145/2810103.2813677

14. Koh, P.W., Liang, P.: Understanding black-box predictions via influence functions. In: International Conference on Machine Learning (2017)

15. McDonald, A.M., Cranor, L.F.: The cost of reading privacy policies. ISJLP **4**, 543 (2008)
16. Veale, M., Binns, R., Edwards, L.: Algorithms that remember: model inversion attacks and data protection law. Philos. Trans. R. Soc. A: Math. Phys. Eng. Sci. **376**(2133), 20180083 (2018)
17. Papernot, N., Song, S., Mironov, I., Raghunathan, A., Talwar, K., Erlingsson, Ú.: Scalable private learning with pate. CoRR abs/1802.08908 (2018)
18. Parkhi, O.M., Vedaldi, A., Zisserman, A.: Deep face recognition. In: British Machine Vision Conference (2015)
19. Salem, A., Zhang, Y., Humbert, M., Berrang, P., Fritz, M., Backes, M.: ML-leaks: model and data independent membership inference attacks and defenses on machine learning models. In: 26th Annual Network and Distributed System Security Symposium (NDSS 2019), February 2019. https://publications.cispa.saarland/2754/
20. Sheffet, O.: Private approximations of the 2nd-moment matrix using existing techniques in linear regression. arXiv preprint arXiv:1507.00056 (2015)
21. Shokri, R., Stronati, M., Shmatikov, V.: Membership inference attacks against machine learning models. In: 2017 IEEE Symposium on Security and Privacy (SP), pp. 3–18 (2017)
22. Srivastava, N., Hinton, G., Krizhevsky, A., Sutskever, I., Salakhutdinov, R.: Dropout: a simple way to prevent neural networks from overfitting. J. Mach. Learn. Res. **15**, 1929–1958 (2014)
23. Tang, J., Korolova, A., Bai, X., Wang, X., Wang, X.: Privacy loss in apple's implementation of differential privacy on MacOS 10.12. CoRR (2017). http://arxiv.org/abs/1709.02753
24. Valentino-DeVries, J., Singer, N., Keller, M.H., Krolik, A.: Your apps know where you were last night, and they're not keeping it secret (2018). https://www.nytimes.com/interactive/2018/12/10/business/location-data-privacy-apps.html?module=inline
25. Yeom, S., Giacomelli, I., Fredrikson, M., Jha, S.: Privacy risk in machine learning: analyzing the connection to overfitting. In: 2018 IEEE 31st Computer Security Foundations Symposium (CSF), pp. 268–282 (2018)
26. Zhu, T., Li, G., Zhou, W., Yu, P.S.: Differentially private deep learning. Differential Privacy and Applications. AIS, vol. 69, pp. 67–82. Springer, Cham (2017). https://doi.org/10.1007/978-3-319-62004-6_7

Risk Assessment

A Multilateral Privacy Impact Analysis Method for Android Apps

Majid Hatamian[1(✉)], Nurul Momen[2], Lothar Fritsch[2], and Kai Rannenberg[1]

[1] Chair of Mobile Business & Multilateral Security, Goethe University Frankfurt,
Frankfurt, Germany
{majid.hatamian,kai.rannenberg}@m-chair.de
[2] Department of Mathematics and Computer Science, Karlstad University,
Karlstad, Sweden
{nurul.momen,lothar.fritsch}@kau.se

Abstract. Smartphone apps have the power to monitor most of people's private lives. Apps can permeate private spaces, access and map social relationships, monitor whereabouts and chart people's activities in digital and/or real world. We are therefore interested in how much information a particular app can and intends to retrieve in a smartphone. Privacy-friendliness of smartphone apps is typically measured based on single-source analyses, which in turn, does not provide a comprehensive measurement regarding the actual privacy risks of apps. This paper presents a multi-source method for privacy analysis and data extraction transparency of Android apps. We describe how we generate several data sets derived from privacy policies, app manifestos, user reviews and actual app profiling at run time. To evaluate our method, we present results from a case study carried out on ten popular fitness and exercise apps. Our results revealed interesting differences concerning the potential privacy impact of apps, with some of the apps in the test set violating critical privacy principles. The result of the case study shows large differences that can help make relevant app choices.

Keywords: Smartphone apps · Case study · Security · Privacy ·
Android · Privacy policy · Reviews · Privacy impact ·
Privacy score and ranking · Privacy risk · Transparency

1 Introduction

Consumers nowadays frequently use smartphone apps to support and organize various parts of their everyday errands, and accordingly, smartphones have become an indispensable part of our lives. Today's smartphones are equipped with sensing and recording capabilities such as camera, microphone, fingerprint recognition, proximity sensors, gyroscope, accelerometer, and more. These are embedded into the hardware made available to apps and the operating system. As a result, they produce a diverse range of information including sensitive

© Springer Nature Switzerland AG 2019
M. Naldi et al. (Eds.): APF 2019, LNCS 11498, pp. 87–106, 2019.
https://doi.org/10.1007/978-3-030-21752-5_7

personal information. Importantly, because of their mobile nature and use of wireless communication protocols (e.g. NFC, Bluetooth, 4G, WiFi) to interact with the environment, they are capable to access, use and transmit such sensitive data to remote servers without user interaction or without user insight into what is being transferred. Such a context-sensitive digital ecosystem is highly at risk to produce privacy violations (e.g. unwanted collection, processing, sharing or invasion [17,35]). This makes it quite challenging and difficult for the users to compare apps' privacy aspects and performance and to protect their own privacy. Thus, it is of particular importance to generate transparency by providing quantifiability and thus comparability of apps in regard to their privacy impact [16].

This paper presents a combined method for app privacy analysis and increased transparency that uses several sets of input data. In a joint effort, two research groups [18,19,24] performed a data collection campaign and combined several analysis approaches into the method presented in this paper. We analyze textual privacy policies from app markets. In addition, we extract the use of so-called "dangerous permissions" from the app metadata. We extract and classify end user information on app threats from public app reviews on the Google Play app store. Finally, we monitor app execution by logging app behavior when showing the dangerous permission credentials to the operating system's access control system before they access data sources. The data from these sources then is analyzed and visualized. The method results in tabular and graphical overlays of the input data that can show deviations among privacy policies, reviews, manifestos and actual app behavior. We developed scoring and ranking schemes to compare the level of personal data usage of apps before installation and during installation. To illustrate the method, we show data from a case study with data captured from a set of ten popular fitness apps. Our results enable both *ex-ante* and *ex-post* transparency in the perspective presented in [25], in order to combine the advantages of both concepts, which allows the incorporation of factual app behavior in app choice decisions and app privacy impact evaluation.

Motivation: Which privacy-sensitive data does a mobile app really aim to extract from smartphones? Does the app behavior correlate with the promises of the privacy policy? What are the user's privacy-invasive experiences with the apps? Do the user's concerns reflect correlated privacy threats? And how will a consumer or a public authority decide which app of a set of possible candidates poses the least or an acceptable privacy risk and impact on its users? To answer these questions, we develop a method that extracts data about apps from several sources and prepares the data to enable comparison of app privacy impact.

Contribution: In this paper, we show how data from various sources can be used to assess the potential privacy impact of mobile apps. We further show results from an application of our method to a case study of apps. We identified several privacy issues visible from the data. By providing an understanding of app privacy behavior through data visualization techniques, we show how the data can easily be visualized with each other.

Outline: The rest of this paper is organized as follows: First, we explain our data acquisition and comparison method for privacy impact assessment of mobile apps in Sect. 2. Section 3 describes our analysis methods used to overlay the data and presents the results of our case study on fitness apps. Then we discuss related work and background relevant for our methodology in Sect. 4. Finally, we conclude this paper and point out directions for future research in Sect. 5.

2 Data Acquisition Methodology

Our multilateral privacy impact analysis is based on a four-pillar methodology as shown by Fig. 1. We acquire and process information relevant for app privacy impact from four sources named A1–A4. The sources of information are related to app vendors, end user feedback and actual app behavior measurements. Our method processes both static and dynamic information about each app's access to personal data. In the following subsections, each pillar is further detailed.

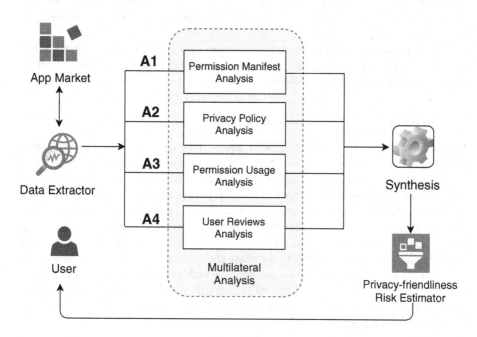

Fig. 1. A high-level overview of our multilateral privacy impact analysis approach.

2.1 Permission Manifest Analysis (A1)

We collect app developers' data access intentions from the apps' Android manifest. In this app metadata, developers declare use of so-called sensitive permissions that grant access to data such as call logs, contact lists, sensors or location tracks on smartphones.

Prior to Android 6.0, users had to grant all the requested permissions at install-time and they were not able to revoke those permissions later. Hence, data access was then unlimited for the future. No information about frequency, volume or amount of personal data retrieved and transferred was provided to the data subjects which is still true to some extent for the post-Marshmallow era. However, in Android 6.0 and later versions, Google initiated a new permission manager system where the users are able to revise/revoke permissions at run-time. Although this was an enhancement to give more privacy controls to the users, but still it was not effective. This is mainly because ordinary users mostly do not understand the technical definitions of permission requests [11]. Also, they sometimes value the use of the apps more than their privacy [10, 34]. Many apps transfer large amounts of data to remote servers. The access permissions are added by app developers, however the privacy policy prose that should be the base of data subject consent upon installing an app is often very difficult to interpret when looking for cues about what personal data will be extracted from a smartphone. In consequence, it is very difficult to assess the actual consumption of personal data carried out by apps, and thus data subject risk assessment or impact assessment is difficult.

The permissions are usually granted for an app on a permanent basis after initial end user approval upon installation. The user will not learn how often which permissions are being used to access data.

2.2   Privacy Policy Analysis (A2)

As mobile apps are directly dealing with users' personal data, they need to fulfill a certain degree of privacy and security regulation imposed by law e.g. the GDPR [2]. Legislation requires app providers to inform users about their data collection and processing practices in a written privacy policy. Hence, privacy policies are the main source for users to inform themselves about how an app deals with their personal information [32]. In our analysis, we pay attention to privacy policy texts to examine the extent to which they are correlated with what the developer's request (in manifest) and what they do (actual permission usage) in reality. Hence, we also check the extent to which the app privacy policies are actually focusing on the app data collection practices, e.g. whether or not the purpose specification of data extraction based on the dangerous permissions is already clear in the policy text.

2.3   Permission Usage Analysis (A3)

Mobile app users trade their data for service usage in non-transparent ways. Accessibility to user data through permissions gives *carte-blanche*[1] access for the app without any constraints. Though the user has the option to revoke granted permissions, the absence of monitoring tools and unexpected consequences such

---

[1] Full discretionary power (Merriam-Webster dictionary), Retrieved on November 22, 2018.

as service exclusion or malfunctions may cause hindrances [5, 12, 36]. So we measure apps' permission access patterns based on the method described in [23]. We argue that such information can reveal apps' behavior and its impact on individual privacy. It has the potential to assist the user to compare apps based on potential privacy impact and to make decisions based on privacy-friendliness. A comparison matrix or ranking will also be helpful for choosing apps with the least impact for delivering a desired service.

2.4   User Reviews Analysis (A4)

User reviews on app market are an additional source of information regarding app properties. Some contain privacy-related complaints from users. Such complaints can reveal actual privacy risks. Therefore, we try to extract such information from the reviews. However, such information is unstructured and it is quite time consuming to manually code thousands of reviews to gain knowledge about the privacy aspects of apps. Therefore, we exploit this important source of information by automatically collecting reviews and then applying machine learning and natural language processing techniques to extract comments on perceived app privacy problems based on the analysis of user reviews. The resulting data is a mapping of apps into a privacy threat classification. We detect not only a privacy and security relevant user review, but also determine the underlying threat. Based on our already proposed threat catalog [18], we use these threats as the input for the classifier as described in Table 1.

3   Multilateral Analysis

This section describes our case study of fitness apps from four different perspectives (A1–A4). It discusses findings and insights gained. Our data collection was performed in October and November 2018. The first two phases of analysis are focused on data sources that are available for ex-ante transparency scenarios. First, apps' metadata is collected from Google Play store to determine the required permissions that are stated ahead of installation. Second, app's privacy policy documents are collected and analyzed to adjudicate the cohesion with technical data access intents (manifest data) as described in Sect. 2.2. The third and fourth phases are focused on the data sources that are accessible through ex-post transparency scenarios. Ten fitness and exercise monitoring apps (called the app set in the remainder of this text) were chosen based on the top search results on the Google Play app store and were installed and dynamically monitored to measure their permission access requests. Such selection is rationalized as follows: (1) Researchers have raised serious privacy and security concerns resulted from using invasive health and fitness related apps [20, 22, 28]; (2) Such apps are sometimes underestimated by the users and we intend to highlight the gap between their perception and reality. User reviews of fitness apps can be treated as complementing factor to the technical properties that is measured, which also supports the emphasis on transparency and intervenability by the

Table 1. Identified threats (shown by T).

#	Threat	Description
T1	Tracking & spyware	Allows an attacker to access or infer personal data to use it for marketing purposes, such as profiling
T2	Phishing	An attacker collects user credentials (such as passwords and credit card numbers) by means of fake apps or (SMS, email) messages that seem genuine
T3	Unintended data disclosure	Users are not always aware of app functionalities. Even if they have given explicit consent, users may be unaware that an app collects and publishes personal data
T4	Targeted ads	Refers to unwanted ads and push notifications
T5	Spam	Threat of receiving unsolicited, undesired or illegal messages. Spam is considered an invasion of privacy. The receipt of spam can also be considered a violation of our right to determine for ourselves when, how, and to what extent information about us is used
T6	General	Comprises all the issues that are not categorized into other threats, such as permission hungry apps, general privacy and security concerns, etc

GDPR [9]. As compared with other popular app categories such as *Lifestyle*, users are not well-aware of the potential negative consequences of using privacy invasive health/fitness-based apps. For instance, in the early 2018, already people were informed about Facebook-Cambridge Analytica data privacy scandal [3]. Hence, it is generally believed that lifestyle-based and social networking apps are the only main potential sources of privacy violations; (3) As a result of extreme proliferation of gadgets and physical activity trackers (such as FitBit), users are currently surrounded by such technologies. Such technological trend is highly dependent on wireless communications between gadgets and smartphones (i.e. health/fitness-based apps) that may potentially impose privacy risks (we can refer to the fitness tracking app gives away location of secret US military bases as a famous example of such dire consequences [4]). The app set is listed on Table 2. Finally, user reviews (collected during the first phase) are analyzed in order to take perceptions and concerns of the user into account. In the following subsections, we explain analysis steps A1–A4 from Fig. 1.

3.1   Step A1: Permission Manifest Analysis

In order to perform tasks in Android, apps can request access to system resources through permissions. The permissions are requested to enable functionality of apps, but they typically exceed this bare-bone minimum requirement, and hence are not privacy friendly. Depending on the resource types, consent from the user is required. There are four types of permissions[2]: *normal, dangerous, signature* and *signatureOrSystem. Normal* level permissions allow access to resources that are considered low-risk, and they are granted during installation of any package requesting them. The *dangerous* level permissions are required to access resources that are considered to be high-risk. In this case, the user must grant permission. So-called *signature* level permissions grant access only to packages with the same author. Finally, *signatureOrSystem* level permissions grant both packages with the same author and packages installed in the system receive permission to access specific resources. Every application or app has a *manifest* file which contains information about that particular app (for example - its name, author, icon, and description). It provides information about the required permissions that are requested by the developer. Analyzing the manifest and corresponding permission list offers the primary insight regarding potential personal data access.

Data Collection. On the Google Play app store, there is made available public information about apps. Once we obtain the apps' url in the Google Play app store web pages, we can gather the information that we are interested in. We used the scraper in [1] and for each app we retrieved its app ID, title, ratings, number of downloads (installs), app category, permission requests and associated user reviews. Our data set comprises the information of 27,356 apps within *Health & Fitness* category from Google Play. In general, there are 142 distinct types of permissions being extracted across 27,356 apps.

Permission Request Analysis. The ten most requested permissions from our app set can be seen in Fig. 2(top). Also, we retrieved the ten most requested permissions corresponding to the ten selected fitness apps (based on the search results, see Fig. 2(bottom)) to examine and compare how different is the requested permissions within the whole category and the chosen app set. As it can be seen, the most and the least widely requested permissions are INTERNET (93.88%) and RECORD_AUDIO (6.55%) respectively. Interestingly, almost all the permission requests (except WAKE_LOCK and VIBRATION) are among dangerous permission requests. When it comes to the chosen set of ten apps, MICROPHONE is substituted by SENSOR. Nevertheless, the rest combination is still intact, however, the percentages and permutations are different.

3.2   Step A2: Privacy Policy Analysis

We also analyzed the declaration of sensitive permission requests by apps to their privacy policy information. For example, we investigated whether or not the app developers claim in their privacy policies that they are going to use a certain sensitive permission. The result is a gap analysis showing the difference between policy declaration and app privileges.

---

[2] https://developer.android.com/guide/topics/permissions/overview; [Accessed: 2018 -11-27].

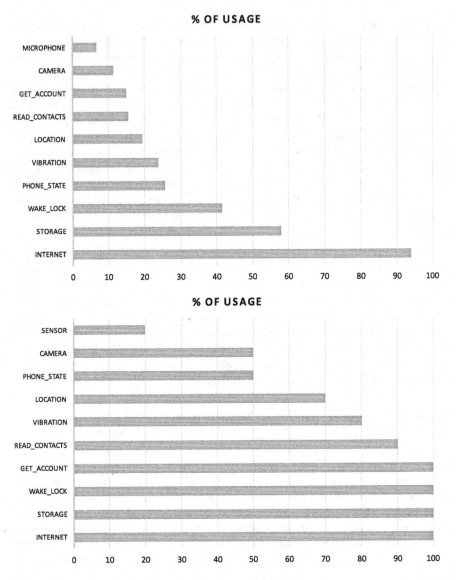

Fig. 2. The 10 most requested permissions in: (Top) *Health & Fitness* category, (Bottom) chosen set of popular 10 apps within *Health & Fitness* category.

Data Collection. We collected the privacy policy texts of the app set. Considering the dangerous sensitive permission request list, two researchers manually coded the data and checked the specification of such permissions in privacy policy texts. Due to frequent evolving nature of apps and their corresponding policies, we archived privacy policy documents of apps on 12 November, 2018.

Table 2. Purpose specification analysis of app privacy policy texts: clarified in the policy: ✓, not clarified: ×, not using that permission: N

App #	CAMERA	SMS	CONTACTS	LOCATION	PHONE	MICROPHONE	SENSOR
Lifesum	×	N	×	N	N	N	×
Endomondo	N	N	✓	✓	✓	N	✓
30dayFitnessChallenge	N	N	×	N	N	N	N
Runkeeper	×	N	×	✓	N	N	N
Pedometer	×	N	✓	✓	×	N	✓
MyFitnessPal	×	N	×	✓	✓	N	✓
Runtastic	N	N	✓	✓	N	×	✓
7minutesWorkout	N	N	N	N	×	N	N
Fitbit	×	×	✓	✓	✓	N	N
Google Fit	N	N	✓	✓	N	N	✓

Purpose Specification Analysis. Art. 5 (1b) GDPR limits the collection and processing of personal data to "specified, explicit and legitimate purposes" and it says: *"personal data shall be collected for specified, explicit and legitimate purposes and not further processed in a manner that is incompatible with those purposes"* [9]. Therefore, it is of particular importance to examine the extent to which the studied mobile apps are fulfilling such requirement. As shown in Table 2, we found 14 incidents where the app developers failed to clarify the need of requesting certain sensitive permissions in their written privacy policy texts (shown by ×).

3.3 Step A3: Permission Usage Analysis

In this section, we present results of a measurement which was conducted in Fall 2018 to determine permission usage patterns of fitness apps in an idle scenario (no user interaction with the app). The app set was installed to observe their activity throughout a period of seven days. In order to do so, apps' permission access log was collected. Apps accessing lower amount of dangerous permissions are assumed as more privacy-friendly.

Data Collection. A prototype probing tool named *Aware* was used for collecting logs of apps' permission usage [24]. It runs as an Android service and documents apps' permission access patterns from Android's AppOpsCommand[3]. Periodically, it checks for the last permission access event by each of the installed apps and writes respective events in a predefined format. Data collection was carried out for one week (starting on 22 October, 2018 and ending on 29 October, 2018). The target apps were installed on a Nokia 5 Android device running

---

[3] https://android.googlesource.com/platform/frameworks/base/+/android-6.0. 1_r25/cmds/appops/src/com/android/commands/appops/AppOpsCommand.java; Accessed: 2018-10-23.

on a vendor stock ROM (Android 7.1.1) which was rooted for monitoring. The apps under investigation were not interacted by any user.

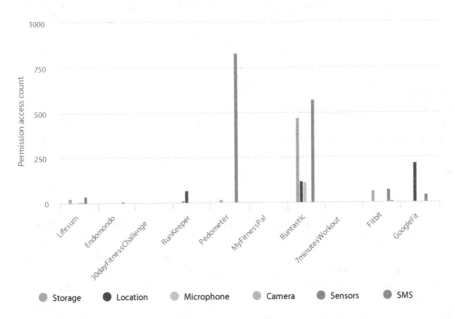

Fig. 3. Permission usage: majority of the fitness apps (7 out of 10) kept accessing dangerous permissions, despite having no user interaction.

Figure 3 shows permission-access activity associated with the unused apps. Accessing to some sensitive permissions such as storage, microphone, SMS and camera while the apps are not being actively used may lead to the following conclusions:

Permission Access Analysis. The collected log indicates the intent to access permissions by apps. As idle-time permission access is depicted in Fig. 3, following observations can be drawn from it:

Data Minimization Principle Violation: the permission access events are supposed to be specific to a particular tasks carried out with an app. We found quite the opposite: throughout the experiment period, apps kept accessing permissions. Even though pseudo user installed the apps, their services were not in use. So, resource access by them indicates potential violation of article 5-1(c) of GDPR which states that personal data shall be *adequate, relevant and limited to what is necessary in relation to the purposes for which they are processed ("data minimization")* [9].

Principle of Least Privilege Violation: principle of least privilege (PoLP) was first proposed as a design principle by Saltzer and Schroeder [33]. According to PoLP, "Every program and every user of the system should operate using the least set of privileges necessary to complete the job." Clearly, this principle is directly connected to "data minimization" principle, as we observed some apps accessing dangerous permissions which are irrelevant to their intended functionality, for instance in Fig. 3, Lifesum's usage of CAMERA and MICROPHONE. Also, the need of requesting and accessing such sensitive permissions was unclear in the examined privacy policy texts.

3.4   Step A4: User Reviews Analysis

Crowdsourced user reviews for apps are an additional reference point for identifying privacy threats. It allows us to take the individual's privacy attitudes into account and map the identified threats to the corresponding cases. We extracted app market user feedback for the app set.

Data Collection. Using the tool in [1], we collected a data set consisting of 44,643 user reviews corresponding to the app set from the Google Play app store (in Nov 2018) with a maximum number of 4,500 reviews per app.

Privacy Relevant Complaints Analysis. Our goal was to understand what users were posting about privacy issues of apps. We were interested to first extract such information, and then, to determine the granularity of privacy relevant statements (to extract potential privacy threats of apps based on the analysis of their user reviews). Based on our previous work [18], we used the collected data as an input for a trained machine learning algorithm (*Logistic Regression (LR)* implemented in scikit-learn [29]). This ultimately led to a smaller result set. In the end, we detected 1,145 privacy and security-based user reviews. We used recall, precision and F-score metrics to evaluate the performance of the classifier. The values of these metrics show how well the classifier's results correspond to the annotated results. The observation is that the overall recall, precision and F-score values are of 78.19%, 86.13% and 81.59%, respectively. As the performance analysis of our classification approach is out of the scope of this paper, in the following we mainly focus on the quality of the results (information) that we gathered out of the user reviews. To gain better understanding of the classified user reviews, Table 3 shows some examples regarding the strength of our analysis in distinguishing different types of user reviews and their relevant threat.

In Table 4 and Fig. 4 we report the identified privacy threats associated to each individual fitness app (✓ represents the identified threats) and the total number of privacy relevant user reviews per app, respectively. As can be seen, Runkeeper and FitBit comprise the highest number of threat-related complaints.

The Most Mentioned Permissions. Overall, we found 240 statements corresponding to ten sensitive permissions while some of the privacy relevant user reviews comprise multiple statements referring to a certain permission. Figure 5

Table 3. An example of classified user reviews.

#	Sample user review	T
1	*You don't need to spy on my activities outside of this app. they don't care about their customers, they want to ruin the device with horrible bloatware spyware*	T1
2	*Im still getting warnings that my phone is infected with virus after i update and scan again. If its not going to work why download it. I have very limited memory to use. No need to download stupid apps that dont work*	T2
3	*SHit!Takes control of device.. why my photo is there??!!*	T3
4	*Ads are terrible Sorry but the ads are comparing to the website really irritating*	T4
5	*Simple interface to use with plenty of features - but pop ups*	T5
6	*Dangerous! requires unnecessary access to sensitive permissions! Uninstalled*	T6

Table 4. List of fitness apps with their respective identified privacy threats (shown by ✓).

No	App name	T1	T2	T3	T4	T5	T6
1	Lifesum	×	×	×	×	×	✓
2	Endomondo	×	×	×	✓	✓	×
3	30dayFitnessChallenge	×	×	×	✓	✓	×
4	Runkeeper	✓	✓	✓	✓	✓	✓
5	Pedometer	×	✓	×	✓	×	×
6	MyFitnessPal	×	×	×	✓	×	×
7	Runtastic	✓	×	✓	✓	×	✓
8	7minutesWorkout	×	×	×	✓	✓	×
9	Fitbit	✓	×	✓	✓	✓	✓
10	Google Fit	×	×	×	✓	✓	×

shows the ten user-mentioned permissions out of our analysis concerning the privacy relevant user reviews. The bar chart depicts that the most mentioned permissions are INTERNET, STORAGE and PHONE_STATE (e.g. complaining about access to outgoing calls, phone numbers) being mentioned 46, 44 and 40 times, respectively. In contrast, CALENDAR, CAMERA and MICROPHONE permissions are the least repetitive permissions.

3.5   Synthesis of Analysis

To achieve an overall app privacy impact analysis, we fused the collected data with a scoring algorithm. We presume all permission accesses to be equally risky for privacy. In addition, we treat the different data sets (A1–A4) as contributing equally to privacy impact when fusing the results. In order to do so, total 36 infraction points were set up for calculating cumulative privacy impact score. We

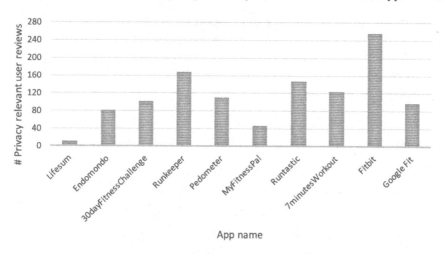

Fig. 4. The total number of privacy relevant reviews per selected app.

assessed the gaps in the privacy policies as defined in Sect. 2.2. In addition, we monitored idle app data access. Both Table 5 and Fig. 6 show our result—ranking of the app set according to the app privacy impact analysis. We acknowledge that the cumulative sum of privacy impact infraction points lacks some obvious factors e.g. dependability on personal context, subjectivity of risk-perception, real-time interaction with apps, individual preferences etc. which remained out of reach for this study due to enormous complexity for adding meaningful weights to impact score and thus, it can be deemed as a limitation.

As the results from four different sources are aggregated into a total privacy impact score as depicted in Table 5, an overall comparison can be drawn from it by ordering from highest to lowest impact score which represents highest to lowest privacy impact. The graphs are presented for each app along with ten dangerous permission groups that could be requested by them (outer blue line in graph). So, an app has the possibility to accumulate total impact score of 36 (10 for requesting permissions, 10 for not clarifying purposes in privacy policy (black segments in graph), 10 for accessing permissions when the app is not in use (red segments in graph) and 6 for identified threats from user review analysis). For instance, in Table 5, Fitbit's privacy impact score is 20 (sum of requested permissions, missing clarifications, usage during idle time and number of identified threats from user review analysis).

From the graphical representation of apps' privacy impact in Fig. 6, it is evident that 30dayFitnessChallenge and 7minutesWorkout are more privacy-preserving choices than the rest of the apps. As it is visualized with blue lines (representing permission groups requested in manifest), they are the least permission hungry apps. On the other hand, Fitbit is the most permission hungry app (it requests for 9 out of 10 dangerous permission groups). However, apps' privacy policies lack declaration of data processing related to permissions. These discrepancies are visualized with black pie-slices which are placed along-

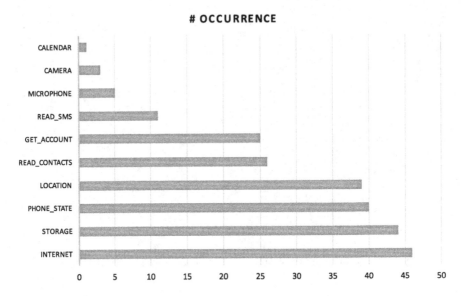

Fig. 5. 10 most user-mentioned permissions in user reviews.

side corresponding permission groups. `Google Fit` and `Endomondo` do not have any discrepancy between their manifest's permission requests and available clarifications in respective privacy policies.

Permission access measured while the app set was installed without user interaction are presented with red areas in the app graphs in Fig. 6. Only three out of ten chosen apps show no idle usage of their listed permissions: `30dayFitnessChallenge`, `7minutesWorkout` and `MyFitnessPal`. The fourth judgment criterion, user review analysis, is not plotted in Fig. 6 due to the fact that it becomes cumbersome for visual representation, but the threat count (T) is considered in total impact score calculation. In Table 5, the identified threats from user review analysis are mapped to the corresponding apps. As it is depicted in the rightmost column for instance, `Runkeeper` is subjected to the most privacy threats that are identified from user reviews, but it ranks second according to the total privacy impact score.

Based on our analysis, an app can be deemed as more privacy-preserving if it requests fewer number of dangerous permissions, has less discrepancy between manifest and available clarification in policy document, has reasonable permission usage during run-time and has fewer threats from user review analysis.

4   Related Work

The assessment of privacy risk and privacy impact suffers from a general shortage of empirical data that provides the basis for privacy risk analysis [13]. Risk calculations are made difficult due to the lack of occurrence and damage information. Analysis therefore looks for other cues, e.g. static properties of program

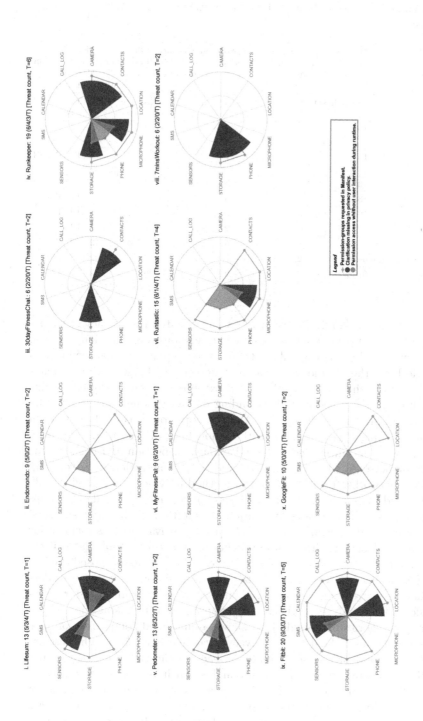

Fig. 6. Visual comparison of apps' privacy impact. Headline: App name, privacy impact score out of 36, (parameters in brackets: permissions declared—blue outline, gaps in privacy policy—black segments, data accessed while unused—red transparent segments and T = threat count which is not plotted in graph). (Color figure online)

Table 5. Synthesis of results from multilateral privacy analysis, ordered by privacy impact score.

App	Privacy impact score (out of 36)	Dangerous Permission Groups Requested (out of 10)	Absent Clarifica-tion in Privacy Policy (out of 10)	Idle Permission Usage (out of 10)	Identified Threats from User Reviews (out of 6)
Fitbit	20 (highest)	9	3	3	5 (T1, T3, T4, T5, T6)
Runkeeper	19	6	4	3	6 (T1, T2, T3, T4, T5, T6)
Runtastic	15	6	1	4	4 (T1, T3, T4, T6)
Lifesum	13	5	3	4	1 (T6)
Pedometer	13	6	3	2	2 (T2, T4)
Google Fit	10	5	0	3	2 (T4, T5)
MyFitnessPal	9	6	2	0	1 (T4)
Endomondo	9	5	0	2	2 (T4, T5)
30dayFitness-Challenge	6 (lowest)	2	2	0	2 (T4, T5)
7minutesWorkout	6 (lowest)	2	2	0	2 (T4, T5)

code or code behavior [26,27]. Enck et al. [8] investigated the privacy of smartphone apps by monitoring a set of sensitive permissions, e.g. location, storage, contacts, phone number. In a sample of 311 of the most popular apps downloaded from Google Play, they found five apps that implement dangerous functionalities, and therefore, should be installed with extreme caution. Followed by this study, Enck et al. [7] aimed at understanding of smartphone apps security by proposing a decompiler which recovers Android apps source code directly from its installation image. They analyzed 21 million lines of recovered code from 1,100 free apps using automated tests and manual inspection and it shows the use/misuse of personal/phone identifiers, and deep penetration of advertising and analytics networks. TaintDroid [6] is a method in which the behavior of 30 popular Android apps is studied. The analysis showed that two-third of the apps show suspicious handling of sensitive data and that 15 of them reported users' location to remote advertising servers. *FAIR* [19] is a privacy risk assessment for Android apps and benefits from an app behavior monitoring tool that collects information about accesses to sensitive resources. The authors proposed the calculation of a privacy risk score using a fuzzy logic-based approach that considers type, number and frequency of accesses on resources according to some predefined rules. Their analysis on the 15 most popular apps by installation within different app categories on Google Play shows a quantified comparison of apps by reporting to the user the detected privacy invasive events. Although these are important works and provide insights for privacy researchers, but they do not consider the importance of app meta data analysis such as user reviews, privacy policy, manifest declaration, etc. In [21], the authors investigated the issue of trust when installing a new mobile app. They considered app ratings, reviews and permissions as trust metrics and assessed the trustworthiness of mobile apps.

Similar to this, Habib et al. [15] proposed an automatic framework to assess the trustworthiness of mobile apps. Their framework is structured on app's reputation and state of the art static analysis tools. They evaluated their framework on a data set of some selected apps from the Google Play store that revealed their approach outperforms the existing methods. Neither of these two works studied the privacy-friendliness aspects of mobile apps. Furthermore, they did not investigate the importance of privacy and security analysis of user reviews and they only considered the sentimental aspects of them. Also, the importance of app privacy policy analysis and the correlation between dangerous permission requests (in manifest) and purpose specification (in privacy policy) was not explored. This is why in our work we consider the importance of such aspects and overcome these limitations.

The concept of privacy transparency, in particular ex-post and ex-ante transparency, are presented in detail in [25]. We derived our combined ex-ante and ex-post approach from the ideas discussed in this paper. The privacy impact analysis relates to the principle of multilateral security, which is a security analysis approach that includes all stakeholders' perspectives and needs in a security analysis [30,31]. The visualization of information is crucial when analyzing and comparing complex information. The data sets in this study are of heterogeneous nature, which poses challenges for visualization. With their systematic overview over visual comparison methods, Gleicher et. al. [14] provided us with useful insights, in particular on overlay encoding of graphs with superposition and explicit encoding.

5   Conclusions and Future Work

In this paper, we presented a method to assess privacy impact of Android apps. The method uses four data sources. We demonstrated the use of the method with a case study performed on ten popular fitness and exercise apps available on the Android app market. Our multilateral methodology allows the assessment and comparison of privacy implication of an app from four different perspectives: (a) comparison of apps' resource requirement, (b) assessment of those requirements based on their corresponding privacy policies, (c) quantification of their permission access efforts during run-time and (d) assessment of privacy concerns raised by users. We combined ex-post and ex-ante transparency perspectives and presented the overlaying results in tabular and graphical overlays as well as in an aggregated privacy impact score which can offer an overview of privacy consequences for a given set of apps. This ranking enables sorting the apps by their potential privacy impact.

The case study found considerable gaps between the privacy policies and the privilege requests and in addition, documented suspicious app behavior of some of the apps in the app set. From this preliminary evidence we conclude that the method has potential in providing transparency about app's actual intentions to consume personal data to both end users and regulators. Table 5 and Fig. 6 both show that there are clear differences between app's access request to data and app vendors' declaration about their data access intentions. Our results can therefore be used as a base for personal decision-making about continued or future app use.

Our future work will test and refine the method by evaluating the method through studies on app sets for various purposes in diverse contexts. We are also interested to investigate the impact of such visualization and privacy impact analysis on users' decision making while choosing an app. These steps could include but are not limited to automation of the procedure, prototype development and usability studies. Possibly, our method in the future can support documentation and regulation of privacy violations.

Acknowledgments. This research is partially supported by the ALerT project, Research Council of Norway, IKTPLUSS 2017–2021 and by the European Union Horizon 2020 research and innovation programme under the Marie Skłodowska-Curie grant agreement No 675730 Privacy&Us.

References

1. Google play scraper. https://github.com/facundoolano/google-play-scraper/
2. Eu general data protection regulation (2016). https://eur-lex.europa.eu/legal-content/en/txt/html/?uri=celex:32016r0679. Accessed 8 Aug 2018
3. Facebook data privacy scandal: A cheat sheet (2018). https://www.techrepublic.com/article/facebook-data-privacy-scandal-a-cheat-sheet/. Accessed 11 Jan 2019
4. Fitness app strava lights up staff at military bases (2018). https://www.bbc.com/news/technology-42853072. Accessed 01 Feb 2019
5. Almuhimedi, H., et al.: Your location has been shared 5,398 times!: a field study on mobile app privacy nudging. In: Proceedings of the 33rd Annual ACM Conference on Human Factors in Computing Systems, pp. 787–796. ACM (2015)
6. Enck, W., et al.: TaintDroid: an information-flow tracking system for realtime privacy monitoring on smartphones. In: the Proceedings of the the 9th ACM USENIX Conference on Operating Systems Design and Implementation, Vancouver, BC, Canada, pp. 393–407 (2010)
7. Enck, W., Octeau, D., McDaniel, P., Chaudhuri, S.: A study of android application security. In: the Proceedings of the the 20th USENIX Conference on Security, San Francisco, CA, USA, p. 21 (2011)
8. Enck, W., Ongtang, M., Mcdaniel, P.: On lightweight mobile phone application certification. In: the Proceedings of the the 16th ACM Conference on Computer and Communications Security, Chicago, Illinois, USA, pp. 235–245 (2009)
9. EU Regulation: 679 of the European Parliament and of the Council of 27 April 2016 on the protection of natural persons with regard to the processing of personal data and on the free movement of such data, and repealing Directive 95/46/EC (General Data Protection Regulation). Off J Eur Union p. L119 (2016)
10. Felt, A.P., Egelman, S., Wagner, D.: I've got 99 problems, but vibration ain't one: A survey of smartphone users' concerns. In: the Proceedings of the 2nd ACM Workshop on Security and Privacy in Smartphones and Mobile Devices, SPSM 2012, New York, NY, USA, pp. 33–44 (2012)
11. Felt, A.P., Ha, E., Egelman, S., Haney, A., Chin, E., Wagner, D.: Android permissions: user attention, comprehension, and behavior. In: the Proceedings of the 8th

ACM Symposium on Usable Privacy and Security, SOUPS 2012, New York, NY, USA, pp. 1–3 (2012)

12. Franzen, D., Aspinall, D.: PhoneWrap-Injecting the "How Often" into Mobile Apps. In: Proceedings of the 1st International Workshop on Innovations in Mobile Privacy and Security co-located with the International Symposium on Engineering Secure Software and Systems (ESSoS 2016), pp. 11–19. CEUR-WS.org (2016)

13. Fritsch, L., Abie, H., Regnesentral, N.: Towards a research road map for the management of privacy risks in information systems. In: Gesellschaft für Informatik eV (GI) publishes this series in order to make available to a broad public recent findings in informatics (ie computer science and informa-tion systems), to document conferences that are organized in co-operation with GI and to publish the annual GI Award dissertation, p. 1 (2008)

14. Gleicher, M., Albers, D., Walker, R., Jusufi, I., Hansen, C.D., Roberts, J.C.: Visual comparison for information visualization. Inf. Vis. **10**(4), 289–309 (2011)

15. Habib, S.M., Alexopoulos, N., Islam, M.M., Heider, J., Marsh, S., Müehlhäeuser, M.: Trust4App: automating trustworthiness assessment of mobile applications. In: 2018 17th IEEE International Conference On Trust, Security And Privacy In Computing And Communications/12th IEEE International Conference On Big Data Science And Engineering (TrustCom/BigDataSE), pp. 124–135. IEEE (2018)

16. Hatamian, M., Serna-Olvera, J.: Beacon alarming: informed decision-making supporter and privacy risk analyser in smartphone applications. In: To be Appeared in the Proceedings of the 35th IEEE International Conference on Consumer Electronics (ICCE), USA (2017)

17. Hatamian, M., Kitkowska, A., Korunovska, J., Kirrane, S.: "It's shocking!": analysing the impact and reactions to the A3: android apps behaviour analyser. In: Kerschbaum, F., Paraboschi, S. (eds.) Data and Applications Security and Privacy XXXII, pp. 198–215. Springer International Publishing, Cham (2018)

18. Hatamian, M., Serna, J., Rannenberg, K.: Revealing the unrevealed: mining smartphone users privacy perception on app markets. Comput. Secur. (2019). https://doi.org/10.1016/j.cose.2019.02.010,   http://www.sciencedirect.com/science/article/pii/S0167404818313051

19. Hatamian, M., Serna, J., Rannenberg, K., Igler, B.: Fair: fuzzy alarming index rule for privacy analysis in smartphone apps. In: Lopez, J., Fischer-Hübner, S., Lambrinoudakis, C. (eds.) Trust, Privacy and Security in Digital Business, pp. 3–18. Springer, Cham (2017). https://doi.org/10.1007/978-3-319-98385-1

20. Hutton, L., et al.: Assessing the privacy of mhealth apps for self-tracking: heuristic evaluation approach. JMIR Mhealth Uhealth **6**(10), e185 (2018). https://doi.org/10.2196/mhealth.9217

21. Kuehnhausen, M., Frost, V.S.: Trusting smartphone apps? to install or not to install, that is the question. In: 2013 IEEE International Multi-Disciplinary Conference on Cognitive Methods in Situation Awareness and Decision Support (CogSIMA), pp. 30–37 (2013). https://doi.org/10.1109/CogSIMA.2013.6523820

22. Martínez-Pérez, B., De La Torre-Díez, I., López-Coronado, M.: Privacy and security in mobile health apps: a review and recommendations. J. Med. Syst. **39**(1), 1–8 (2015)

23. Momen, N.: Towards Measuring Apps' Privacy-Friendliness (licentiate thesis). Ph.D. thesis, Karlstads universitet (2018)

24. Momen, N., Pulls, T., Fritsch, L., Lindskog, S.: How much privilege does an app need? investigating resource usage of android apps. In: 2017 15th Annual Conference on Privacy, Security and Trust (PST), pp. 268–2685. IEEE (2017)

25. Murmann, P., Fischer-Hübner, S.: Tools for achieving usable ex post transparency: a survey. IEEE Access **5**, 22965–22991 (2017). https://doi.org/10.1109/ACCESS. 2017.2765539. http://ieeexplore.ieee.org/document/8078167/

26. Paintsil, E., Fritsch, L.: A Taxonomy of privacy and security risks contributing factors. In: Fischer-Hübner, S., Duquenoy, P., Hansen, M., Leenes, R., Zhang, G. (eds.) Privacy and Identity 2010. IAICT, vol. 352, pp. 52–63. Springer, Heidelberg (2011). https://doi.org/10.1007/978-3-642-20769-3_5

27. Paintsil, E., Fritsch, L.: Executable model-based risk analysis method for identity management systems: using hierarchical colored petri nets. In: Furnell, S., Lambrinoudakis, C., Lopez, J. (eds.) TrustBus 2013. LNCS, vol. 8058, pp. 48–61. Springer, Heidelberg (2013). https://doi.org/10.1007/978-3-642-40343-9_5

28. Papageorgiou, A., Strigkos, M., Politou, E., Alepis, E., Solanas, A., Patsakis, C.: Security and privacy analysis of mobile health applications: the alarming state of practice. IEEE Access **6**, 9390–9403 (2018). https://doi.org/10.1109/ACCESS. 2018.2799522

29. Pedregosa, F., et al.: Scikit-learn: machine learning in python. J. Mach. Learn. Res. **12**, 2825–2830 (2011)

30. Rannenberg, K.: Recent development in information technology security evaluation - the need for evaluation criteria for multilateral security. In: Proceedings of the IFIP TC9/WG9.6 Working Conference on Security and Control of Information Technology in Society on Board M/S Illich and Ashore, pp. 113–128. North-Holland Publishing Co., Amsterdam (1994). http://dl.acm.org/citation.cfm?id=647317. 723330

31. Rannenberg, K.: Multilateral security a concept and examples for balanced security. In: Proceedings of the 2000 Workshop on New Security Paradigms. pp. 151–162. NSPW 2000, ACM, New York (2000). https://doi.org/10.1145/366173.366208, http://doi.acm.org/10.1145/366173.366208

32. Reidenberg, J.R., Breaux, T., Carnor, L.F., French, B.: Disagreeable privacy policies: Mismatches between meaning and users' understanding. Berkely Technol. Law J. **30**(1), 39–68 (2015)

33. Saltzer, J.H., Schroeder, M.D.: The protection of information in computer systems. Proc. IEEE **63**(9), 1278–1308 (1975). https://doi.org/10.1109/PROC.1975.9939

34. Solove, D.J.: Nothing to Hide: The False Tradeoff between Privacy and Security. Yale University Press, New Haven (2011)

35. Solove, D.J.: A taxonomy of privacy. U. Pa. L. Rev. **154**, 477 (2005)

36. Van Kleek, M., Liccardi, I., Binns, R., Zhao, J., Weitzner, D.J., Shadbolt, N.: Better the devil you know: exposing the data sharing practices of smartphone apps. In: Proceedings of the 2017 CHI Conference on Human Factors in Computing Systems, pp. 5208–5220. ACM (2017)

Re-using Personal Data for Statistical and Research Purposes in the Context of Big Data and Artificial Intelligence

Yordanka Ivanova[✉]

Sofia University "St. Kliment Ohridski", Sofia, Bulgaria
d_mintcheva@abv.bg

Abstract. This paper analyzes the purpose limitation principle under the General Data Protection Regulation and the opportunities for re-using personal data, in particular for statistical and research purposes. It examines the conditions and the scope of application of the research exemption and the safeguards that must be in place for organisations to be able to re-use personal data without asking for consent from individuals. In general, it is argued that the research exemption could have a rather broad interpretation and application, including in the context of Big Data and Artificial Intelligence. The creation of privacy "regulatory sandboxes" is also proposed as a new form for cooperation between innovators and regulators which could enable the development of privacy-designed innovation products and projects, while keeping supervisory authorities abreast of the risks and impacts posed by the emerging technologies to individuals' privacy and the society at large.

Keywords: Data protection · Purpose limitation · Research exemption · Big data · Artificial intelligence · Privacy regulatory sandbox

1 Introduction

As of 25 May 2018, the General Data Protection Regulation (GDPR)[1] is the single applicable EU legal framework for data protection which imposes a wide range of obligations on public and private organizations processing personal data ("controllers") and respectively envisages high fines for those who fail to comply with them[2]. Amongst its numerous regulations, a key legal hurdle for many controllers, especially for tech companies and other innovators, represents the "principle of purpose limitation" and the degree of flexibility allowed for the re-use of personal data for a purpose, different from the purpose for which the data has been initially collected[3]. The strict application of this principle has been opposed by some Member States in favor of innovation[4] as well as by some scholars who have criticized the obstacles it poses and its incompatibility with Big

---

[1] See Regulation (EU) (2016/679).

[2] Article 83 of the GDPR envisages administrative fines of up to 20 000 000 EUR, or 4% of the total worldwide annual turnover of the controller, whichever is higher.

[3] Article 5(1)(b) of the GDPR.

[4] E.g. Germany during the negotiations process of the revision of the GDPR.

© Springer Nature Switzerland AG 2019
M. Naldi et al. (Eds.): APF 2019, LNCS 11498, pp. 107–135, 2019.
https://doi.org/10.1007/978-3-030-21752-5_8

Data and other technological advances.[5] Nevertheless, albeit with some changes, the principle of purpose limitation has been maintained in the GDPR which may pose challenges for controllers, working in the field of research or in innovative fields such as Big Data analytics, Artificial Intelligence (AI) and other emerging technologies.

The importance of this principle for the lawfulness of the processing activities under GDPR must be also placed in the context of the ambition of the EU and many of its member states to reap the benefits of the data-driven economy and roll out trustworthy AI applications[6] which, can produce many benefits for the society, but may also pose certain risks to privacy and other fundamental rights. In this context, the aim of this paper is to examine the opportunities for re-using personal data for statistical and research purposes and the conditions which the controllers must satisfy to benefit from the research exemption, in particular in the context of Big Data and Artificial Intelligence.

The paper examines, first, the main components of the principle of purpose limitation and arguably the challenges it faces and poses in a world of Big Data and technological innovation. Secondly, it analyzes the conditions and the scope of application of the research and statistical exemption in the context of the re-use of personal data as well as the other derogations it enables from other GDPR provisions. It is generally argued that the principle of purpose limitation allows a margin of flexibility, especially in the context of research, which could in fact make GDPR sufficiently adaptable to the needs and realities of the emerging technologies, not stifling but, on the contrary, enabling privacy-friendly innovation. Still, the flexibility of this principle increases generally the legal uncertainty for the controllers how strictly this principle will be actually applied by the regulators. As a solution to this problem, the paper proposes in the end an innovative approach already initiated by the UK Information Commissioner's Office, notably the creation of privacy "regulatory sandbox(es)" that could be also embraced by the EU and its member states. It is argued that such regulatory sandboxes could provide added value to both regulators and innovators by enabling the development of privacy-designed innovation products and projects, while keeping supervisory authorities abreast of the risks and impacts posed by the emerging technologies to privacy and the society at large.

2   The Purpose Limitation Principle in the Context of Big Data/AI

2.1   The Principle of Purpose Limitation

The principle of purpose limitation is a fundamental principle of data processing enshrined in all major legal acts in Europe[7] which regulate the processing of personal data, including in Article 5(1)(b) of the GDPR. Its rationale resides in the need that any

---

[5] See Zarsky (2017, 2015); Rubinstein (2013); Custers and Uršič (2016).

[6] The EU has set the ambition to become a global leader in Trustworthy Artifitial Intelligence and roll it out in both public and private spheres. See Communication from the European Commission (2018).

[7] Article 9 of the Convention 108, Council of Europe (1981); Paragraph 9–10 of the OECD (1980); Article 8(1) of the Charter of Fundamental Rights of the European Union (2012).

interference with the fundamental rights to privacy and data protection[8] should have a legal basis which pursues a legitimate purpose and represents a necessary and proportionate restriction in a democratic society[9].

The principle has two main building blocks: the personal data must be collected for "specified, explicit and legitimate" purposes (purpose specification) and not "further processed in a way incompatible" with those purposes (compatible use).[10] It therefore seeks to enhance predictability for the data subject how his or her personal data will be processed once collected, while at the same time leaving a degree of flexibility for its potential re-use by the controller.

First, the purpose specification requires controllers to specify the purpose(s), which are intended to be served with the collected data prior to, and in any event, not later than the time when the collection of the personal data occurs.[11] The purpose must be:

(a) **Specific** which means precise enough to determine what processing is and is not included within the specified purpose and to allow assessment of the compliance with the law and the necessary data protection safeguards. Specificity largely depends on the context and the envisaged activities by the controller, but it is not permissible in principle to use too vague or very general descriptions in order to have a broader scope of manoeuvre.[12] As a general rule, the more the data subject is affected by the envisaged processing, the more detailed the purpose specification should be[13].

(b) **Explicit** which means that the specification of the purpose must be clearly explained or expressed in an intelligible form. The ultimate objective is to ensure that the purposes are specified without vagueness or ambiguity as to their meaning or intent[14]

(c) **Legitimate** which requires a legal basis for the processing[15] and compliance with all applicable laws as well as codes of conduct, ethics and contractual arrangements.

---

[8] The EU Charter of fundamental rights (2012) provides for two distinct rights to private life and data protection enshrined respectively in article 7 and article 8 of the Charter of fundamental rights. See more about the distinction in Gonzales Fuster and Gutwirth (2013).

[9] Article 52(1) of the EU Charter of Fundamental Rights (2012).

[10] See Article 29 Working Party (WP29): Opinion (2013), p. 29.

[11] See Article 29 Working Party (WP29): Opinion (2013), p. 15.

[12] See Article 29 Working Party (WP29): Opinion (2013), p. 16.

[13] See Forgó et al. (2017), p. 31.

[14] WP29 Opinion on Purpose Limitation (2013), p. 17.

[15] This means that the data controller should obtain the personal data on one of the legal grounds provided for in Article 6(1) of the GDPR: (a) consent of the data subject; (b) contract with the data subject; (c) legal obligation under EU or national law, (d) to protect the vital interests of the data subject or of another natural person, (e) for a task carried out in the public interest or in the exercise of official authority, or (f) legitimate interests of the controller or a third party, except where such interests are overridden by the interests or fundamental rights and freedoms of the data subject. Specific legal grounds are also envisaged for the processing of "sensitive" data under Article 9 and Article 10 of the GDPR.

Secondly, the controller may re-use the data for another purpose, if a compatibility assessment shows that the purpose for the secondary use can be considered *compatible* with the initial one, taking into account a number of criteria[16] that mainly seek to respect the data subjects' reasonable expectations about *how* and *by whom* their data will be processed. If the assessment shows that the secondary purpose for the re-use of the personal data is incompatible, the controller must ask for consent from the data subject before processing with the re-use[17]. There is a legal presumption that further processing for archiving purposes in the public interest, scientific or historical research purposes, if done in accordance with the safeguards in Article 89, shall not be considered incompatible with the initial purposes[18].

2.2   Challenges to the Purpose Limitation Principle in a World of Big Data/AI

With the digital revolution and the radical transformation of our daily lives, Big Data[19] technologies have allowed for new uses of huge amounts of data in real time from a vast variety of sources (IoT sensing devices, smart grids, digital services, social applications, mobile video, etc.) which have led to the creation and aggregation of gigantic digital datasets held by corporations, governments and other organisations[20]. Artificial Intelligence,[21] which may be trained on this data or analyze it for other purposes, offer novel opportunities to re-use and extract value from these large datasets, identifying correlations and conceiving new and unanticipated uses. Big Data and AI finds applications in many sectors of our everyday life and may provide numerous benefits for the economy and the society at large e.g. from saving lives, to discovering cures for chronic diseases, managing threats to security etc.[22] At the same time, many scholars have rigorously criticized Big Data and the new digital technologies which also pose risks and

---

[16] Article 6(4) of the GDPR.

[17] Ibidem.

[18] Article 5(1)(b) of the GDPR.

[19] Big data is usally decribed by 3 or more Vs, incluidng **Volume** - the quantity of generated and stored data. The size of the data determines the value and potential insight, and whether it can be considered big data or not; **Variety** - the type and nature of the data. This helps people who analyze it to effectively use the resulting insight. **Velocity** - the speed at which the data is generated and processed as Big data is often available in real-time. **Veracity** - It is the extended definition for big data, which refers to the data quality and the data value which can be drawn from it.

[20] The European Union Agency for Network and Information Security (ENISA) (2015).

[21] Artificial intelligence (AI) refers to systems that display intelligent behaviour by analysing their environment and taking actions – with some degree of autonomy – to achieve specific goals. AI-based systems can be purely software-based, acting in the virtual world (e.g. voice assistants, image analysis software, search engines, speech and face recognition systems) or AI can be embedded in hardware devices (e.g. advanced robots, autonomous cars, drones or Internet of Things applications). See Communication from the European Commission: Artificial Intelligence for Europe (2018).

[22] See, for example, a document prepared by the European Commission on Artifitial Intelligence: Real Benefits, https://ec.europa.eu/digital-single-market/en/news/communication-artificial-intelligence-europe.

interfere significantly with individuals' right to privacy given that most of that data is personal through which directly or indirectly an individual can be identified[23].

The application of GDPR to these digital technologies and Industry 4.0. poses certainly limitations to the processing of the personal data, while traditional privacy concept and principles are also strained by the far-reaching technological and societal transformations. One particular challenge for controllers to comply with the principle of purpose limitation is that often it is not possible to know in advance the predictions Big Data/AI will make, so it is hard to define in sufficient detail the purpose of the re-use to assess whether it is compatible or not. It is often the case that the purpose may also change as the machine learns and develops or the controllers involved in the Big Data value chain change it over time, depending on the results and the needs.[24] The principle of purpose limitation prevents thus the free re-use of the data and may therefore constrain Big Data/AI applications because one of the methods to leverage value from Big Data is to use data and further process datasets for different purposes as well as to analyze the data in a way that may not have been envisaged at the time the data was first collected[25]. It may also restrict the use of the personal data as training data which is still highly indispensable for the continuous learning and improvement of the AI. Some scholars highlight also that in today's non-linear and highly decentralized environment, the different types of data processing occur simultaneously or parallel and are intertwined, with the information constantly retrieved. Consequently, the information depends, more than before, on the corresponding context of usage which requires new contextual understanding of how to apply the purpose specification principle in practice[26].

However, these challenges could be also seen as opportunities that, if appropriately handled, could build trust in the AI and Big Data ecosystem and create innovation technologies that incorporate privacy safeguards and thus benefit individuals, the technological industry and the society at large. The following section of the paper will examine in particular the key conditions and safeguards that must be in place when personal data is re-used for a secondary statistical or research purpose in the context of AI and Big Data in compliance with the GDPR requirements.

3 The Research and Statistical Exemption Under GDPR

Article 5(1)(b) of GDPR envisages a privileged rule for the re-use of personal data by controllers, stipulating that further processing for scientific or historical research purposes or statistical purposes shall, in accordance with Article 89(1), *a priori* be considered compatible with the initial purposes[27]. In practice, that would allow companies, public authorities and other organizations to freely re-use personal data, if the following conditions are fulfilled:

---

[23] E.g. Richards and King (2013); Rubinstein (2014).

[24] See Norwegian Data Protection Authority: Artificial Intelligence and Privacy (2018).

[25] See Forgó et al. (2017), p. 20.

[26] Von Grafenstein (2019), p. 103.

[27] Article 5(1)(b) of the GDPR.

(1) The personal data has been collected transparently[28] and lawfully at the first place for a specific, explicit and legitimate purpose on one of the legal bases under Article 6(1) of the GDPR[29];

(2) The data will be re-used for a statistical or research purpose;

(3) The controller has put safeguards for the data subjects' rights and freedoms, including technical and organizational measures, in particular in order to respect the principle of data minimization, and uses techniques such as anonymization or pseudonymization provided that the research or statistical purposes can be fulfilled in that manner.[30]

If these conditions are fulfilled, the controller could re-use the personal data and lawfully process it for research or statistical purposes, relying on the same legal basis on which the personal data has been originally collected without asking for an additional or new consent from the data subjects[31].

3.1 Scope of Application

It is important to note that the research and statistical exemption applies to both non-sensitive and sensitive data[32] and its application in the context of AI/Big Data could be quite extensive. Statistical purposes, in particular, cover a wide range of processing activities, from commercial purposes such as analytical tools of websites or Big data applications aimed at market research[33] to public interests e.g. statistical information produced from data collected by medical clinics or public authorities. GDPR also introduces a broad interpretation of the notion "scientific research", including *inter alia* studies conducted in the public interest, technological development and demonstration, fundamental research, applied research and privately funded research[34]. This would

---

[28] Article 13 of the GDPR obliges controllers always to provide certain information to data subjects when they are collecting their data from them, including the purpose of the intended uses, the categories of personal data, the legal basis for processing, the storage period and the security measures, the third parties with whom the data will be shared, the existence of automated-decision making, the transfer of the data outside the EU etc.

[29] See Article 6(1) of the GDPR and (no. 16) above. If the processing is based on consent in particular, Recital 33 of the GDPR recognizes that it is often not possible to fully identify the purpose of personal data processing for scientific research purposes at the time of data collection. Therefore, data subjects should be allowed to give their consent to certain areas of scientific research when in keeping with recognized ethical standards for scientific research. They should also be able to consent only to certain areas of research or parts of research projects to the extent allowed by the intended purpose.

[30] Article 89(1) of the GDPR.

[31] Recital 50 of the GDPR.

[32] This covers data revealing racial or ethnic origin, political opinions, religious or philosophical beliefs, or trade union membership, and the processing of genetic data, biometric data for the purpose of uniquely identifying a natural person, data concerning health or data concerning a natural person's sex life or sexual orientation which Article 9(2)(j) of the GDPR explicitly allows to be processed for statistical and research purposes subject to the safeguards envisaged in Article 89(1) of the GDPR.

[33] WP29 Opinion on Purpose Limitation (2013), p. 29.

[34] Recital 159 of the GDPR.

enable, for example, research institutes, public authorities and companies to re-use personal data in Big Data Analytics for discovering trends and correlations between large datasets. The research exemption can be also relied upon to feed personal data for training and development of AI/Machine and Deep Learning models. Still, its application may be controversial, if the personal data is used by an AI model not only for training purposes, but also to support decisions about the individuals whose data has been collected. The difficulty to differentiate between these two stages is notably highlighted by the Norwegian Data Protection Authority which remains vague how far the research exemption can be applied in such circumstances[35]. While Recital 162 states that processing for statistical purposes should not be used in support of measures or decisions regarding any particular natural person, such prohibition does not exist in relation to research.

In such instances, the clear limit for re-use of the data for research purposes is the prohibition of solely automated decision-making, including profiling, if it produces legal or similarly significant effects on the data subject (e.g. assessing the suitability of a job applicant or one's right to residence or social benefits, credit-scoring etc.[36]) except where the data subject has given an explicit consent or there is another legal basis[37]. Still, whether this prohibition can be applied also to less significant effects in the research context is unclear. On one hand, one could argue that supporting decisions vis-à-vis the data subjects based on knowledge inferred from the research would go beyond the research purpose and would be against the data subjects' reasonable expectations and the "functional separation"[38] principle which aims to avoid negative impacts on individuals and clearly separate research from other functions. Such restrictive interpretation is in line with the guidance of the Article 29 Working Party[39] and the limitations introduced in some national legislations which transpose Article 89 of the GDPR.[40] On the other hand, it is important also to note that GDPR has not kept

---

[35] The Norwegian Data Protection Authority (2018) (no. 25), p. 18.

[36] Article 29 Working Party (2017), 17/EN WP 251, p. 10.

[37] Article 22 of the GDPR prohibits solely automated decision-making with legal or similarly significant effects except where it: (a) is necessary for entering into, or performance of, a contract between the data subject and a data controller; (b) is authorised by Union or Member State law to which the controller is subject and which also lays down suitable measures to safeguard the data subject's rights and freedoms and legitimate interests; or (c) is based on the data subject's explicit consent. See also WP29 Guidelines on Automated Decision-Making and Profiling (2017).

[38] Article 29 Working Party is the EU body comprising all national data protection authorities now replaced by the European Data Protection Board envisaged in Article 68 of the GDPR. For the guidance about the functional principle see WP29 Opinion on Purpose Limitation (2013), p. 30.

[39] Ibidem. Article 29 Working Party has also emphasized that even when data is properly anonymized, using such information (often in combination with other data) for taking decisions that produce effects (albeit indirectly) on individuals should be avoided. See WP29 Opinion 05/2014 on Anonymization Techniques, 0829/14/EN WP216, p. 11.

[40] For example, Section 19 of the 2018 UK Data Protection Act restricts the processing for research purposes where the processing causes substantial damage or distress to the data subject, or where the processing is to support a decision being made about a particular data subject unless it is carried for the purposes of ,'approved medical research'. Cyprus has also introduced a general restriction to use research results in support of decisions regarding individuals in Article 31 of the Cypriot Law No. 125 (I)/2018 on the Protection of Natural Persons Against the Processing of Personal Data and on the Free Movement of Such Data.

the text of Recital 29 of the repealed Directive 95/46/EC which in the context of research required explicitly before to *"rule out the use of the data in support of measures or decisions regarding any particular individual"*. On the contrary, Recital 159 of the GDPR now states that *"if the result of scientific research in particular in the health context gives reason for further measures in the interest of the data subject, the general rules of this Regulation should apply in view of those measures"*. This novel provision raises the question how far may this new rule be applied in case of Big Data/AI models which play today increasingly important role in many sectors of scientific research?

In this context, we must recall that while article 5(1)(b) of the GDPR establishes a legal presumption for compatibility, according to WP29 *"this should not be read as providing an overall exception from the requirement of compatibility, and it is not intended as a general authorisation to further process data in all cases for historical, statistical or scientific purposes"*[41]. The controllers must therefore still consider the overall compatibility between the research and the other intended purposes with the original purpose for which the personal data has been collected. This assessment should be done on the basis of Article 6(4) of the GDPR which introduces a set of substantive criteria for this compatibility test, including:

- the link between the original and the secondary purposes;
- the context, in particular the relation between the controller and the data subject;
- the nature of the personal data, in particular if processing concerns "sensitive" data under Article 9 and Article 10 of the GDPR;
- the possible consequences of the intended further processing for the data subjects, and
- the existence of appropriate safeguards, which may include encryption or pseudonymisation.

The global multi-criteria assessment for the compatibility of the re-use should balance and consider the different weight of each criteria. Particular importance has the last criteria, notably the safeguards given that these could compensate for some of the deficiencies of the other criteria[42]. As a "rule of thumb", the re-use would be compatible, if it respects the reasonable expectations of the data subjects and treat them fairly[43]. In general, the more severe or unexpected the consequences for the data subjects and the more sensitive the data processed, the more rigorous the safeguards should be (see more for safeguards in point Sect. 3.2. below). Transparency also plays a key role to ensure respect of the data subjects' reasonable expectations as it provides

---

[41] WP29 Opinion on Purpose Limitation (2013), p.28.

[42] WP29 Opinion on Purpose Limitation (2013), p.26.

[43] The UK Information Commissioner's Office (ICO) (2017), p. 38, https://ico.org.uk/media/for-organisations/documents/2013559/big-data-ai-ml-and-data-protection.pdf.

them with predictability what to expect regarding the processing of their personal data.[44] However, in research it is often difficult to define in advance the research purposes or these may often change in the course of a project. This is also the case in Machine Learning or open-ended Big Data applications where the analysis gives answers to questions that have not been asked before which face certain limits in this respect[45]. According to WP29, if the purposes have changed or have not been specified clearly, a first necessary (but not always sufficient) condition towards ensuring compatibility of the re-use is to re-specify the purpose once it is known. Often it is also necessary to provide additional notice to the data subjects and – depending on the circumstances and the legal basis of the further processing – it may be necessary to allow them to opt-in or opt-out.[46] If the processing is based on consent, in particular for research purposes, GDPR allows a more general consent to be given by the data subjects to certain areas of scientific research in keeping with recognized ethical standards for scientific research[47]. Data subjects should also be able to consent only to certain areas of research or parts of research projects to the extent allowed by the intended purpose. If any measures or decisions are to be taken based on the results from the research, this can only be done if these treat the data subjects fairly, respect their reasonable expectations and are clearly in their interests as required by Recital 159 of the GDPR.

Before the adoption of the GDPR, WP29 specifically called attention to *"some of the challenges in applying the compatibility test to Big Data requiring, more so than elsewhere, a rigorous but balanced and flexible application of the compatibility test to ensure it can be applied in our modern, networked society"*. WP29 provided two examples of big data applications: (1) finding trends and correlations which it considered as compatible re-use as long as the functional separation principle is applied, and (2) gaining information about certain individuals and making decisions affecting such individuals which it considered as incompatible and almost always requiring an opt-in consent. At the same time, the UK Information Commissioner's Officer seems to follow a more flexible approach when assessing compatibility of the re-use, considering largely whether the re-use treat fairly the data subjects and respect their reasonable expectations[48].

This paper suggests that given the broadened notion of "research" and the new Recital 159 of the GDPR, there is an opportunity for a more flexible approach in assessing Big data/AI applications when these are able to infer information about individuals or possibly even in some instances support decisions about them, but only if such decisions and measures are in the data subjects' interests and respect their reasonable expectations. At least, GDPR leaves open such possibility which leaves a margin of discretion to the national data protection authorities whether to follow a stricter or more flexible approach in the application of the GDPR. Of course, whether the purpose(s) of the re-use would be considered compatible would be a result of the

---

[44] WP29 Opinion on Purpose Limitation (2013), p. 13.

[45] Forgó et al. (2017).

[46] WP29 Opinion on Purpose Limitation (2013), p. 26.

[47] Recital 33 of the GDPR.

[48] ICO (2017), p. 37.

overall assessment of the compatibility test, taking all criteria into consideration and, in particular the safeguards for the data subjects' rights and freedoms. It is clear that tracking users' behavior and profiling them in order to micro-target them with manipulative advertisements would be certainly incompatible and require consent, but there may well be instances where a beneficial research Big Data/AI project could support policy decisions or measures that may be also in the interests of the data subjects, respect their reasonable expectations and treat them fairly. In this context it is interesting to note that in its recent opinion on clinical trials, the successor of WP29 – the European Data Protection Board - recognizes that consent may not always be the right legal basis for research, but controller may better rely on the public interest or the legitimate interests, in particular in circumstances where there are structural imbalances which imply that the consent cannot be "freely given".[49]

Besides the nominal changes introduced in the GDPR with regard to research, there are also practical arguments which call for a more flexible approach in the application of the compatibility assessment for the possible re-use of the personal data. It should be recalled that the re-use of the data and the principle of purpose limitation was one of the most contentious issues during the legislative process when the GDPR was adopted and will certainly remain one of the first points to be considered in the forthcoming review of the regulation. A more flexible and context-specific assessment may thus better compensate the deficiency of a strict procedural approach in the enforcement of the GDPR, especially in times of rapidly changing technological developments which also transform social values and norms. It could also ensure a more context and value-based approach in line with Helen Nissenbaum's concept of "contextual integrity of privacy"[50] which highlights in particular that that the purpose rather needs to reflect the context of the processing. She also emphasizes the need for flexibility *"where science and technology enable disruptions of entrenched norms, a heuristic supported by contextual integrity sets entrenched norms as default, but allows that if novel practices are more effective in promoting interests, general moral and political values, and context-specific ends, purposes, and values, they should be favored over the status quo*[51]*"*. Some rationale in such more flexible interpretation of the compatibility assessment could be also found in the need to find a fair balance between individuals' rights to privacy and data protection which must be also reconciled with the freedom of the sciences, enshrined in article 13 of the EU Charter of fundamental rights and other competing fundamental rights such as the right to conduct business. Pre-defined strictness of the application may pose thus difficulties to both the innovators who need to implement the new requirements and the regulators who risk, on the other hand, to lag behind the real impact that emerging technologies already have on the society and our fundamental rights.

Finding the fair balance between privacy and innovation and setting the appropriate safeguards in a Big data and algorithmic world is however also a challenging task. The next section of the paper will examine what are the key pre-conditions that must be in

---

[49] European Data Protection Board (2019), pp. 4–8.

[50] Nissenbaum (2004).

[51] Barocas and Nissenbaum (2014), p. 48.

place as a minimum to enable re-use of the data for research purposes, while the third section will propose an innovative form of cooperation between regulators and inno-vators to ensure enforcement of the GDPR, while enabling privacy-friendly innovation in times of rapidly emerging technologies.

3.2 Safeguards for Data Subjects' Rights and Freedoms

A fundamental pre-condition for the research and statistical exemption to apply are the safeguards for data subjects' rights and freedoms which controllers must put in place as required under Article 89(1) of the GDPR.

3.2.1 Principle of Data Minimization

Article 89(1) requires first technical and organizational measures, in particular to respect the *principle of data minimization* according to which the personal data should be adequate, relevant and limited to what is necessary for achieving the purpose for which it is processed[52]. Still, this principle also faces significant challenges in the context of Big Data/AI which, on the contrary, require as much data as possible. Not knowing in advance the purpose for the re-use or its subsequent re-purposing in the process of learning or within the Big Data value chain also make it hard to define in advance which data is really necessary and relevant. To ensure minimization, con-trollers should therefore thoroughly examine the intended area of application of the Big Data/AI model to facilitate selection of relevant data necessary for the purpose[53] and also continuously monitor and review the input and output data throughout the different stages of the Big Data value chain[54]. But data minimisation requires also more than just limiting the amount of the detail included. The controller must also consider how to achieve the objective in a way that is least invasive for the data subjects' privacy which requires restriction of the degree of individuals' identification by both the quantity and the nature of the information used, bearing in mind the risk of inferences. Appropriate assessment must be therefore made to review the input data in the light of the potential inferences and put in place anonymization, pseudonymization or/and encryption techniques which protect the data subject's identity and help limit the extent of intervention.

---

[52] Article 5(1)(c) of the GDPR.

[53] The Norwegian Data Protection Authority: Artificial Intelligence and Privacy (2018), p. 18.

[54] **Data Acquisition/Collection:** gathering, filtering and cleaning data before it is put in a data repository or any other storage solution. **Data Analysis:** combining data from different sources and making the "raw" collected data amenable for decision-making as well as domain specific usage. **Data Curation:** the active management of data over its lifecycle to ensure it meets the necessary quality requirements for effective usage. A main aspect in that respect is the need to assure the reusability of the data, not only within their original context but in many different contexts. **Data Storage:** storing and managing data in a scalable way satisfying the needs of applications/analytics that require access to the data. **Data Usage:** covers the use of the data by interested parties and is very much dependent on the data processing scenario.

3.2.2   Use of Techniques Such as Anonymization or Pseudonymization

Data controllers are specifically obliged to use anonymization or pseudonymization techniques insofar the research or statistical purposes can be fulfilled in that manner. Full or partial anonymization, in particular, can be relevant to the safe use or sharing of data within organisations, particularly large ones, or in the context of Big Data/AI where a number of different controllers/processors are involved at different stages of the Big Data value chain with varying obligations and controls over the data and the processing operations. Anonymization requires the personal data to be rendered irreversibly anonymous for the controller and all other third parties in such a manner that the data subject is not or no longer identifiable[55]. Adequate risk assessment will need to carefully consider the risk of re-dentification and what a human and an algorithm could uncover from the data not only now, but also in the future[56].

Depending on the purpose of the processing and the context, controllers may use a mixture of techniques to effectively anonymize the data, while taking due account of their shortcomings[57]. A promising anonymization technique is "differential privacy"[58] under which datasets are provided to authorized third parties in response to a traceable specific query rather than through the release of a single dataset. The primary setting of differential privacy was to anonymize the answers to interactive queries submitted to a database, rather than anonymizing datasets, which makes it particularly useful for research and Big data,[59] but only if combined with strong traceable logs and controls to continuously re-assess the risks. It is still an open research issue to find a good interactive query-response mechanism which is at the same time capable of answering any questions fairly accurately (meaning in the less noisy way), thus preserving utility while simultaneously protecting privacy[60]. To address these shortcomings, several new techniques have been proposed, combining differential privacy with aggregation such

---

[55] Recital 26 of the GDPR. The following criteria must be simultaneously fulfilled for the personal data to be effectively anonymized: (1) it must not be possible to *single out* an individual, e.g. to isolate some or all records which identify an individual in the dataset; (2) it must not be possible to *link* records relating to an individual (from at least two datasets); (3) it must not be possible to *infer* information concerning an individual, e.g. to deduce, with significant probability, the value of an attribute from the values of a set of other attributes. See also WP29 Opinion on Anonymization Techniques (2018).

[56] Recital 26 of the GDPR specifically requires the risk of re-dentification to be assessed, considering all the means reasonably likely to be used, taking into account all objective factors, such as the costs of and the amount of time required for identification, taking into consideration the available technology at the time of the processing, but also technological developments.

[57] WP29 (2014) and ENISA (2015) have provided a thorough review of the two main families of anonymization techniques and their shortcomings with recommendations how to apply them in practice including in the context of Big data.

[58] This privacy model was proposed for the first time by Dwork (2006), pp. 1–12. Based on this concept, several proposals have been made to generate differentially private data sets which follow two main approaches: (i) create a synthetic (simulated) data set from an ε-differentially private for the data (usually from a differentially private histogram), or (ii) add noise to mask the values of the original. See more in ENISA Report on Big data (2015), p. 31.

[59] ENISA Report on Big Data (2015).

[60] WP29 Opinion on Anonymisation Techniques (2014), p. 15.

as *crowd-blending privacy, blowfish* etc. that could be applied in combination also with encryption techniques and/or decentralized anonymization[61].

Still, the anonymization techniques may well not be fully applicable in the context of Big Data/AI due to their inherent shortcomings which are further exacerbated by the massive collection and aggregation of large digital datasets in dynamic environments. As highlighted in a report of the EU Agency for Network and Information Security (ENISA)[62], complete anonymization in the context of Big Data has become very difficult in practice. This is exemplified by numerous cases of high-dimensional datasets which have led to re-identification of individuals e.g. in the context of mobile phones, internet of things, public transportation, genetics, credit card, or wearable devices. AI's growing power to make inferences and correlations makes it also increasing difficult to calculate and avoid the risk of re-identification or inferences. For example, recent cases have shown that someone's personality could be deduced from seemingly innocuous mobile phone data or one's sexual orientation from a number of Facebook "likes".[63] The notorious Facebook/Cambridge Analytica scandal further highlights the serious risks inferences can cause on data subjects' fundamental rights where only a number of Facebook "likes" may be sufficient for AI to create extensive psychographic profiles of users which may be later used for voters' microtargeting and unlawful interference with national elections[64]. These challenges may thus require design of new anonymization privacy models and methods from scratch with Big data and AI precautions in mind.

When full anonymization is not feasible or the research objective cannot be achieved in this manner, data will often at least need to be partially anonymized (e.g. pseudo-anonymised, key-coded, and stripped of direct identifiers, muted with 'noise' etc.) to reduce the risk that the data subjects can be re-identified[65]. GDPR expressly introduces *pseudonymization* as a security measure which enables data processing in a manner that the personal data can no longer be attributed to a specific data subject without the use of additional information, provided that such additional information is kept separately and is subject to technical and organisational measures to ensure that the personal data are not attributed to an identified or identifiable natural person.[66] Some of the most used pseudonymization techniques are encryption with secret key, hash function, keyed-hash function with stored key, tokenization and others[67]. The controller processing the personal data should specifically indicate within the organization the authorized staff who has the key[68].

Bearing in mind the challenges to anonymization outlined above, controllers should in all cases avoid "release and forget approach" in disclosing the anonymized or

---

[61] ENISA Report on Big Data (2015), p. 32.

[62] Ibidem.

[63] Ibidem.

[64] See, for example UK Information Commissioner's Office's Report to the Parliament (2018).

[65] WP29 Opinion on Purpose Limitation (2013), p. 30.

[66] Article 4(5) of the GDPR.

[67] WP29 Opinion on Anonymization Techniques (2014), pp. 20–23.

[68] Recital 29 of the GDPR.

pseudonymized data. They must continuously identify new risks of re-dentification and regularly re-evaluate the residual risk(s), taking into account the identification potential of the non-anonymized portion of a dataset, especially when combined with the anonymized portion, and the potential correlations between attributes[69]. It is equally important to assess whether the controls for identified risks suffice and adjust accordingly as well as to monitor and control these risks.

Finally as regards anonymization, it is also very important to emphasize that even when individuals are not 'identifiable' and the GDPR does not apply, they may still be 'reachable', or comprehensibly represented in records that detail their attributes and activities, and thus may be subject to consequential inferences and predictions taken on that basis[70]. These further effects on individuals' right to privacy and social values, especially in the case of profiling and Big Data Analytics, must be therefore carefully considered as part of the contextual compatibility assessment and the Data Protection Impact Assessment which aims to assess the risks and incorporate safeguards for individual data subjects, but also for groups and the society at large as examined in the other safeguards described below.

3.2.3 Other Safeguards for Data Subjects' Rights and Freedoms

Even if data controllers use anonymization and/or pseudonymization (insofar the research purpose can be fulfilled in this manner), these techniques should not be regarded as a data protection guarantee *per se*. They are rather a primary component in a picture which must already incorporate lawful and transparent processing and be complemented with other safeguards in order to adequately protect the data subjects and avoid any unaniticipated harms for the individuals and the society at large. In general, the more sensitive the data and the more consequential potential adverse impact on the data subject, if identified would be, the more additional safeguards would be required[71].

A primary additional safeguard is the fundamental security technique of encryption which transforms data in a way that only authorised parties can read it. Its role can be integral in Big data, as long as it is performed using suitable encryption algorithms and key sizes, and the encryption keys are adequately secured[72]. While symmetric encryption schemes are widely used in big data and cloud environments, there are some concerns related to secure and scalable key management, as well as to the possibility to perform certain functionalities without disclosing the secret key[73]. On top of the "traditional" local encryption solutions, new promising techniques aimed at allowing

---

[69] WP29 Opinion on Anonymization Techniques (2014), p. 24.

[70] See Barocas and Nissenbaum (2014).

[71] WP29 Opinion on Purpose Limitation (2013), p. 32.

[72] See ENISA Report on Big Data (2015), pp. 38–42 for a full review of the existing encryption techniques and their application in the context of Big Data and AI.

[73] See ENISA Report on Big Data (2015), p. 38.

more flexibility regarding access and retrieval of encrypted data include attribute-based or functional encryption and others offering encrypted search and computations such as homomorphic encryption, secure multi-party computation etc.[74].

Depending on the context, WP29[75] recommends considering also the following appropriate safeguards which may bring additional protection:

- entering into a trusted third party (TTP) arrangement in situations where a number of organizations each process the personal data they hold for use in a collaborative project;[76]
- restricting access to personal data only on a need-to-know basis, carefully balancing the benefits of wider dissemination against the risks of inadvertent disclosure of personal data to unauthorized persons. This may include, for example, creating secure research enclaves or allowing read-only access on controlled premises. Alternatively, arrangements could be made for limited disclosure in a secure local environment to properly constituted closed communities.
- placing legally enforceable obligations on the recipients of the data, including for confidentiality and prohibiting publication of identifiable information.

In particular in the context of Big Data, ENISA recommends also a number of security and accountability controls that may be appropriate to enhance security e.g. secure computations in distributed programming frameworks, secure data storage and transaction logs, end-point input validation/filtering, real-time security/compliance monitoring, scalable and composable privacy-preserving data mining and analytics, cryptographically enforced access control and secure communication, granular access control, granular audits and data provenance[77]. The shortcomings of the exiting "notice and consent mechanism" in the digital environment could be also compensated by other innovative ways for enhancing data subjects' control over how and by whom their personal data are processed by means of personal data stores, privacy preferences and sticky policies, dynamic consent etc.[78].

Given the fact that AI learns from humans and is prone to biases, controllers must also pay specific attention in particular to comply with the "principle of fairness"[79] which requires fair treatment of data subjects and avoidance of any discriminatory or arbitrary results. Appropriate safeguards are therefore needed to regularly test the algorithms for biases and discriminatory results and to use appropriate mathematical or statistical procedures. Factors which result in inaccuracies in personal data must be corrected and the risk of errors minimized. Automated decision-making and profiling based on special categories of personal data should be allowed only under specific

---

[74] See ENISA Report on Big Data (2015), pp. 39–40.

[75] WP29 Opinion on Purpose Limitation (2013), p. 32.

[76] As pointed out by WP29, this model is increasingly being used to facilitate the large-scale research using data collected by a number of organisations. Trusted third parties can be used to link datasets from separate organisations, and then create anonymised records for researchers. E.g. the Norwegian research project http://raird.no/.

[77] ENISA Report on Big Data (2015), p. 42.

[78] ENISA Report on Big Data (2015), pp. 46–48.

[79] Article 5(1)(a) of the GDPR.

conditions[80], taking also due account of the risk that such data can be inferred from other non-sensitive information.

Equally important is also the obligation of the controller to respect the principle of accountability[81] which also implies algorithmic accountability and explainability which are both fields of intensive research and experimentation[82]. The new concept of "privacy by design and by default"[83] as an umbrella obligation for the controller to embed privacy measures and privacy enhancing technologies (PETs) directly into the design of systems, products and processes will be also of key importance to safeguard data subjects' rights and freedoms and ensure the least invasive interference with their privacy. While "privacy by design" faces certainly significant challenges in the Big Data/AI context, its integration into these applications is all the more important and both practitioners and researchers work hard to find practical "privacy by design strategies and measures" to be integrated in all different phases of the AI/Big Data value chain[84]. Compliance with the controller's obligation to carry out a Data Protection Impact Assessment (DPIA) when the processing involves sensitive data at large scale or use of new technologies, including profiling,[85] will also play a crucial role to ensure that innovation does not come at the expense of privacy, but supports it. The DPIA must consider in particular not only the risks to data subjects' privacy posed by the processing activity, but also to other fundamental rights (e.g. dignity, non-discrimination, right to free expression and information, due process etc.) and to address these risks at sufficiently early stage. As suggested by some scholars, the DPIA can thus become the primary tool for monitoring the technological developments and their impacts on the data subjects, but also on the society at large, taking due account of the wider human rights, social and ethical implications in order to ensure value-based and ethic-driven technological innovation[86].

3.2.4 Big Data and AI Ethics

While GDPR does not require explicitly compliance with ethical rules in order to benefit from the research exemption, it is argued in this paper that this is implied in the requirement for the legitimacy of the research purposes. Controllers must therefore adhere to existing ethical norms when relying on the research exemption and Member States' legislation may also explicitly envisage this as one of the safeguards for the research exemption to apply. In this respect, there are a number of existing ethical rules, in particular in the medical field[87]. The Convention on Human Rights and Biomedicine

---

[80] Recital 71 and Article 22 of the GDPR.

[81] Article 5(2) of the GDPR.

[82] Castelluccia and Le Métayer (2019), pp. 47–56.

[83] Article 25 of the GDPR.

[84] See very practical recommendations and technologies how to integrate privacy by design in Big Data in ENISA Report on Big Data (2015).

[85] Article 35(1) and (3) of the GDPR. See also WP29 Opinion on Automated-Decision Making (no. 37) and WP29 Guidelines on Data Protection Impact Assessment (DPIA) (2017).

[86] E.g. Mantelero (2018).

[87] See WMA General Assembly (2013), WHO (2008).

or the Oviedo Convention is also meant to address the ethical issues raised by research within the framework of the protection of human rights and to set common standards for all members of the Council of Europe[88]. Many of the existing ethical frameworks fail however to address properly the rapid technological changes which have transformed the society over the last years. To address this gap, new ethical frameworks are under development in the context of Big Data and AI. For example, the EU is in process of adopting Ethical rules for Trustworthy Artificial Intelligence[89] and Big Data Analytics in European Statics[90] and the European Data Protection Supervisor (EDPS) has recently launched a process for developing a new framework for digital ethics[91]. Other ethical guidelines and principles have been also proposed such as the 40th ICDPPC Declaration on Ethics and Data Protection in Artificial Intelligence,[92] the Asilomar Principles[93] on the safe, ethical, and beneficial use of AI etc. The increasing emphasis on ethic-based innovation and research is driven by the challenges which the core principles of research ethics (informed consent, anonymity, respect for privacy) face today and the need for new ethical approaches that could enable innovation, while at the same time address in an appropriate manner the far-reaching effects of AI and Big Data on the society at large and on traditional human values and rights, including the right to privacy[94].

3.2.5   Derogations from Other GDPR Obligations

If appropriate safeguards for the data subjects' rights are in place, controllers can not only re-use the personal data for research and statistical purposes, but also benefit from other derogations from the GDPR. First, controllers may derogate from the *"storage limitation principle"* which will allow them to store the personal data for a longer period (beyond what is necessary for the initial purpose of collection) insofar as the personal data will be re-used or processed at a later stage solely for research or statistical purposes[95]. Secondly, controllers may also rely on exemption from their *obligation to inform the data subject* where the personal data is obtained from other sources or new knowledge in the form of "inferences" is produced about the data subject[96]. In particular, controllers are not obliged to inform the data subjects about the purpose of the intended re-use of the data, the categories of the data not provided by the data subject (e.g. inferences made by the Big Data Analytics or input data from other sources), the third parties to whom the data will be disclosed, the existence of automated-decision making etc. This can be, however, done only insofar the provision

---

[88] Council of Europe (2010), pp. 5–6.

[89] Draft Ethics Guidelines For Trustworthy Artifitial Intelligence (2018).

[90] Draft Ethical guidelines for the use of Big Data in European statistics (2017).

[91] See Euroean Data Protection Supervisor (2018). Ethics Report of the Advisory Group to the EDPS (2018).

[92] 40th International Conference of Data Protection and Privacy Commissioners (2018).

[93] https://futureoflife.org/ai-principles/?cn-reloaded=1.

[94] See, for example, Richards and King (2014); Barocas and Nissenbaum (2014), pp. 44–75; Zimmer (2018); Tene and Polonetsky (2016).

[95] Article 5(e) of the GDPR.

[96] See for criticism about all these derogations from the data subjects' rights Wachter and Mittelstadt (2018, forthcoming).

of such information proves impossible or would involve a disproportionate effort, in particular for processing for research or statistical purposes. Thirdly, controllers may also benefit from derogations from the data subjects' *"right to be forgotten"* and reject a request for deletion, if this is likely to render impossible or seriously impair the achievement of the research or statistical objectives of the processing[97].

In addition, Member States may adopt national laws which could further provide for derogations from other data subjects' rights, notably the *right to access, correction, restriction of processing and objection* insofar such rights are likely to render impossible or seriously impair the achievement of the specific research or statistical purposes, and such derogations are necessary for the fulfilment of those purposes.[98] Certain Member States have already introduced in their national data protection laws certain derogations from the requirements of the GDPR in relation to data subjects' rights, including the United Kingdom[99], France,[100] Germany[101], Czech Republic,[102] Latvia,[103] Poland,[104] Romania[105], Slovakia[106] and

---

[97] Article 17(3)(d) of the GDPR.

[98] The right to access (Articles 15), correction (Article 16), restriction of processing (Article 18) and right to object (Article 21). Given that article 16(3)(d) provides for general exemption from "the right to be forgotten", in fact the only applicable right in the context of the research and statistical purposes remains the right not to be subject to decision-making, taken by solely automated means, including profiling (Article 22).

[99] Part 6, Schedule 2 of the UK Data Protection Act provides derogations from the rights to access, correction, restriction and objection to the extent that the application of these rights would prevent or seriously impair the achievement of the statistical or research purposes in question.

[100] The French Act No 2018-493 of 20 June 2018 modifying Act No. 78-17 of 06 January 1978 relating to information technology, data files and liberties as amended provides restrictions to the right of access (Article 39, II, (2)) and possibility to retain personal data beyond time necessary to fulfil historical, statistical, scientific purposes for which they are processed (Article 36(1)).

[101] Section 27(2) of the German Federal Data Protection Act of 30 June 2017 provides derogations from the right to object and the right to access if the exercise of these rights is likely to render impossible or seriously impair the achievement of research or statistical purposes. Access can be denied also if this would involve disproportionate effort for the data controller.

[102] E.g. Czech Republic's Act No. 499/2004 Coll. on Archiving and Records Management.

[103] Section 29 and Section 31 of the Latvian Personal Data Protection Act of 21 June 2018 provides derogation from the right to access, correction, erasure and objection to the processing when data is processed for research and statistical purposes.

[104] Poland provides derogations from the rights to access, correction, restriction and objection, but only for research carried out by Research Institutes, Higher Education and the National Academy of Science. See Polish Act of 30 April 2010 on Research Institutes, Act of 27 July 2005 on Higher Education, the Act of 30 April 2010 on the Polish Academy of Sciences.

[105] Article 8(1) of the Romanian Act No. 190 of 18 July 2018 on the Implementation of the GDPR provides derogations from the rights to access, correction, restriction and objection to the processing subject to the conditions under Article 89 of the GDPR.

[106] The Slovak Act No. 18/2018 Coll. on Protection of Personal Data provides derogations from the right to access, correction, restriction and objection to the processing subject to the conditions under Article 89 of the GDPR.

Bulgaria[107]. Given the significant burden which compliance with data subjects' rights poses on controllers, research activities in Big Data/AI would be significantly easier in these EU countries, making them eventually more attractive for investments in research and innovation.

Still, it must be pointed out that reliance by the controllers on any of these derogations must be compensated with strong safeguards for data subjects' rights and freedoms, so as to ensure in the end respect for their reasonable expectations - otherwise the re-use of the data for statistical or research purposes would not be considered compatible. Where re-use of the data serves at the same time another purpose, including when the results of the research may be used to support measures or decisions regarding the data subjects, the derogations from the obligations in relation to the data subjects' rights can apply only to the processing for the research or statistical purpose[108].

4 Privacy "Regulatory Sandboxes" to Enable Innovation Under GDPR

Based on the analysis in the previous section, it can be concluded that GDPR generally leaves sufficiently wide scope for research and innovation to take place, while ensuring also protection of individuals and their fundamental rights against the actual risks caused by innovation. Still, it must be also confessed that GDPR as a principle-based framework, which notably aims to enable flexibility and context-specific application, increases legal uncertainty for controllers who do not know how exactly these principles would be applied in concrete cases and whether the solutions found meet the regulators' expectations. One trade-off is that this uncertainty and complexity may create chilling effect for companies and start-ups to innovate, especially for smaller ones who lack the expertise of the big tech companies dominating the market or who cannot afford to bear the risk of the potential high fines in case of non-compliance. In response to a survey whether GDPR is perceived as a barrier to innovation, the overwhelming majority of responses pertained notably to lack of understanding what the correct application and interpretation of GDPR should be in particular contexts and hence what should be permitted in challenging areas related to innovation such as re-purposing in AI context, sharing of data in dynamic environment across numerous actors, application of emerging technologies etc.[109] Consequently, as the German scholar Franzius stresses individuals and the regulators have to start an interactive and transparent process reconstructing together the certainty of the legal rules.[110]

On the other hand, the regulators also face certain difficulties in applying the new legal framework to rapidly emerging technologies and in supervising effectively their

---

[107] Article 25 m of the Bulgarian Data Protection Act (OJ No. 17 from 26 February 2019) on the implementation of the GDPR provides derogations from the rights to access, correction, restriction and objection to the processing, but only when the data is processed for statistical purposes, and not for research purposes.

[108] Article 89(4) of the GDPR.

[109] See UK Information Commissioner's Office's Call (2018).

[110] Franzius (2012).

actual impact which transforms the society and revolutionizes traditional concepts and values. It is thus recognized that legislators should not repeat again the mistake done before in leaving unattended the digital technologies for too long and addressing them only post-factum when they have already rolled out into the market in massive use. This calls the regulators to have immediate or "hands-on" experience in their supervision which requires a sort of an "early warning mechanism" to address quickly and effectively any potential risks, including by means of anticipatory regulations which may prove necessary.

To respond to these challenges faced by both innovators and regulators, this paper suggests that the EU must establish new forms of engagement between the controllers and regulators and closely monitor the risks of these emerging technologies for the data subjects' rights and the society at large, while enabling innovation to take place in compliance with existing rules. One opportunity to achieve both these goals could be the creation of privacy "regulatory sandboxes" where under the close supervision of the national data protection authorities (DPAs) the controllers could experiment safely with innovative projects which are in public interest and bring clear benefits for the data subjects and the society. Such "regulatory sandboxes" have already had great success in the field of financial technology[111] and the UK Information Commissioner's Officer (ICO) has recently announced launching a similar privacy "regulatory sandbox"[112] which is expected to kick off in April 2019. In line with its ambition to stimulate innovation and become a leader in truswothy AI, this paper suggests that the EU should also embrace this initiatve and support the creation of similar regulatory sandboxes in the member states which are interested to participate, including at cross-border regional and EU level.

4.1 Benefits and Opportunities

Some of the key benefits of the privacy "regulatory sandbox" would be that it would encourage privacy-friendly innovation and advances in technologies, because the national data protection authorities could provide the controllers with effective guidance about how to address data protection risks arising from technology and mitigating design risk at early stages of product and service development. Secondly, it will provide a new form of cooperation between controllers and the supervising authorities which will help them solve challenges and come to a common understanding about how to apply the GDPR in an open and collaborative spirit. This will reduce the regulatory uncertainty about the application of the GDPR and will also address the chilling effect it may create to innovators, while guaranteeing that the new services or projects benefit from strong privacy safeguards and controls for compliance with the GDPR. The sandbox will also provide a key opportunity for the supervisory authorities to keep abreast of rapidly emerging technologies and gain valuable insights into the

---

[111] See UK Financial Conduct Authority (2017).

[112] See UK Information Commissioner's Office's Call (2018).

risks and the impacts posed by them to the right to privacy and the society at large. It will also allow testing approaches to address these challenges in specific contexts or sectors which could then inform the creation of topic or sector-specific guidance/codes of conduct and provide good practice examples in areas such as AI, Big Data, IoT, blockchain etc. Last but not least, experience from the sandbox could also inform future legislative revision about gaps or key changes to be made when reviewing the GDPR or designing any future regulatory framework for specific contexts or technologies which turns out to be necessary (e.g. automated vehicles, AI, facial recognition etc.).

When calling for views about such privacy regulatory sandbox, the ICO as a pioneer launching this initiative received strong support from many companies, research organisations and public authorities who addressed various aspects of its most useful set-up and potential added value[113]. While this is certainly an innovative idea which still needs testing and further detailed rules, it could be an appropriate new way to reconcile the ambition of the EU to reap the benefits of the data-driven economy and AI, while also ensuring strong protections against the risks posed by them to individuals' rights and the society at large. Switching from a reactive and sanctioning approach, the sandbox will thus enable also a preventive and incentivizing engagement of the DPAs with interested innovators and tech companies. The sandbox could in this way help to address more effectively the disruptive potential of the new technologies and the shortcomings of any regulatory framework that inevitably lags behind the rapid technological advances. The regulatory sandbox will also enable the DPAs to test the more flexible approach proposed in this paper in applying the context-specific compatibility assessment for the re-use as one of the key hurdles to innovation and why not even to inform specific derogations from the purpose limitation principle in specific national or EU legislation – an opportunity currently left open now in Article 6(4) of the GDPR.

4.2 Challenges and Risks

On the other hand, there are also a number of challenges for the implementation of such regulatory sandboxes that must be thoroughly considered and addressed to avoid any unanticipated risks or negative impacts for both the DPAs and the controllers participating in the sandbox. The first one is to clearly avoid the risk of loosening the strictness of the control and the sandbox becoming a rubber stamp for free-riders or non-compliance. That is why it is important to ensure from the start that a primary objective of the sandbox is not to exempt, but to ensure that the participating innovation projects fully comply with the GDPR requirements. As noted by the ICO, the sandbox should not be a way to derogate from the application of the GDPR, but to ensure that innovation takes place in compliance with it[114]. This will thus require robust safeguards to ensure that the corrective and sanctioning powers of the DPAs are not compromised in relation to the participants in the sandbox and there are clear terms and conditions, specifying also the consequences of any non-compliance, while

---

[113] See summary of the responses above.

[114] UK Information Commissioner's Office's Call (2018).

ensuring also certain comfort for the companies to experiment. Another major concern highlighted by companies has been also the necessary protection of the commercial confidentiality and trade secrets, whilst DPAs must also meet the requirements under public access to information acts. Last but not least, a key problem for practical implementation will be most probably the lack of resources and the overburden given that many DPAs face shortages in staff to carry out their primary role, what to say about an extra task of supervising participants in the sandbox, which albeit wishful, may be impossible in practice.

4.3 Addressing the Challenges and the Practicalities of the Set-up

While certainly valuable concerns, all the challenges highlighted above could be addressed and become in fact opportunities for the DPAs to even further strengthen their growing powers, if support for the regulatory sandboxes is provided at EU level by the European Commission and/or the Europan Data Protection Board (EDPB). Certainly, only DPAs who are interested will take part and these will be most probably countries like UK which have set the ambition to become hubs for innovation and new technologies. In fact, there are currently no legal hurdles in the GDPR which would prevent the creation of such regulatory sandboxes. On the contrary, some of the DPAs' tasks could in fact be carried out in the context of the sandbox, notably monitoring and enforcing the application of the GDPR, providing advice and promoting awareness about controllers' obligations, monitoring relevant developments affecting the protection of personal data[115]. As ICO highlights, the creation of the sandbox will be an enhancement of its role as regulator and not a substitution of its other powers or the 'constructive engagement' based activity.

The major problem related to the financial and human resources faced by many DPAs could be, on the other hand, solved with financial support from the European Commission which could probably also provide some EU "sandbox" coordination framework and platform for interested DPAs to cooperate and develop together the initiative with common rules and sharing of best practices. In this respect, the involvement of the EDPB will be crucial to ensure consistency in the rules that must be applied by the national/EU sandboxes and also coherence between the sandbox and the DPAs' primary role as supervisory authorities for the enforcement of the GDPR. Lessons learnt from the EU Fintech regulatory sandboxes, which have proven to be a huge success in 5 EU member states, have shown that common framework and consistency in the application is key to avoid discrepancies and varying level of enforcement of existing rules[116]. Thus, the sandbox may in fact enhance not only financially the DPAs with new staff, but also increase consistency and lead to common evaluation and monitoring frameworks for the supervision and auditing of algorithms, big data applications and other emerging technologies. In this context, it is also very important to ensure synergies with the EU ethical guidelines on Trustworthy AI that the European Commission is in process of developing and plans to test with companies

---

[115] Article 57(1)(a), (d) and (i) of the GDPR.
[116] European Supervisiory Authorities (2019).

later on this year. Many of the requirements in the ethical AI guidelines are directly linked to concrete provisions of the GDPR that must be also fulfilled which calls for a systematic methodological framework to ensure companies experimenting with AI comply with both ethical rules and the GDPR. As GDPR and ethics must go hand in hand, with an EU-wide regulatory sandboxes the EU would have the unique opportunity to apply consistently not only its binding data protection legislation, but also its newly designed ethical rules on AI and digital ethics[117].

Depending on the priorities and the demand on the market, the scope of application of the sandbox could vary from the whole spectrum of innovative projects to specialization in only certain fields or technologies such as AI, autonomous machines, big data applications, blockchain etc. In terms of timeline, it could be left open on an ongoing basis or based on calls for proposals published at regular intervals. The second option may prove to be a good way to kick off the initiative through a beta phase, as envisaged by the ICO, but then open it permanently to provide flexibility and address the variability of development cycles.

The ICO has already published its discussion paper[118] how the beta phase of the sandbox will work expecting around 10 organisations to involve of different types and sizes ideally from across the private, public and third sectors. Specific threshold eligibility criteria for projects have been also designed, notably the project must present: (1) genuine innovation; (2) public interest; (3) data protection maturity and robust accountability and control framework, while other factors will be also taken into account as part of the overall project evaluation[119]. The sandbox mechanism itself will be structured around advisory and collaborative processes and will be developed for each participant in a bespoke sandbox plan with defined objectives and timescales. Such mechanism will be drawn from an indicative list, including phased or iterative advice, supervised product or service testing; process walkthroughs, advice on risk mitigation at design stage and others. Within such plans ICO plans to permit a testing which makes use of live data if all the requirements are fulfilled within the plan and the DPIA has shown that the risks have been properly mitigated. The sandbox is expected to be a structured journey through a number of defined stages over around 15 months period, but allowing flexibility for individual organisations to exit before, depending on their specific journey.

---

[117] See Draft Ethics Guidelines for Trustworthy Artifitial Intelligence (2018) and European Data Protection Supervisor (2018).

[118] Information Commissioner's Office (2019).

[119] These factors include: a. A balance of size, sector and type of organisation to ensure a broad mix of organisations. b. Any recent data protection incidents or ICO enforcement action. While previous enforcement action or reported incidents are not a clear-cut bar to entry to the sandbox, their severity and relevance to the application will be taken into account. c. Whether and what data innovation challenge they are planning to address. d. ICO's own resources, priorities and capabilities, including expertise on a particular technology. e. Other regulatory remits, in particular where products and services are in any associated processes. f. The viability of proposed sandbox plans, including issues such as what risk assessment the applicant would undertake and the controls in place, what the exit strategy will be, and how data subjects' rights will be protected. See ICO Sandbox Beta Phase discussion paper (2019), p. 8.

Successful applicants must comply with terms and condition of participation which will clearly stipulate their obligations and detail how GDPR requirements will be implemented through the sandbox e.g. prior consultation of DPIAs, breach notifications, the corrective and sanctioning powers of the ICO etc. To ensure added value and certainty for participants to engage in the new initiative, the ICO has designed also two flexible mechanisms:

- Comfort from enforcement for participants on entry, provided they are taking appropriate steps to try to comply. Any accidental breach of data protection legislation during the sandbox process will not lead immediately to enforcement action subject to organisations maintaining a productive dialogue with the ICO throughout the sandbox process;
- Letters of negative assurance on exit, assuming all conditions set out within the sandbox plan have been met. These letters would be issued to successful participants on exiting the sandbox and would confirm that at the point the relevant product or service transitioned out of the sandbox, nothing indicates its operation would breach data protection legislation and any potential areas of concern or potential breaches were resolved. Still, ICO will retain the right to change its view and to revoke this confirmation based on future legal or market developments, or if it is made aware of information not previously seen. If the product breaches data protection laws in the future, then all liability would sit with the organisation and not the ICO.

5 Conclusion

The analysis in first two parts of the paper shows that there are important new provisions in the GDPR which allow a rather broad interpretation and application of the priviliged research and statistical exemption, including in the context of Big Data/AI. This exepmtion could enable controllers to re-use personal data which has been collected initially for one purpose for secondary research or statistical purposes and, in addition, derogate from a number of other provisions of the GDPR in relation to the data subjects' rights and the storage limitation period. If the appropriate safeguards for data subjects' rights envisaged in Article 89(1) are in place, the processing for research and statistical purposes could be, in principle, considered as a compatible re-use and the controller would not need to ask for consent from the data subjects. This exemption is, however, not an absolute authorization and the controllers should still have due regard to the criteria introduced in Article 6(4) of the GDPR which require a context-specific assessment of the compatibility to ensure that data subjects' reasonable expectations are respected and they are treated fairly. In this respect, a key question is how far results from the research can be used to support decisions vis-a-vis the data subjects which is of particular importance in the context of Big Data/AI applications that are increasingly used nowadays to infer knowledge. It is argued in this paper that GDPR leaves open the possibility for controllers to use inferred knowledge from the research to support decisions or measures vis-a-vis the data subjects, but only if these are in the interests of the data subjects, they are treated fairly and their reasonable expectations are respected, taking due account of the necessary safeguards for their rights and freedoms. Before the Court of Justice of the EU rules on the exact remits of the application of the research exemption, national DPAs could follow a stricter or more flexible approach in its application. This may enable innovation and larger application of Big Data/AI, but only if appropriate safeguards for data subjects' rights are in place in compliance with article 89(1) of the GDPR which are all the more important in the Big data and rapidly changing technological era. Such safeguards should include not only measures to minimize the impact on data subjects' privacy with techniques such as anonymization and pseudonimization (insofar the research or statistical purpose can be fulfilled in that manner), but also additional safeguards especially considering the risks posed by Big data and AI as emerging technologies. In addition, it is suggested that compliance with existing and new ethical rules, in particular, in relation to digital and AI ethics, should be also a pre-condition for the controllers to be able to rely on the research exemption.

Still, the flexibility of the purpose limitation principle inevitably increases also legal uncertainty for controllers who do not know how exactly these principles would be applied in concrete cases and whether the solutions found meet the regulators' expectations. As a solution to this problem, the paper proposes in the end an innovative approach already initiated by the UK Information Commissioner's Office, notably the creation of privacy "regulatory sandbox(es)" that could be also embraced by the EU and its member states. While still an innovative and debatable idea subject to further concretization, such privacy regulatory sandboxes could provide safe environment for controllers to experiment safely with innovation under the strict supervision of national data protection authorities (DPAs). It is argued that such regulatory sandboxes could provide added value to both regulators and innovators by enabling the development of privacy-designed innovation products and projects, while keeping supervisory authorities abreast of the risks and impacts posed by the emerging technologies to privacy and the society at large. The debate is now open to the European Commission and the national DPAs if and how to implement such a new form of regulatory monitoring and compliance in line with the EU ambition to become a global leader in Trustworthy AI and digitalization in a human rights-based and privacy-friendly manner.

Bibliography

Legalislation

International Conventions

Council of Europe: Convention 108 (1981) Convention for the Protection of Individuals with regard to Automatic Processing of Personal Data (1981)
Council of Europe: Biomedicine and human rights – The Oviedo Convention and Its Additional Protocols (2010)
Council of Europe: European Convention on Human Rights (1950)

European Union Legislation

Charter of Fundamental Rights of the European Union, OJ C 326, pp. 391–407, 26 October 2012

Regulation (EU) 2016/679 of the European Parliament and of the Council of 27 April 2016 on the protection of natural persons with regard to the processing of personal data and on the free movement of such data, and repealing Directive 95/46/EC (General Data Protection Regulation) (Text with EEA relevance) OJ L 119, pp. 1–88, 4 May 2016

National Legislation

Bulgarian Data Protection Act (No. 17 of 26 February 2019)

Cypriot Data Protection Act (No. 125 (I)/2018)

Czeck Republic's Act on Archiving and Records Management (No. 499/2004)

French Act (No. 2018-493 of 20 June 2018) modifying Act No. 78-17 of 06 January 1978 relating to information technology, data files and liberties

German Federal Data Protection Act of 30 June 2017

Latvian Data Protection Act of 21 June 2018

Polish Act of 30 April 2010 on Research Institutes, Act of 27 July 2005 on Higher Education, the Act of 30 April 2010 on the Polish Academy of Sciences

Romanian Data Protection Act No. 190 of 18 July 2018

Slovak Act No. 18/2018 on Protection of Personal Data

UK Data Protection Act (2018). http://www.legislation.gov.uk/ukpga/2018/12/contents/enacted

Official Non-bidning Documents: Official EU Documents

Article 29 Data Protection Working Party: Opinion 4/2007 on the Concept of Personal Data, 01248/07/EN WP 136

Article 29 Data Protection Working Party: Opinion 03/2013 on Purpose Limitation, 00569/13/EN WP 203

Article 29 Data Protection Working Party: Opinion 05/2014 on Anonymization Techniques, 0829/14/EN WP216

Article 29 Data Protection Working Party: Guidelines on Automated Individual Decision-Making and Profiling for the Purposes of Regulation 2016/679, 17/EN WP 251, 03 October 2017

Article 29 Data Protection Working Party: Guidelines on Data Protection Impact Assessment (DPIA) and determining whether processing is "likely to result in a high risk" for the purposes of Regulation 2016/679, 17/EN WP 248, 4 April 2017

Communication from the European Commission: Artificial Intelligence for Europe, COM/2018/237 final (2018)

Draft Ethics Guidelines For Trustworthy Artifitial Intelligence, 18 December 2018. https://ec. europa.eu/digital-single-market/en/news/draft-ethics-guidelines-trustworthy-ai

Draft Ethical Guidelines for the use of Big Data in European Statistics, 3 June 2017. https://ec. europa.eu/eurostat/cros/system/files/draft_ethical_guidelines_final.pdf

Ethics Report of the Advisory Group to the European Data Protection Supervisor (2018). https:// edps.europa.eu/sites/edp/files/publication/18-01-25_eag_report_en.pdf

European Data Protection Supervisor: Public Consultation on Digital Ethics, Summary Results (2018). https://edps.europa.eu/sites/edp/files/publication/18-09-25_edps_publicconsultationdigitalethicssummary_en.pdf

European Data Protection Board: Opinion 3/2019 concerning the Questions and Answers on the Interplay between the Clinical Trials Regulation (CTR) and the General Data Protection regulation (GDPR) (art. 70.1.b)), pp. 4–8, 23 January 2019. https://edpb.europa.eu/our-work-tools/our-documents/opinion-art-70/opinion-32019-concerning-questions-and-answers-interplay_en

European Supervisiory Authorities: FinTech: Regulatory Sandboxes and Innovation Hubs, JC 2018 74, January 2019. https://eba.europa.eu/documents/10180/2545547/JC+2018+74+Joint+Report+on+Regulatory+Sandboxes+and+Innovation+Hubs.pdf

European Union Agency for Network and Information Security (ENISA): Privacy by Design in Big Data (2015). https://www.enisa.europa.eu/publications/big-data-protection

European Commission on Artifitial Intelligence: Real Benefits. https://ec.europa.eu/digital-single-market/en/news/communication-artificial-intelligence-europe

Official International Documents

OECD: Annex to the recommendation of the Council of 23 September 1980: Guidelines. Governing the protection of privacy and transborder flows of personal data (1980)

WMA General Assembly: WMA Declaration of Helsinki—Ethical Principles for Medical Research Involving Human Subjects, Council for International Organizations of Medical Sciences (CIOMS) (2013)

WHO: International Ethical Guidelines for Biomedical Research Involving Human Subjects (2008)

40th International Conference of Data Protection and Privacy Commissioners: Declaration on Ethics and Data Protection in Artifitial Intelligence, 23 October 2018

Official National Documents

Norwegian Data Protection Authority: Artificial Intelligence and Privacy (2018). https://www.datatilsynet.no/globalassets/global/english/ai-and-privacy.pdf

UK Financial Conduct Authority: Regulatory Sandbox Lessons Learned Report (2017). https://www.fca.org.uk/publication/research-and-data/regulatory-sandbox-lessons-learned-report.pdf

UK Information Commissioner's Office (ICO): Guidance on Big data, Artificial Intelligence, Machine-Learning and Data Protection (2017). https://ico.org.uk/media/for-organisations/documents/2013559/big-data-ai-ml-and-data-protection.pdf

UK Information Commissioner's Office's report to the Parliament: Investigation into the Use of Data Analytics in Political Campaigns, 6 November 2018. https://ico.org.uk/media/2260277/investigation-into-the-use-of-data-analytics-in-political-campaigns-20181107.pdf

UK Information Commissioner's Office: Call for Views on Building a Sandbox: Summary of Responses and ICO Comment (2018). https://ico.org.uk/media/about-the-ico/consultations/2260322/201811-sandbox-call-for-views-analysis.pdf

UK Information Commissioner's Office: Sandbox Beta Phase discussion paper, February 2019. https://ico.org.uk/media/2614219/sandbox-discussion-paper-20190130.pdf

Articles

Barocas, S., Nissenbaum, H.: Big data's end run around anonymity and consent. In: Lane, J., Stodden, V., Bender, S., Nissenbaum, H. (eds.) Privacy, Big Data, and the Public Good Frameworks for Engagement, pp. 44–75. Cambridge University Press (2014). http://dx.doi.org/10.1017/CBO9781107590205.004

Castelluccia, C., Le Métayer, D.: Understanding algorithmic decision-making: opportunities and challenges. In: European Parliamentary Research Service, Scientific Foresight Unit (STOA) PE 624.261, pp. 47–56, March 2019. http://www.europarl.europa.eu/RegData/etudes/STUD/2019/624261/EPRS_STU(2019)624261_EN.pdf

Custers, B., Uršič, H.: Big data and data reuse: a taxonomy of data reuse for balancing big data benefits and personal data protection. In: International Data Privacy Law Advance. Oxford University Press (2016). http://data-reuse.eu/wp-content/uploads/2016/01/International-Data-Privacy-Law-2016-Custers.pdf

Dwork, C.: Differential privacy. In: 33rd International Colloquium, ICALP Venice, pp. 1–12 (2006). https://www.microsoft.com/en-us/research/wp-content/uploads/2016/02/dwork.pdf

Forgó, N., Hänold, S., Schütze, B.: The principle of purpose limitation and big data. In: Corrales, M., Fenwick, M., Forgó, N. (eds.) New Technology, Big Data and the Law. PLBI, pp. 17–42. Springer, Singapore (2017). https://doi.org/10.1007/978-981-10-5038-1_2. https://www.google.com/search?q=Forg%C3%B3%2C+N.%2C+H%C3%A4nold%2C+S.%2C+Sch%C3%BCtze%2C+B%3A+New+Technology%2C+Big+Data+and+the+Law.&rlz=1C1EJFA_enBG729BG743&oq=Forg%C3%B3%2C+N.%2C+H%C3%A4nold%2C+S.%2C+Sch%C3%BCtze%2C+B%3A+New+Technology%2C+Big+Data+and+the+Law.&aqs=chrome.69i57.217j0j4&sourceid=chrome&ie=UTF-8#

Franzius, C.: Modalitäten und Wirkungsfaktoren der Steuerung durch Recht. In: Hoffmann-Riem, W., Schmidt-Aßmann, E., Voßkuhle, A. (eds.) Grundlagen des Verwaltungsrechts – Band I "Methoden – Maßstäbe – Aufgaben – Organisation", 2nd edn. C.H. Beck, München (2012)

Gonzales Fuster, G., Gutwirth, S.: Opening up personal data protection: a conceptual controversy. In: Computer Law and Security Review (CLRS), vol. 29, pp. 531–539 (2013). https://www.researchgate.net/publication/259123304_Opening_up_personal_data_protection_A_conceptual_controversy

Mantelero, A.: AI and big data: a blueprint for a human rights, social and ethical impact assessment. Comput. Law Secur. Rev. **34**, 754–772 (2018). https://papers.ssrn.com/sol3/papers.cfm?abstract_id=3225749

Nissenbaum, H.: Privacy as contextual integrity. Wash. L. Rev. **79**(1), 119–158 (2004). https://www.researchgate.net/publication/228198982_Privacy_As_Contextual_Integrity

Richards, N.M., King, J.: Three paradoxes of big data. Stanford Law Rev. **66**, 41 (2013). https://ssrn.com/abstract=2325537

Richards, N.M., King, J.: Big data ethics. Wake Forest Law Rev. (2014). https://ssrn.com/abstract=2384174

Rubinstein, I.: Big data: the end of privacy or a new beginning? IDPL **3**, 74 (2013). https://papers.ssrn.com/sol3/papers.cfm?abstract_id=2157659

Rubinstein, I.: Voter privacy in the age of big data. Wisconsin Law Rev. (2014). https://ssrn.com/abstract=2447956 or http://dx.doi.org/10.2139/ssrn.2447956

Tene, O., Polonetsky, J.: Beyond IRBS: ethical guidelines for data research. Wash. & Lee L. Rev. **72**, 458 (2016). https://scholarlycommons.law.wlu.edu/wlulr-online/vol72/iss3/7

Von Grafenstein, M.: The Principle of Purpose Limitation in Data Protection Laws, p. 103 (2019). https://www.nomos-elibrary.de/10.5771/9783845290843.pdf?download_full_pdf=1

Wachter, S., Mittelstadt, B.: A right to reasonable inferences: re-thinking data protection law in the age of big data and AI. In: Columbia Business Law Review (2018, forthcoming). https://ssrn.com/abstract=3248829

Zarsky, T.: Incompatible: the GDPR in the age of big data. Seton Hall Law Rev. **47**, 995–1020 (2017). https://scholarship.shu.edu/cgi/viewcontent.cgi?article=1606&context=shlr

Zarsky, T.: The privacy-innovation conundrum. Lewis & Clark L. Rev. **19**(1), 160 (2015). https://papers.ssrn.com/sol3/papers.cfm?abstract_id=2596822

Zimmer, M.: Addressing conceptual gaps in big data research ethics: an application of contextual integrity. Soc. Media+ Soc. 1–11 (2018). https://journals.sagepub.com/doi/pdf/10.1177/2056305118768300,

IoT Security and Privacy Labels

Yun Shen[1](✉) and Pierre-Antoine Vervier[2]

[1] Symantec Research Labs, Reading, UK
{yun_shen,pierre-antoine_vervier}@symantec.com
[2] Symantec Research Labs, Sophia Antipolis, France

Abstract. IoT devices are riddled with vulnerabilities and design flaws. In consequence, we have witnessed the rise of IoT specific malware and botnets with devastating consequences on the security and privacy of consumers using those devices. Despite the growing attacks targeting these vulnerable IoT devices, manufacturers are yet to strengthen the security posture of their devices and adopt best-practices and a security by design approach. To this end, we devise an concise, informative IoT labelling scheme to convey high-level security and privacy facts about an IoT device to the consumers so as to raise their security and privacy awareness.

1 Introduction

The Internet of Things (IoT) market has taken off. There are hundreds of thousands of connected IoT devices available for the consumers ranging from fitness tracking devices, security webcams to smart home appliances. However, despite their increasing acceptance by consumers, recent studies of IoT devices [5] demonstrated that "security" is not a word that gets associated with this category of devices, leaving consumers potentially exposed to massive attacks [24]. In consequence, we have witnessed the rise of IoT specific malware such as Mirai [1], Brickerbot [7], Tsunami [8] and a series of high profile incidents involving IoT devices in recent years [10].

Common mistakes that we have seen in these devices that lead to the aforementioned incidents include the use of unencrypted network communications, hardcoded username/password (which is prone to brutal force attack), lack of strong authentication mechanism, etc. For example, Symantec reported that almost two out of ten mobile apps used to control the tested IoT devices did not use Secure Sockets Layer (SSL) to encrypt communications to the cloud. That being the case, it is inevitable that attacks on Internet of Things (IoT) devices will increase dramatically due to the accelerated growth in the number of internet-connected smart devices/appliances without security by design.

It is important to note that most IoT devices are closed, i.e., their software and hardware designs are proprietary. In addition, most of these devices have limited processing capability and storage capacity. These factors render conventional security techniques less feasible. For example, customers cannot install

M. Naldi et al. (Eds.): APF 2019, LNCS 11498, pp. 136–147, 2019.
https://doi.org/10.1007/978-3-030-21752-5_9

additional security software into these devices like what they could do with PCs. Given the close coupling of hardware and software in the IoT model, one approach to strengthen the security posture in the IoT is "security by design", where security is built into IoT devices so that they are secured at various system levels. For example, IoT device makers should require encryption and authentication for devices to know whether or not they can trust a remote system. Depending on the processing capability of a device, they can also leverage host-based protection to provide various security functionalities including hardening, lockdown, whitelisting, sandboxing, network facing intrusion prevention, etc.

Another important aspect relating to IoT security is the end users. Most IoT devices are designed to provide the end-users with a small number of functions to accomplish a specific goal, e.g., fitness tracking, remote monitoring, etc. In turn, they offer a limited user interface. Lacking of keyboards or effective input mechanisms, the device makers are prone to take shortcuts and make the implementation of authentication mechanisms weak by default, for instance, by hindering or preventing the update of the password in a password-based authentications. Rooting upon the aforementioned 'closed' characteristic, the end users are not always aware of the cybersecurity risk associated with a given IoT device, nor there exists any standardized format/metrics to inform the end users about such risk. In many cases, well informed consumers are capable of understanding the threat posed by IoT devices. For example, after the Mirai attack, considerable number of consumers changed default passwords of these affected devices and reduced the risk of compromise.

The question that motivated our work is: "can we devise an concise, informative format to convey high-level security and privacy facts about an IoT device to the consumers?" To address this question, we developed a security and privacy label for IoT devices to improve consumers' purchasing decisions. "Nutrition Facts" label was designed by the FDA to reveal sources of information as to the contents of food. From this label we can ascertain the breakdown of ingredients including fat, carbohydrates, vitamins etc., and some crucial information such as allergy advice, dosage. *So what factors would go into a security and privacy label for IoT devices? How should we organize these factors so that they can easily be understood by consumers*, especially in light of the new best-practice recommendations [17] published by ENISA in 2017?

2   Related Work

IoT security and privacy label is a relatively new idea. In this section, we aim to review all related work in the literature.

Kelley *et al.* [18] is one of the very first research effort on designing a privacy label which presents to consumers the ways organizations collect, use, and share their personal information. Centering on the goal to create an informational design that improves the visual presentation and comprehensibility of privacy policies, the authors iteratively experimented with three privacy label designs: Platform for Privacy Preferences (P3P) expandable grid, P3P simplified grid and privacy nutrition label. They performed a 24-participant laboratory user study comparing a standard natural language privacy policy with privacy policies presented in their privacy nutrition label. The experimental results demonstrated that the participants using the privacy nutrition label design could consistently select the companies that had strong privacy policies, in contrast to those using natural language privacy policies.

Following this effort, Kelley *et al.* [19] carried out an online user study of 764 participants on testing five privacy policy formats: standardized table, standardized short table, standardized short text, full policy text, and layered text. Note that the first two designs are inherited from Kelley *et al.* [18]. The authors crafted seven blocks of questions (e.g., single policy likability, policy comparison likability, etc.) to study the effectiveness of these five designs. Based up on the experimental results, the authors concluded that policy formats do have significant impact on users' ability to both quickly and accurately find information, and on users' attitudes regarding the experience of using privacy policies. The authors claimed that the standardized table and standardized short table overall outperformed the rest of the designs.

More specifically, for IoT devices, there is a need for transparency, control, and new tools to ensure that individual privacy requirements are met. Therefore, it is important to better understand people's perception on the privacy implications of using IoT devices and how they prefer to be notified about data collection [21]. To this end, Naeini *et al.* [20] conducted a 24-participant semistructured interview study followed by a 200-participant MTurk survey to study consumers' knowledge, and pre- and post-purchase behavior regarding IoT security and privacy. The authors revealed that security and privacy were factors that would influence consumers' purchase decisions if IoT devices may collect sensitive information. Building on top of these survey results, the authors also evaluated a prototype privacy and security IoT label. In addition to the conclusions presented in [18,19], the authors observed that such IoT security and privacy labels need to be widely used and convey accurate information (e.g., definitions of the terms). Additionally, an interactive online label can be helpful for the users to obtain additional information.

These previous literature leans toward privacy policies, explaining how data would be collected, used and shared. However, privacy should not be considered as a standalone factor when designing such an IoT label. For example, a security flaw of an IoT device can lead to private information leakage. Based on previous research on attacks against IoT devices as well as on system-level IoT device security, our work embraces a holistic approach to devise an concise, informative format to convey high-level security and privacy facts about an IoT device to the consumers.

3   Design of Security and Privacy Labels

As we have seen in the previous Section, both consumers and the cyber security and privacy actors have expressed the need for independent quality metrics, à la "food nutrition facts" for IoT devices. We refer to these as "IoT facts" in the reminder of this document. Designing such device factors is a delicate process, which brings up several challenges.

- The first challenge consists in **defining** the device factors and associated terms, taking into account that they need to convey an *concise and informative* yet complete *security and privacy* assessment of an IoT device to the consumers.
- The second challenge is related to the **implementation** of the device factors. In order for consumers to rely on device factors in the buying process, these factors must be *accurately* set and properly kept *up-to-date* throughout the device lifetime. It must also be possible to *verify* the correctness of these factors. Given the high heterogeneity in IoT devices hardware and software, developing techniques to profile and accurately extract detailed information about these devices is a challenging task, which requires further research.

In the reminder of this section (i) we present a list of device factors that concern consumers the most, (ii) we propose two layouts to visualize these device factors, and (iii) we elaborate on the existing and potential, yet to be researched, new techniques to populate and verify the device factors.

3.1 Device Factors

Considering the fact that most consumers don't have excessive knowledge in technology, it is vital for the proposed security and privacy factors to capture the essential factors that may offer the most assistance to consumers' purchase decision. Additionally, these factors must reliably reflect the device's resilience to cyber attacks as well as its ability to keep the consumer's data safe. To this end, we propose five label categories: (i) *system (security)*, (ii) *communication (security)*, (iii) *sensory (privacy)*, (iv) *data (privacy)* and (v) *connectivity (information)*.

System (Security). This category gives a basic set of guidelines to consumers to consider from their perspective in terms of device security. These fundamentals will greatly improve the consumers' security awareness of any IoT product. For example, this category will cover if a device has (in)sufficient authentication, or if a device uses encrypted communication when backing up data, secure firmware/OTA update, etc. A list of factors within this category is shown below.

- *Certificates:* certifications granted to the device by 3rd party certification authorities;
- *Secure boot:* prevents booting from a unsigned/modified device firmware;
- *Firmware/software update:* describes the device's supported firmware update methods;
- *Password:* characteristics and update mechanisms of potential passwords used;
- *Authentication:* available authentication mechanisms when accessing the device;

- *Remote Access:* device's ability to be accessed remotely, for instance via an application on a mobile phone, from the home network or the internet.

Communication (Security). One of the most interesting features for consumers is the ability to directly interact with IoT devices they deploy on their home network through network communication channels. Unfortunately, this feature also creates an attack vector for cybercriminals. IoT devices' capabilities to secure their communication is thus key to preserving users privacy and devices security. We provide the list of factors for this category in the list below.

- *Encryption:* whether the network communications involving the IoT device are encrypted and the characteristics of the encryption used;
- *Internet access:* whether the device requires access to the Internet to work properly;
- *Talk to other devices:* whether the device is intended to communicate with other devices on the local network.

Data (Privacy). Privacy is one of the most important factors in terms of IoT devices. The motivation behind this category is that the proposed device factors should inform the consumers if any personal information/anonymous diagnostic data is collected by an IoT device; if any local/remote data storage is supported by this device, etc. The list of considered factors within this category is shown below.

- *Personal information:* informs whether personal information is collected by the device and, if yes, describes the type of information;
- *Telemetry data:* informs the user whether anonymous telemetry data, such as usage statistics or threat monitoring alerts, is collected and potentially reported back to the manufacturer;
- *Data storage:* describes the different types of storage supported and used by an IoT device so that the user is aware of where the data is stored, if policy guarding the data storage is GDPR compatible, etc.

Sensory (Privacy). In general, a sensor is an electronic component designed to detect events or changes in its environment and send the information to other electronics. With advances in micro-machinery and easy-to-use micro-controller platforms, it is easy to integrate various sensors in IoT devices. Due to the fact that most IoT devices' design are proprietary, it is critical to enumerate all the sensors that are used by an IoT device, especially given the privacy aspect of the data these sensors might collect. The list of factors within this category is shown below.

- *Audio:* whether the device has audio capturing capabilities;
- *Video:* whether the device is equipped with a camera;
- *Motion:* whether the device embeds a motion sensor;
- *Location:* whether the device has geolocation capabilities;
- *Environment:* whether the device captures any other aspect of its environment, such as the temperature, humidity level, etc.

Connectivity (Information). IoT devices can be classified in two basic categories [5]. One category, which includes TV set-top boxes, uses already-existing networking technologies such as Wi-Fi and Ethernet connections.

The other category, which includes sensors, may use different wireless technologies that better suit some of the devices' needs, such as lower energy consumption or ad-hoc network coverage. The list of factors within this category is shown below.

- Ethernet/LAN
- Wi-Fi
- Bluetooth
- ZigBee
- Z-Wave

3.2 Visual Layouts

Two visual layouts are proposed in this section. The first candidate (Fig. 1) is close to the design of the FAD nutrition facts label using a similar design strategy to convey aforementioned device factors to the consumers. We use the common knowledge color system - red and yellow - to highlight severe and cautious security and privacy factors. The second candidate (Fig. 2) leverages icons with text to convey high-level information to the consumers. This design is motivated by the fact that considerable consumers have smartphones and may be responsive to icons. Similarly we use the same color system to highlight security and privacy factors. Note that we leave the user study of these two visual layouts as part of future work.

3.3 Implementation

Extracting information from IoT devices to populate or verify already populated device factors can be achieved using essentially three different techniques: (i) passive discovery, (ii) active probing (fuzzing) and (iii) hardware and software analysis.

Passive discovery techniques consists in deploying the device in a realistic smart home environment testbed and observing the behavior resulting from a normal use of the device. This way we can uncover various communication-related aspects of the device, such as the network protocols it uses, whether the traffic is encrypted or what kind of data is exchanged between the device and the Internet. Existing tools, such as Wireshark [4] and the Nessus Network Monitor [23] are commonly used to passively extract intelligence from network traffic [9]. Some research has also been performed to extract intelligence from passive network communication monitoring, for instance by analyzing patterns in network traffic [11]. However, passive discovery cannot explore all possible behaviors an IoT device can possibly exhibit. Moreover, it provides limited information for IoT devices that generate few or no network traffic or when network communications are encrypted.

Alternatively, *active probing (or fuzzing)* consists in actively testing the device against different inputs in order to trigger as many behaviors as possible. This approach is thus complementary to the passive discovery one. Some existing tools, such the Nessus Scanner [3] or OpenVAS [2] are available and

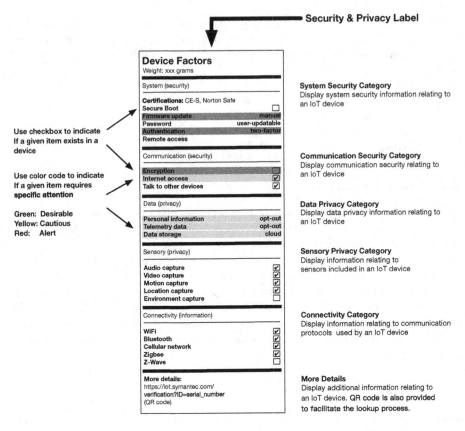

Fig. 1. Candidate visual layout 1: leverage the design concepts of food nutrition facts.

the research community has also been working on IoT-specific fuzzing techniques [14]. However, the peculiarities of IoT devices, for instance the over-presence of sensors [22], tend to significantly increase the attack surface to analyze and usually require fuzzing techniques to be adapted for the assessment of IoT devices.

Finally, *hardware and software analysis* techniques help uncover lower-level characteristics of IoT device systems that can hardly by observed otherwise. For instance, the presence of some sensors, such as a GPS chip, can only be found by inspecting the firmware or even the hardware of a device. Determining whether user data stored on the device is properly handled and is not transmitted back to the manufacturer without the user consent may also require a thorough review of the device firmware. Techniques such as static and dynamic analysis of device firmware, reverse engineering of embedded applications and automated code review are often used in this scenario. While research to uncover vulnerabilities in IoT device firmware [13,15,16,25] or privacy data leaks [12] has already been carried out in this area, some problems remain to be solved and require further research. Moreover, this task is more challenging in the IoT world due to the heterogeneity of IoT device hardware architectures and operating systems.

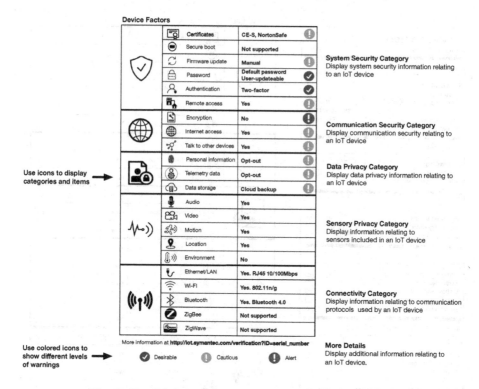

Fig. 2. Candidate visual layout 2: leverage icons and text.

4   Case Study - TVT DVR

TVT Digital Technology Co., Ltd is the manufacturer of over 70 white-labelled Digital Video Recorders (DVRs) for different companies. Its DVR series was found to be [6] and remains as of today [8] vulnerable to attacks from the Mirai botnet and its variants (e.g., Tsunami) according to the latest research. Several factors contributed to its poor security posture. First of all, the TVT DVR series doesn't enforce encrypted communication allowing the attackers to eavesdrop on video feeds (i.e., privacy leakage) and steal login credentials (i.e., security breach). Secondly, it doesn't enforce password change during the setup process even though the users can update the password afterwards. More importantly, it doesn't support over-the-air (OTA) firmware update. The customers have to update the firmware manually. This manual update process is not scalable nor automated, hence the manufacturers cannot roll out critical patches to the customers in a timely manner. Finally the manufacturer doesn't provide clear information on potential private and telemetry data collection.

How can our proposed IoT security and privacy labels help in this particular case? We demonstrate our labels in Fig. 3a and b. These two candidates are able to capture and flag several severe security and privacy problems - unencrypted communication and manual firmware update. These fields are accord-

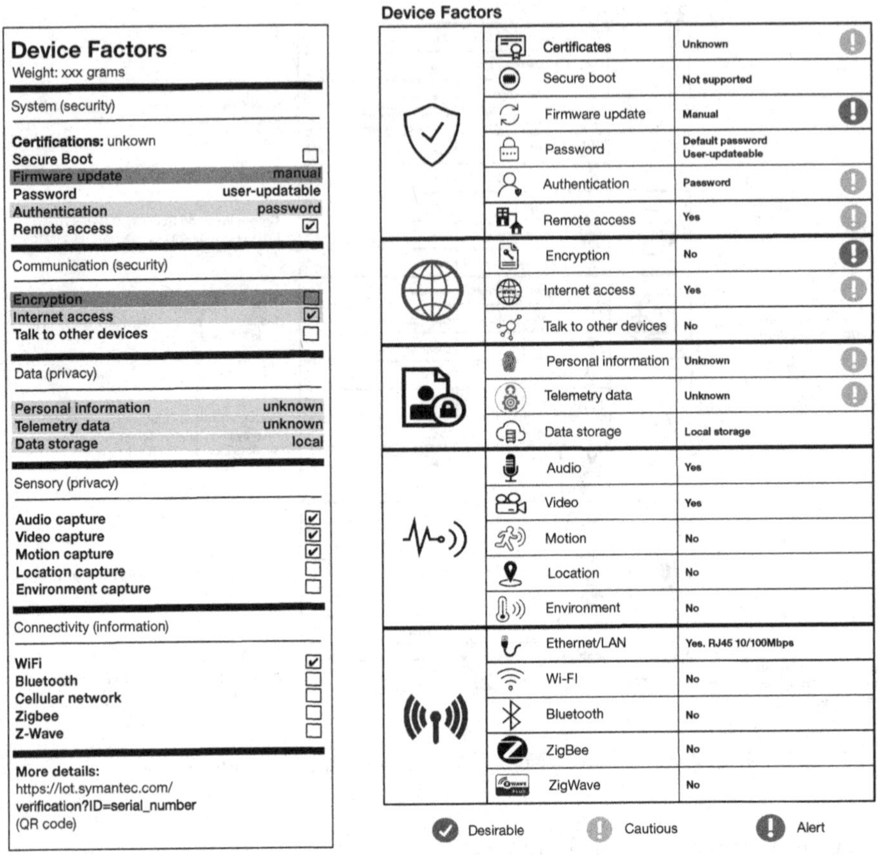

(a) Candidate layout 1.

(b) Candidate layout 2.

Fig. 3. Device factors: TVT DVR. (Color figure online)

ingly highlighted in red. These labels also notify the potential consumers that there are some undesirable factors highlighted in yellow/amber, e.g., password-based authentication and remote access from the Internet is enabled, the data collection procedure is not disclosed, certificates coming with the system are not disclosed, etc.

5 Discussion

In Sect. 3, we presented the IoT factors designed to help consumers in their purchasing of IoT devices. We described the different factors devices should be evaluated against and we elaborated on the implementation of the whole system. In this Section we further discuss some challenges faced in the design, implementation, maintenance and adoption of the IoT device factors.

The device factors presented in Sect. 3.1 constitute a tradeoff between providing an as thorough as possible security and privacy posture of an IoT device and providing a high-level enough summary of this posture. However, IoT security and privacy factors would ideally provide different levels of technical details so consumers with different levels of expertise would find the relevant information they need.

Additionally, we focused on designing device factors that are persistent and have a long validity period. That means that factors shall not change over the course of the device lifetime. However, given the rapidly evolving IoT threat landscape [24] IoT devices should be updated frequently to maintain the highest level of security. Such updates to the devices firmware are likely to change their posture with respect to the security and privacy factors. This introduces the challenge of updating IoT factors. Consequently, a single IoT device could have a different security and privacy posture over time depending on the release of software updates that would fix previously uncovered issues. This could have a cascading effect in the event IoT factors would be printed on the device packages; multiple packages for the same device potentially exhibiting different factors depending on when they were manufactured. A solution to that problem would be to provide additional information through an online service thus ensuring always up-to-date data.

Here above we discussed the motivation behind defining long-lived or "static" device factors. However, as we have seen, these factors are limited to capture "static" aspects of IoT devices. Extending this model to dynamic factors – which would likely vary much more across time and depending on a device usage and environment – would enable a more thorough and fine-grained security and privacy assessment of the device. For instance, software vulnerabilities are regularly uncovered in IoT device firmware, which turns out to be the main attack vector to infect and compromise IoT devices. Such vulnerabilities can include faulty applications, weak authentication mechanisms, use of outdated or broken encryption algorithms, etc. These vulnerabilities then need to be fixed through software updates, which is handled more or less diligently by the different manufacturers. Including such a software vulnerability assessment in the factors would thus provide a very informative assessment of a device's security posture.

Recently, the European Union Agency for Network and Information Security (ENISA) published a report [17] on best practices for the development and deployment of IoT devices. While these guidelines are seldom followed in practice, they should be reflected in the factors and used to evaluate the security and privacy posture of IoT devices. One feasible strategy is making ENISA best practices enforceable. All IoT devices must be certificated following its guidance through a rigorous procedure. In this way, the manufacturers are responsible to produce factual security and privacy labels. In turn, these labels produced by the IoT device manufacturers can be verified and tested by third party watchdogs and hold them accountable if any violations are identified.

Finally, one of the reasons why IoT devices are riddled with vulnerabilities and design flaws is the pressure manufacturers have to flood the market with new devices providing an ever growing set of functionalities. This aggressive development often comes at the price of poorly manufactured devices. We believe that the introduction of IoT labels is likely to motivate manufacturers to improve their products in order to keep them competitive.

6   Conclusion

In response to the increasing number of attacks against IoT devices and the rampant poorly manufactured devices that offer poor or no protection to their users, we propose IoT security and privacy fact labels. These labels aim at offering consumers a high-level assessment of the security and privacy posture of IoT devices to help in the buying process. We introduce a classification of IoT device factors that we believe offer a good tradeoff between simplicity and completeness. We also provide two possible layouts for a quick and easy visualization of a device security and privacy posture. Finally, we elaborate on the challenges to be faced to implement these IoT device factors. Indeed, while the information provided in the device factors is summarized and high-level, populating these factors requires further research to perform in-depth profiling and exploration of IoT devices hardware and software.

References

1. Mirai: what you need to know about the botnet behind recent major DDoS attacks. https://www.symantec.com/connect/blogs/mirai-what-you-need-know-about-botnet-behind-recent-major-ddos-attacks
2. OpenVAS - Open Vulnerability Assessment System. http://openvas.org/
3. The Nessus Scanner. https://www.tenable.com/products/nessus/nessus-professional
4. Wireshark. https://www.wireshark.org/
5. Insecurity in the Internet of Things (2015). https://www.symantec.com/content/en/us/enterprise/iot/b-insecurity-in-the-internet-of-things_21349619.pdf
6. Remote Code Execution in CCTV-DVR affecting over 70 different vendors (2016). http://www.kerneronsec.com/2016/02/remote-code-execution-in-cctv-dvrs-of.html
7. "BrickerBot" Results In PDoS Attack (2017). https://security.radware.com/ddos-threats-attacks/brickerbot-pdos-permanent-denial-of-service/
8. New IoT/Linux Malware Targets DVRs, Forms Botnet (2017). http://researchcenter.paloaltonetworks.com/2017/04/unit42-new-iotlinux-malware-targets-dvrs-forms-botnet/
9. Alrawi, O., Lever, C., Antonakakis, M., Monrose, F.: SoK: security evaluation of home-based IoT deployments. In: IEEE S&P (2019)
10. Antonakakis, M., et al.: Understanding the mirai botnet. In: USENIX Security (2017)
11. Apthorpe, N., Reisman, D., Feamster, N.: A smart home is no castle: privacy vulnerabilities of encrypted IoT traffic. In: DAT (2017)
12. Celik, Z.B., et al.: Sensitive information tracking in commodity IoT. In: USENIX Security (2018)

13. Chen, D.D., Woo, M., Brumley, D., Egele, M.: Towards automated dynamic analysis for Linux-based embedded firmware. In: NDSS (2016)
14. Chen, J., et al.: IoTFuzzer: discovering memory corruptions in IoT through app-based fuzzing. In: NDSS (2018)
15. Costin, A., Zaddach, J., Francillon, A., Balzarotti, D.: A large scale analysis of the security of embedded firmwares. In: USENIX Security (2014)
16. Costin, A., Zarras, A., Francillon, A.: Automated dynamic firmware analysis at scale: a case study on embedded web interfaces. In: ASIACCS (2016)
17. ENISA. Baseline Security Recommendations for IoT (2017). https://www.enisa.europa.eu/publications/baseline-security-recommendations-for-iot
18. Kelley, P.G., Bresee, J., Cranor, L.F., Reeder, R.W.: A nutrition label for privacy. In: USENIX SOUPS (2009)
19. Kelley, P.G., Cesca, L., Bresee, J., Cranor, L.F.: Standardizing privacy notices: an online study of the nutrition label approach. In: CHI (2010)
20. Naeini, P.E., Agarwal, Y., Cranor, L., Dixon, H.: Exploring how privacy and security factor into IoT device purchase behavior. In: USENIX SOUPS (2017)
21. Naeini, P.E., et al.: Privacy expectations and preferences in an IoT world. In: USENIX SOUPS (2017)
22. Sikder, A.K., Petracca, G., Aksu, H., Jaeger, T., Uluagac, A.S.: A Survey on Sensor-based Threats to Internet-of-Things (IoT) Devices and Applications (2018). https://arxiv.org/pdf/1802.02041.pdf
23. Tenable: Nessus Network Monitor (2018). https://www.tenable.com/sites/drupal.dmz.tenablesecurity.com/files/datasheets/Tenable2018_DS-Nessus-Network-Monitor.pdf
24. Pierre-Antoine, V., Shen, Y.: Before toasters rise up: a view into the emerging IoT threat landscape. In: RAID (2018)
25. Zaddach, J., Bruno, L., Francillon, A., Balzarotti, D.: Avatar: a framework to support dynamic security analysis of embedded systems' firmwares. In: NDSS (2014)

Applications

Digital Forensics and Privacy-by-Design: Example in a Blockchain-Based Dynamic Navigation System

David Billard[(⊠)] and Baptiste Bartolomei

Geneva School of Business Administration, HES-SO, Geneva, Switzerland
{david.billard,baptiste.bartolomei}@hesge.ch

Abstract. This research presents an experimental model and prototype to exploit digital evidence in Internet of Things (IoT). The novelty of this research is to consider new data privacy mechanisms that should be implemented in IoT, in compliance with the GDPR regulation, and their impact on digital forensic processes. The testbed is an innovative project for car navigation [1, 2], GDPR compatible, which offers users the possibility to submit their GPS position into a blockchain for obtaining road traffic information and alternative paths. The vehicles are communicating among themselves through IoTs and circumvent the use of third-party services. We propose a solution for forensic investigations of such a service by building a solid case thanks to the non-repudiable, immutable, identifiable as current and authentic properties of data logged into the blockchain. This solution applies to criminal and insurance cases, where law enforcement and individuals need to prove their claims.

Keywords: Forensics · IoT · Blockchain · Privacy · Insurance · Hyperledger Fabric · Proximity storage

1 Introduction

Internet of Things (IoT) is an ongoing technological revolution, which enables small devices to act as intelligent objects thanks to their sensors and tends to make life easier and more dynamic [3]. The model behind IoT is often a sensor (or set of sensors) submitting data to a service provider which turns data into meaningful information, transmitted to the user's phone or dedicated device. IoT may also be active and can act on its environment.

While some service providers tend to use the data of their clients to produce augmented services by using AI technology or simple algorithms, we witness a contradictory use of data. On the one hand, personal data might be used unfairly by some companies and exposed in the process. On the other hand, data that can be useful in forensic cases remain out of reach to investigators (law enforcement) or users (for their own defense).

M. Naldi et al. (Eds.): APF 2019, LNCS 11498, pp. 151–160, 2019.
https://doi.org/10.1007/978-3-030-21752-5_10

If we take a broader picture, nowadays IoT is composed of millions of machines and objects such as smart cars, smart watches, smart cameras, smart refrigerators or smart coffee makers. IoT is used in fields as different as e-health, smart cities, home automation, social fields and the quantified-self which generate huge amounts of data. This number increases steadily and in 2020, more than 20 billion devices will be connected to the Internet [3]. Table 1 shows the number of IoT devices from 2014 to 2020, classified by category [4]. This development will bring a certain comfort in our daily life but will also create privacy problems.

Table 1. Number of IoT by category (by million)

Category	2014	2015	2016	2020
Consumer	2,277	3,023	4,024	13,509
Business: cross-industry	632	815	1,092	4,408
Business: vertical-specific	898	1,065	1,276	2,880
Grand total	3,807	4,902	6,392	20,797

Unfortunately, privacy problems often lead to security problem: every technology is exposed to cybercriminality because some of this technology (IoT) is not designed with privacy in mind. And it is also true the other way around: security flaws jeopardize privacy and even safety.

According to MELANI's semi-annual report concerning IoT [5], different malwares may take over control of IoT's vulnerable devices by creating armies of zombies launching attacks to paralyze Internet service providers like Dyn in 2016 [6].

Last year, the US Food and Drug Administration (FDA) issued a warning concerning series of pacemakers (a device that sends electrical impulses to the heart in order to regulate its rates) which are vulnerable to hackers. That means in fact that users of the system may be exposed to suffering or death if the system becomes the target of a hacker who may be able to control the pacemaker [7]. This risk was unacceptable, so the FDA called back 464,000 pacemakers.

These examples demonstrate why IoT must solve three categories of problems: security, confidentiality and trust.

The project presented in this paper focuses on confidentiality and trust: the solution does not compromise data privacy by avoiding the use of third-party services but in the same time allows for a voluntarily and spontaneous release of data for forensic purposes. In addition, the data collected by our smart car's solution offers the possibility to better understand the environment of a crime scene.

Whereas security is a much active research field for IoT, confidentiality and trust are quite absent from contemporary researches in IoT model. By using local, or proximity, storage and processing, we overcome the need of data being collected by IoT providers. These providers deal with the privacy of users for personal, commercial or other purposes [8] even though the new General Data Protection Regulation (GDPR), which became effective March 2018, reinforces the protection of the user's data [9].

As a matter of fact, data collected by IoT providers are used by providers for conducting their own business and are seldom readily available for law enforcement forensic purposes. By offering a proximity storage and processing, users have a better hold on their own data.

We propose such a privacy-protecting solution in the framework of an innovative navigation project, which offers users the possibility to submit their GPS position for obtaining road traffic information and alternative paths, using a blockchain technology solution.

The blockchain is an information storage and transmission technology, transparent, secure, and functioning without a central control organ [10]. The blockchain provides the *non-repudiable*, *immutable*, *identifiable as current* and *authentic* properties of data logged. In addition, the blockchain helps in resolving the issues associated with the interchange of information inside the network.

The HACIT project [1, 2] therefore proposes to rely on a distributed system of IoT to supply a higher-level service to the final user. Instead of feeding a central system with data collected at the IoT level, an IoT is able to collect partial knowledge from other IoTs in the vicinity and provides the best possible service to the user. The HACIT project also evokes a solution for gathering forensic policies that may reveal useful for the police authorities, or the user himself.

This forensic solution is the subject of this paper which is organized as follows: in Sect. 2 we present related work on blockchain and forensics. Then the forensic capabilities are detailed in Sect. 3. Section 4 concludes this work and opens venues for future works.

2   Related and Previous Work

This paper proposes a better understanding of the forensic capabilities at work in the Hardened and Collaborative Internet of Things project (HaCIT). It proposes a GPS navigation application using the blockchain technology, which allows users to use the navigation service without compromising privacy. An overview of the project can be found in [1, 2].

This innovative project uses IBM blockchain framework [11] on top of Hyperledger Fabric developed by Linux Foundation [12], which offers an extensive framework for blockchain technology implementation. Hyperledger Fabric (HF) proposes a framework for developing permissioned blockchain technology. Contrary to Bitcoin, access to the blockchain is controlled by an entity called the Membership Service Provider (MSP) [13], which guarantees access for its users and the peers with the help of cryptographic material (certificate and keys) delivered by a certificate authority (CA).

The blockchain includes a ledger of transactions but also a representation of the global state through a key-value database. Access, queries, modifications and Smart Contracts are deemed to use the blockchain rule called Chaincode [14]. This allows efficient querying and modification of the dataset without having to analyze the entire chain of data transactions. In order to set up the project, we used an external device such as Raspberry Pi to delegate the computing and the storage of the peer clients' data.

Furthermore, we added the OpenStreetMap files [15], the GraphHopper Java library [16] as well as OSMAnd Android library [17] which are used respectively for the map file, the graph handler and the dynamic navigation UI on Android.

Finally, this innovating approach offers forensic capabilities for our application. Indeed, data is stored at multiple places in proximity of the IoT. Therefore, any legal officer may have access to a navigation path in the immutable ledger without violating user anonymity. The aim of this work is to extend the comprehension of our model and to explore its forensic capabilities [11].

The problem of navigation in Vehicular Ad-Hoc Network (VANET) using only local information has been well studied in recent years. For example, [18] proposes a dynamic routing application and [19] offers a suboptimal offline rerouting solution while addressing the communication problems that might arise in VANET. In addition, [20] provides an anonymous and secure navigation system in VANET.

Although these works satisfy most requirements for security and privacy, they still need to rely on third parties in order to remove the anonymity of vehicle ID. However, all the aforementioned papers use direct communication between vehicles (via Wi-Fi or radio) in a dynamic ad-hoc network. As a result, only partial and local traffic information is shared between moving nodes, as opposed to a system centralizing all traffic information such as Google Map.

To the best of our knowledge, although the security in VANET is a well-researched field [21], no paper takes care of the privacy and forensic capabilities. Indeed, no publication offers a system which allows dynamic rerouting and forensics for the mobile devices using a fully implemented blockchain technology. For instance, the Sharma [22] and Leiding [23] projects use the blockchain technology in VANET. However, they use it for monetary applications such as an automatic smart contract for insurance or tolling and uses Ethereum to host smart contracts.

3   Forensic Capabilities

The judiciary inquiries have undergone many changes since the beginning of the 1900s. In fact, traces of fingerprints started being used at this period. The investigators had to adapt to the new traces to make proper use of them. As of 1985, the first use of DNA in the Pitchfork case in the United Kingdom [24] allowed to exclude a suspect.

Following the year 2000, data on mobile phones created a shock in the forensic field, with many new data attached to a user now available for investigations. As a consequence, the judiciary inquiries had to change their methods and processes.

In 2007, the smartphone revolution changed the society and with this change, new data had to be explored again. As a matter of fact, smartphones reveal more on one individual's life than the home computer.

Today, multimedia, artificial intelligent and IoT have brought totally new data to be explored by the investigators. We speak today of Big Data and the three V (Volume, Variety and Velocity) and new dimensions appear like Value and Validity [20].

It is a challenge and a necessity for forensics to manage the volume of these new traces. Everything change quite rapidly and the exponential changes have a strong influence on the functioning of inquiries that are based on new types of data. We are talking about a new magnitude in scale [25].

Furthermore, most data are not always available to law enforcement, due to different country laws, inadequate regulations or absence of treaties.

In this paper, we mainly focus on data present in IoT, and more specifically in our project, which is exploitable in a forensic field as digital evidence.

3.1 HACIT Project

The architecture of the proposed application allows every user to have access to the history of transactions and thus enables forensics inquiries.

Each user holds a *UserId* and each transaction of the user is logged into the system through its *UserId*. He is the only one to know his *UserId* and can thus recover the history of his transactions.

Hyperledger Fabric stores a database system (asset, e.g. *RoadAsset*) and a transaction blockchain. Both are permissioned, so anyone with rights has access to these two entities, atomic and immutable. Therefore, anyone with rights may have access to the submitted transaction list. For the time being, our application registers only transactions when there is a traffic jam since the application is initially a dynamic navigation application before being a forensic tool. However, we can easily force the user to regularly submit his speed and therefore reveal his position via the *RoadId*.

3.2 Hurdles on the Way

In this section, we present the several barriers that can be considered as impediments to our proposed solution. We show that some solutions exist to overcome most of the difficulties.

Security

First, the evidence collected by IoT devices could be modified or removed due to lack of security, which could make the evidence invalid in court. That is why our solution is based on blockchain technology. It provides confidence since its data is immutable and authenticated. Therefore, the evidence cannot be tampered with.

However, our solution supposes that calculated information is accurate with can be proved wrong is the user has submitted faked information before the incident. The way this is actually achieved is not investigated in this paper.

Authenticity and veracity

Since the data is immutable and authenticated, it is necessary to question the authenticity and veracity of the data stored in the blockchain. Indeed, a corrupt system could submit false transactions. The solution to this problem would be to have the transactions validated by other peers and encourage the users not to cheat. For instance, data can be used for the user's defense in case of a road accident. Of course, it will be always possible for a user to submit false information, so this must be costly for the user and the benefit of submitting correct information should always be much higher than submitting faked ones. In addition, some safe guards must be implemented in the system in the future in order to detect abnormal behavior.

In addition, our blockchain can achieve consensus without computationally expensive proof-of-work, for instance with a Practical Byzantine Fault Tolerance (PBFT) algorithm [26].

Privacy

The last problem is the question about data protection since data are not anonymous but pseudonymous. Anonymous data do not allow to find the identity of the person while the pseudonymous data can potentially allow it. In fact, thanks to patterns, it is possible to find the user's identity. Suppose we know the itinerary of a user; we could check the transactions and find his UserId and discover all the transactions he made.

However, the risk is low since we are using a permissioned blockchain, and users must have permission to read and write in the blockchain. A public blockchain allows everyone to view the transactions, whereas in a permissioned blockchain, a specific permission must be given [27]. Therefore, the number of people with access to the ledger is less than in a public blockchain. Although the risk is lower, the problem remains the same.

From the point of view of Swiss law, it is necessary to protect the data which is pseudonymized which makes it potentially possible to retrieve the personal data of the user [28]. These data are sensitive if they provide information about religious opinions or activities, health, privacy, intimate sphere, race, social assistance, criminal or administrative prosecutions or sanctions. We must therefore pay attention to this information.

The data collected by our system do not directly affect a priori the categories listed above. However, they can be attached to it. Take for instance a person who goes every Sunday morning with his car to a worship center to practice his religion. Thus, the personal data of this user may become sensitive and therefore need a different treatment.

At this stage of the project, we yet don't have total anonymity but only a strong pseudonymity. It is planned to use temporal *UserId*, which means the *UserId* is randomly changed after a predefined period of time. Only the user keeps track of its succession of *UserId* (and the timestamp when it changed).

3.3   Forensic Investigation

Each IoT device provides important information that could assist in the investigation process.

Our system brings brand-new digital traces that can be used in the judicial field. The data, which can be given to the investigators, are those that have been sent to the blockchain in transactions like speed of the car, road, traffic jams, etc.

These data may help investigators to understand and reconstitute road accidents. Furthermore, this information may also be used for prevention purposes, since the investigators can recognize the problems of the road and can set up different processes to mitigate the risk of accident.

Investigations concerning car accidents are very complicated and often differ from one canton to the other in Switzerland. Indeed, each police has its own specialist team and its own investigative habits [29]. Our system could help the investigation service in standardizing its procedures by having access to the data stored on the blockchain and using the same method of analysis.

Moreover, real-world application is problematic for the judiciary examiner, especially with respect to the location of data and the heterogeneous nature of IoT devices such as differences in operating and communication systems. Our project provides solutions to these problems but does not solve all of them effectively.

In our case, the data may be used in forensic investigation because it may be connected via a UserId directly to the user.

However, a problem remains: the fact that the data collected is associated to a device and not directly to a user may be problematic to investigators. This can lead to several problems such as the veracity of these data. Indeed, the system can validate that the device (Raspberry Pi) was well on this road (RoadId), at a precise hour (Timestamp) and at a certain speed (Speed), but it cannot validate that the user providing the data to the administration was the user driving the vehicle.

Even with blockchain technology which offers transparency of transactions or with a private key system that could validate the identity of the user, nothing prevents this user from sharing his private key or devices (Raspberry Pi) with another person.

A validation should be added to prove that the person was driving the vehicle. For instance, the identification to the Android application with fingerprints. Of course, other ways to validate the user can be installed. There are therefore several means of proof that can be put in place and prove the identity of the user.

However, this is a common problem in forensic science: the attribution of fact to an individual. Unfortunately, no universal solution exists, in digital forensics or other related disciplines.

3.4 Forensic Insurance

Concerning insurance companies, data protection is also to be taken into account. Swiss insurance companies may ask their customer for agreement to implement a system which will harvest personal data on the activities of their customer [30]. The law on data protection in Switzerland [28] and more generally the GDPR in Europe [9] puts a point of honor on the protection of individuals. This is why such follow-ups are only possible with the customer's consent. However, the purpose of collecting and processing these data must be clearly defined and not be used for other purposes than those originally defined in the contract. Insurance companies may therefore use this system.

In a centralized system, insurance companies have access to all the information collected from the user: journeys, speed limits (respected or not), ignored stop signs, addresses, etc. This is a massive intrusion on individual privacy and collected data can serve to other purposes than to verify the validity of insurance claims.

If the centralized system is also owned by the same actor than the medical centralized system storing the health information of the individual, the possibility to use both data is tempting. This case is not entirely fictional, since it is now known that Google has been "*accused of breaking promises to patients, after the company announced it would be moving a healthcarefocused subsidiary, DeepMind Health, into the main arm of the organisation*" [31].

With our decentralized system, data stay within the car IoT, and the other car IoTs that shared traffic information. The data will not be available to the insurance companies until a situation arises and a case is opened. These data are then used by the insurance companies to process the case.

The data that could be used by insurance companies are the same than in the legal field but their use will have a different purpose. This system will benefit insurance companies as much as their customers. In fact, insurance companies will have more information on the cause of an accident and will be able to fight fraud more effectively. For instance, between 2014 and 2016, more than 24 million Swiss Francs of insurance fraud were discovered in Switzerland [32]. Conversely, customers could take advantage by paying lower premiums.

Our system allows insurance companies to have a follow-up of their clients like travel, speed, distance, etc. This follow-up may provide useful data, which will help to understand how users behave just prior to an accident. Indeed, the insurance must protect the victims and predict the risks involved. These risks may be more or less predictable depending on the data collected. Our system collects many data that allow insurance companies to anticipate risks and avoid them as much as possible.

Insurance companies are already in the field of IoT. As an example, the life insurance giant John Hancock asked customers to wear an electronic bracelet for being able to follow their activity. In that manner, John Hancock will have information on their global health and will modulate premiums accordingly [33]. This insurance may also favor sporting activities such as running that allows its customer to take advantage of lower premiums. Of course, the user should be free to accept or decline the use of such devices.

Finally, our system may profit to the customer. On many occasions, it is very difficult for an individual to prove his good faith, that he was not at fault or did not violate the law, for example by speeding.

4   Conclusion and Future Works

In this paper, we have presented the digital forensic capabilities of an experimental project by exploiting digital evidence in Internet of Things (IoT). The novelty of this research is to consider new data privacy mechanisms that should be implemented in IoT, following the GDPR regulation, and their impact on digital forensic processes.

The testbed is an innovative project for car navigation where vehicles are communicating among themselves through IoTs in order to determine the best route. The project circumvents the use of third-party services by relying only on inter-vehicle exchanges and submission of GPS position into a proximity blockchain for obtaining road traffic information and alternative paths.

Data privacy is well respected in this model, which is GDPR compatible, but poses new challenges for digital forensics. This paper presents the difficulties of conducting a forensic investigation and the solutions implemented in the model. The explored forensic scenarii are traffic police and insurance.

Our solution provides forensic investigations with a solid case thanks to the *non-repudiable*, *immutable*, *identifiable as current* and *authentic* properties of data logged into the blockchain. These data can be used indiscriminately by law enforcement agencies, insurance companies and individuals who need to prove their claims. The solution respects the privacy of the user's data since law enforcement agencies and insurance companies have access to the basic set of data needed to process a case, but not the whole life of the user.

Future works on health care data privacy are currently envisioned. The purpose of these works is to allow health care while restricting access to health data for non-medical bodies.

References

1. Decoster, K., Billard, D. (eds.): HACIT: a privacy preserving and low cost solution for dynamic navigation and forensics in VANET. In: 2018 4th International Conference on Vehicle Technology and Intelligent Transport Systems (VEHITS) (2018)
2. Kevin, D., David, B.: HACIT2: a privacy preserving, region based and blockchain application for dynamic navigation and forensics in VANET. In: Zheng, J., Xiang, W., Lorenz, P., Mao, S., Yan, F. (eds.) ADHOCNETS 2018. LNICST, vol. 258, pp. 225–236. Springer, Cham (2019). https://doi.org/10.1007/978-3-030-05888-3_21
3. Gartner: Leading the IoT e-Book. https://www.gartner.com/en/publications/iot-business. Accessed 31 Oct 2018
4. Rioche, J.: L'enjeu de la sécurité des objets connectés, I2D – Inf. Données Doc., vol. 54, no. 3, pp. 64–65, October 2017
5. Reporting and Analysis Centre for Information Assurance (MELANI): Data leaks, crimeware and attacks on industrial control systems – topics in the MELANI semi-annual report. https://www.melani.admin.ch/. Accessed 31 Oct 2018
6. The DDoS Attack Against Dyn One Year Later. https://www.forbes.com/sites/davelewis/2017/10/23/the-ddos-attackagainst-dyn-one-year-later/#44f2b8311ae9. Accessed 31 Oct 2018
7. C. for D. and R. Health: Safety Communications - Firmware Update to Address Cybersecurity Vulnerabilities Identified in Abbott's (formerly St. Jude Medical's) Implantable Cardiac Pacemakers: FDA Safety Communication, 29 August 2017
8. Beresford, A.R., Stajano, F.: Mix zones: user privacy in location-aware services. In: 2004 Proceedings of the Second IEEE Annual Conference on Pervasive Computing and Communications Workshops, pp. 127–131 (2004)
9. P.O. of the E. Union: Regulation (EU) 2016/679 of the European Parliament and of the Council of 27 April 2016 on the protection of natural persons with regard to the processing of personal data and on the free movement of such data, and repealing Directive 95/46/EC (General Data Protection Regulation) (Text with EEA relevance), 27 April 2016
10. Guegan, D.: The Digital World: II – Alternatives to the Bitcoin Blockchain?, June 2018
11. IBM: IBM Blockchain Platform (2017). https://ibm-blockchain.github.io/develop/. Accessed 04 Oct 2018
12. Linux Foundation: HyperLedger Fabric docs (2016). https://hyperledger-fabric.readthedocs.io/en/release/. Accessed 26 Sept 2018
13. Hyperledger-fabric: Membership Service Providers (MSP)—hyperledger-fabricdocs master documentation (2018).. https://hyperledger-fabric.readthedocs.io/en/release-1.3/msp.html. Accessed 31 Oct 2018

14. Hyperledger-fabric: Chaincode tutorials - hyperledger-fabricdocs master documentation (2018). https://hyperledger-fabric.readthedocs.io/en/release-1.3/chaincode.html. Accessed 31 Oct 2018

15. OpenStreetMap: OpenStreetMap (2018). https://www.openstreetmap.org/. [Accessed: 31-Oct-2018]

16. GraphHopper: GraphHopper Directions API with Route Optimization," GraphHopper Directions API (2018). https://www.graphhopper.com/. Accessed 31 Oct 2018

17. OsmAnd: OsmAnd - Offline Mobile Maps and Navigation (2018). https://osmand.net/. Accessed 31 Oct 2018

18. On the effectiveness of an opportunistic traffic management system for vehicular networks. IEEE J. Mag. https://ieeexplore.ieee.org/document/5970119. Accessed 15 Nov 2018

19. Garip, M.T., Gursoy, M.E., Reiher, P., Gerla, M.: Scalable reactive vehicle-to-vehicle congestion avoidance mechanism. In: 2015 12th Annual IEEE Consumer Communications and Networking Conference (CCNC), pp. 943–948 (2015)

20. Wang, L., Liu, G., Sun, L.: A secure and privacy-preserving navigation scheme using spatial crowdsourcing in fog based VANETs. Sensors 17(4), 668 (2017)

21. Raya, M., Hubaux, J.-P.: Securing vehicular ad hoc networks. J. Comput. Secur. 15(1), 39–68 (2007)

22. Sharma, P.K., Moon, S.Y., Park, J.H.: Block-VN: a distributed blockchain based vehicular network architecture in smart city. J. Inf. Process. Syst. 13(1), 184–195 (2017)

23. Leiding, B., Memarmoshrefi, B., Hogrefe, D.: Self-managed and blockchain-based vehicular ad-hoc networks. In: Proceedings of the 2016 ACM International Joint Conference on Pervasive and Ubiquitous Computing: Adjunct, New York, NY, USA, pp. 137–140 (2016)

24. Aronson, J.D.: DNA fingerprinting on trial: the dramatic early history of a new forensic technique. Endeavour 29(3), 126–131 (2005)

25. Stoney, D.A., Stoney, P.L.: Critical review of forensic trace evidence analysis and the need for a new approach. Forensic Sci. Int. 251, 159–170 (2015)

26. Bahsoun, J., Guerraoui, R., Shoker, A.: Making BFT protocols really adaptive. In: 2015 IEEE International Parallel and Distributed Processing Symposium, pp. 904–913 (2015)

27. Zheng, Z., Xie, S., Dai, H.N., Chen, X., Wang, H.: Blockchain challenges and opportunities: a survey. Int. J. Web Grid Serv. 14(4), 352 (2018)

28. CC 235.1 Federal Act of 19 June 1992 on Data Protection (FADP), 19 June 1992. https://www.admin.ch/opc/en/classifiedcompilation/19920153/index.html. Accessed 31 Oct 2018

29. Hafsi, S.: L'exploitation des traces dans les accidents de la circulation. University of Lausanne, Lausanne (2011)

30. RS 221.229.1 Loi fédérale du 2 avril 1908 sur le contrat d'assurance (Loi sur le contrat d'assurance, LCA), 02 April 1908. https://www.admin.ch/opc/fr/classifiedcompilation/19080008/index.html. Accessed 31 Oct 2018

31. Hern, A.: Google 'betrays patient trust' with DeepMind Health move, The Guardian, 14 November 2018

32. ASA: Versements évités de 24 millions de francs d'indemnités injustifiés, ASA (2018). https://www.svv.ch/fr/newsroom/versements-evites-de-24-millions-de-francs-dindemnites-injustifies. Accessed 31 Oct 2018

33. Gershgorn, D.: A life insurance giant is asking customers to wear health trackers," Quartz. https://qz.com/1396035/lifeinsurance-giant-john-hancock-is-asking-customers-to-wear-healthtrackers/. Accessed 31 Oct 2018

A Data Protection by Design Model for Privacy Management in Electronic Health Records

Giorgia Bincoletto[1,2]([⊠])

[1] University of Bologna - CIRSFID, 40121 Bologna, Italy
`giorgia.bincoletto2@unibo.it`
[2] University of Luxembourg - FDEF, Luxembourg City, Luxembourg

Abstract. Privacy by design (PbD) is considered an international principle for privacy protection. For understanding and applying a PbD legal provision, the context of the data processing is essential. This paper intends to analyse the data protection by design (DPbD) legal obligation in the European framework and investigate how it can be implemented in the context of e-health for Electronic Health Records. The PbD approach may play a pivotal role in this sector to fulfil the requirements of the law and to better protect the rights of the data subjects. To fulfil these goals, to understand the deeper meaning of the concept and to evaluate the approach itself, the paper conducts a theoretical legal analysis on PbD and critically compares the edges, the benefits, the challenges and the disadvantages. As the chosen legal framework is that of the European Union, the DPbD legal obligation established by the GDPR will be examined. The paper first gives a brief overview of the applicable EU legal framework for EHRs. Settled this context, the paper proposes a comprehensive DPbD model for the privacy management with technical and organisational measures to be implemented in EHRs. The purpose is to provide more guidance for data controllers and developers on how to comply with the DPbD obligation.

Keywords: Privacy by design · Data protection by design ·
Electronic Health Records · Privacy management

1 Introduction

In the digital age a growing number of new technologies has been developed in the health care sector. The term "e-health" identifies a range of services or systems that connects health care and information technology. Digital technologies for health care offer the opportunity to reduce administrative costs, deliver health care services at a distance, avoid unnecessary duplicate examinations and obtain medical information more easily [1]. These technologies can help to improve people's health because the access to care is simplified [2]. Typical examples are Electronic Health Records (hereinafter EHRs) which are used by public authorities and private companies to process citizens personal health data.

© Springer Nature Switzerland AG 2019
M. Naldi et al. (Eds.): APF 2019, LNCS 11498, pp. 161–181, 2019.
https://doi.org/10.1007/978-3-030-21752-5_11

An EHR is defined as "a comprehensive medical record or similar documentation of the past and present physical and mental state of health of an individual in electronic form and providing for ready availability of these data for medical treatment and other closely related purposes" [3]. In the past, all patient's information was collected on paper records, while it is now digitalized on EHRs. These digital records provide opportunity for accessing ubiquitously to health information. Thus, the entire patient's medical history is available online: all diagnoses, prescriptions, laboratory exams are collected and registered in a system. EHRs contain information from all health care providers involved in the patient's care. The digital collection helps clinicians to better manage care for patients with accurate, up-to-date and complete information, and to enable quick access to the record for more effective diagnoses and more reliable prescribing[1].

However, enhancing privacy and security of patient data is one of the key issues for an EHR. Such a tool has to be developed with full respect for data protection rules [2]. Data protection and information security are important to maintain public confidence and trust in digital health services [4]. Moreover, data collected in a health care system represent highly sensitive information concerning a data subject. Every year, both in the United States and in Europe, an increasing number of data breaches involving health record systems occur[2]. A data breach consists in a high risk both for the data controller and the data subject. On one hand, the supervisory authorities could impose serious administrative fines in case of infringement[3]. On the other, potential discrimination of employees and insurances' speculations are possible and dramatic consequences for a data subject. It is necessary to find a way to avoid these risks. Personal health data need an higher level of protection[4]. This is the approach of the General Data Protection Regulation, which includes data concerning health in the special categories of personal data[5].

A considerable amount of literature has been published on how to protect personal data in the context of e-health. The protection of personal sensitive data is widely investigated by the academic community. Nevertheless, few studies have investigated the relation between the principle of privacy by design (from now PbD) and the e-health context. The concept of PbD is one of the most discussed approaches for data protection. PbD may play a pivotal role in the context of health care to fulfil the requirements of the law and to protect more the rights

---

[1] See the official website of the Office of the National Coordinator for Health Information Technology (ONC) in the United States. https://www.healthit.gov/faq/what-are-advantages-electronic-health-records, last accessed 10th Mar 2019.

[2] For example, see in the United States Healthcare Informatics at https://www.health care-informatics.com/news-item/cybersecurity/2017-breach-report-477-breaches-56 m-patient-records-affected. last accessed 10th Mar 2019: "in 2017, there were 477 healthcare breaches reported to the U.S. Department of Health and Human Services (HHS) or the media, and information available for 407 of those incidents, which affected a total of 5.579 million patient records".

[3] For example, article 83 GDPR.

[4] Recital 53, GDPR.

[5] Article 9 (1), GDPR.

of data subjects. It is hoped that this work will contribute to the line of research that investigates the interactions between PbD and health care.

The traditional way of protecting privacy is by regulation. However, the existing privacy regulations and policies alone are not sufficient to safeguard privacy [5]. Technology will instead provide appropriate rules to regulate "as a code" this constantly innovating domain [6]. Thus, the PbD approach has as its main goal to design and develop a system, a product or a service in a way that supports and applies privacy principles, rules and values.

This paper investigates the data protection by design (DPbD) legal obligation in the European framework and how it can be implemented in the context of e-health for Electronic Health Records. The paper critically conducts a theoretical legal analysis on PbD and makes a comparison between the edges, the benefits, the challenges and the disadvantages, in order to understand the deeper meaning of the concept and to evaluate the approach. The chosen legal framework is that of the European Union. So, the DPbD legal obligation established by the GDPR will be analysed. The GDPR states that the data controller shall implement data protection by design and by default technical and organisational measures [7]. So, once examined this binding obligation and the context of e-health, this paper provides a DPbD model for privacy management with technical and organisational measures to be applied in the EHRs. Throughout the pages, the term "privacy" will refer to "data protection".

A cross-disciplinary approach is a fundamental tool for this research. PbD is a principle that requires a constant dialogue between law and technology. The author collaborates with an Italian company active in the sector of EHR software in a project dedicated to implement PbD solutions. As the research is based on the theoretical results of this partnership, on literature review, legal analysis and investigation on the existing technical solutions, the paper will use an interdisciplinary approach.

Following this introduction, the theoretical Sect. 2 will revolve around the approach of PbD. Given the history and philosophy of the principle, the section compares critically and theoretically the advantages and the disadvantages of PbD. So, a critical perspective on PbD will be provided. Then the paper investigates how far privacy by design is a legal requirement for data protection law in the European Union analysing the data protection by design obligation. Section 3 will focus on Electronic Health Records in the light of the European Union framework. Section 4 will propose a comprehensive model for privacy management with technical and organisational measures to be implemented in the EHRs. Conclusions are presented in Sect. 5.

2 The Approach of Privacy by Design

This Section introduces the concept of PbD and aims at defining it in more concrete terms and makes a comparison between the edges, the benefits, the challenges and the disadvantages through a theoretical analysis. Then, the data protection by design legal obligation established by the GDPR will be analysed.

2.1   The Origins of PbD and Its International Recognition

In a broad definition, the principle of PbD has the goal to build privacy into the design and the architecture of systems and technologies.

In 1997 the Privacy Commissioner of Ontario Ann Cavoukian theorised the PbD principle as a proactive framework that seeks to embed privacy into the design specifications of information technologies, networked infrastructure and business practices. PbD aims to achieve the strongest protection possible for personal data by proactive rather than reactive measures to anticipate and prevent privacy invasive events before they happen. Ann Cavoukian wrote, as a mantra, that "Privacy by Design comes before-the-fact, not after" [8]. The former Commissioner conducted a productive scientific research in various application areas, as RFIDs and sensor technologies and remote home health. Moreover, she elaborated seven Privacy by Design's Foundational Principles [9]. The approach aims at anticipating privacy risks identifying them in the design stage and suggests not only technological measures. In fact, the organisational set-up has a fundamental role for the implementation [9]. Embedding measures into the technical design means that privacy becomes a functional component of the system. How to make it possible without diminishing the functionality is a key question. In general, the approach is applied to the entire life-cycle of the personal data from their collection to their erasure. As stated in Cavoukian's principles, the data subject should be aware of the collection and of its purposes. User interests should be central.

In October 2010, during the International Conference of Data Protection Authorities and Privacy Commissioners at Jerusalem, the "Resolution on privacy by design" recognised PbD as an essential component of fundamental privacy protection. The Resolution expressed that existing privacy regulation and policy alone were not enough to safeguard privacy. A more robust approach was required to address the ever-growing and systemic effects of Information and Communication Technologies (ICT) [5]. So, according to the Resolution, embedding privacy as the default into the design, the operation and the management of ICT and systems, was and is necessary to fully protect privacy. The Privacy Commissioners encouraged the adoption of PbD Foundational Principles, fostered the incorporation of these principles in the formulation of privacy policies and legislation and proactively encouraged scientific research on PbD [5]. Even though the Resolution was not binding, it is possible to say that PbD became a pillar of data protection in 2010. PbD was added to the agendas of events on data protection all over the word. In fact, data protection authorities have a crucial role to promote and to formulate privacy policies and legislation within their respective jurisdictions.

In 2012 the U.S. Federal Trade Commission included PbD as one recommended practice for protecting online privacy in the report "Protecting Consumer Privacy in an Era of Rapid Change, Recommendations for Businesses and Policymaker" [10]. As defined in the FTC Report, the framework of best practices applies to all commercial entities that collect or process consumer data that can be reasonably linked to a specific consumer, computer or other device, unless the entities collect only non-sensitive data from fewer than 5,000 consumers per year and do not share the data with third parties [10]. However, FTC recommended US companies to promote consumer privacy throughout their organisations at every stage of the development of their products and services and to incorporate substantive privacy protections into their practices [10]. This is the FTC concept of PbD: a best practice that companies shall maintain throughout the life cycle of their products and services. This best practice is not merely a soft law because US companies take seriously FTC statements and reports. They are not just settlements, but softer kind of rules [11]. It is argued that FTC has a very influential role to promote good practices [12].

Even so, PbD is not a binding rule in the United States and it is limited to consumer privacy protection. On the contrary, in the European Union according to the GDPR, as Sect. 2.3 will highlight, DPbD is now one of the mandatory principles of EU data protection law and, as "data protection by design", a general obligation for the data controller[6] [7].

To better appreciate the approach for a practical implementation, the following section critically provides an overview of the advantages and the challenges of the concept.

2.2 A Critical Perspective on Privacy by Design

As stated above, Pbd is a legal principle that needs a practical implementation. Thus, applying a privacy by design requirement means to put privacy protection into context and design for privacy [13]. Conducting a theoretical and critical analysis on PbD to evaluate the approach, this paper suggests the advantages and the disadvantages collected in the following table.

The statements have been elaborated through a legal analysis on the concept of PbD. Then, the analysis was based on the remarks made by prominent scholars on Lessig's approach of "code is law" and on the PbD principle [14–34]. Overall, the studies highlight the effects of PbD on the digital economy, on technology and innovation, on the theories of law, on the rights and the duties and on democracy. Every advantage is been compared with an equivalent disadvantage and vice-versa (Table 1).

PbD is a process involving various technological and organisational components, which implement privacy and data protection principles [35]. Systems and devices become "privacy-aware" and "privacy-friendly" [15].

Although PbD has several challenges and problems, it gives the opportunity to implement principles, values and rights. From a societal and individual perspective this is very useful. Beyond the legal requirements, PbD fits under the umbrella of the Value Sensitive Design approach, which intends to design technology accounting for human values [16]. The human values under PbD are the privacy principles. On one hand, having regard to European Union, these

---

[6] Article 25, GDPR.

Table 1. Classification of the advantages and the challenges

Advantages and goals	Disadvantages and challenges
PbD legal requirement is flexible and applicable to various contexts	A broad definition means difficult implementation
PbD improves the effectiveness of the law and empowers the rights of the data subject	Translating principles, values and rights into machine-readable language is a challenge
PbD promotes proactive and preventive measures	The State delegates privacy regulation to companies. Private self-regulation may be incompatible with the democratic procedures of lawmaking and law enforcement
PbD prevents privacy breaches before they happen	Every embedded technical solution is rigid. Therefore, it is necessary to update measures frequently
PbD aims at implementing rules, principles and values	Legal interpretation is flexible and dynamic. It is hard to define common principles in different legal frameworks. Conflicts between values are possible in the design stage
PbD requires effective measures and less bureaucratic solutions	PbD implementation demands investments and allocated resources
PbD can increase privacy culture in the society	There is a difficulty of comprehension for the everyman on the topic
PbD can increase trust and confidence in products and services	In the society there is an information asymmetry and a widespread lack of knowledge on design strategies
PbD increases consumer satisfaction and could be an opportunity for business	Collecting and commercialising personal data are the core business of many companies
PbD legal requirement is technologically neutral	Specific solutions must be provided for each technical context
There is a business opportunity for certifications and standards	Certification does not automatically means compliance with the law
PbD fosters the design of new privacy friendly technologies	Adapting the existing technologies is not easy
There will be a control and ethics over the technology	There will be barriers to innovations
PbD requires concrete organisational measures	Companies sometimes lack of knowledgeable organisation
PbD aims at implementing user-centric technologies	There might be increasing costs for having access to digital technologies
PbD is a global approach	Building privacy is critical for developers and not possible in every situation. All the provisions of data protection cannot be automated

principles are expressed in the GDPR[7]. On the other hand, the internationally recognised values and standards about personal information are Fair Information Practices (FIPs) [36]. In 1973 the U.S. Department of Health, Education and Welfare defined the fundamental principles of Fair Information Practices that govern the conduct of a personal-data record-keeping systems [37]. Then, the FIPs played a significant role in the development of the international guidelines for privacy protection (i.e. the OECD Guidelines on the Protection of Privacy and Transborder Flows of Personal Data) [38]. The definitions of FIPs are also formulated by the legal doctrine. Given all the obstacles, the PbD methodology requires that developers and legal practitioners work together to design privacy solutions in a specific context on a case-by-case analysis. Balancing different interests means that stakeholders have to consider the state-of-the-art of the technology, the cost of the implementation, the various rights involved as the GDPR states.

The European Data Protection Supervisor suggests that organisations can only have benefits from adopting the PbD approach [39]. The EDPS encourages PbD strategies as priorities of the EU Agenda. Moreover, an effective implementation of PbD is an opportunity to boost the respect to ethics in technology [39]. From an economic viewpoint, privacy and trust are closely linked because the first can positively influence the second [13].

Engineering PbD requires a specific type of expertise: developers must be informed about state-of-the-art research in security, privacy technologies and legal frameworks [27]. Moreover, a public debate on design practises could inform people of abusive or deceptive methods and could push actors to change the "dark design patterns" in order to avoid the phenomena of "market punishment" [40]. Such a debate is a prerogative of legislators, regulators, authorities, academics, associations and citizens globally.

Given the previous theoretical analyse, the following section will analysis the data protection by design obligation prescribed by the GDPR.

2.3 Data Protection by Design

Before the GDPR, Article 29 Data Protection Working Party declared that users of ICT services were not able to take relevant security measures by themselves and that services and technologies should be designed with privacy by default settings and the legal framework should include a binding provision of a consistent PbD principle [41]. This provision should be expressed in a technologically neutral way and should be flexible enough to be translated into concrete measures.

On May 25th, 2018 the GDPR entered into force. This Regulation introduces a specific legal requirement on PbD in the article 25, defining a "data protection by design obligation". The GDPR states that to demonstrate compliance with

---

[7] Article 5, GDPR: lawfulness, fairness and transparency, purpose limitation, data minimisation, accuracy, storage limitation, integrity and confidentiality, accountability.

the norms, the controller should adopt internal policies and implement measures which meet the principles of data protection by design and data protection by default[8]. In recital 78, the measures suggested are: the minimisation of the processing of personal data; the pseudonymization of the personal data from the beginning of the data processing; the transparency regarding the functions and processing; the monitoring of the processing by the data subject, the creation of security features[9]. Controllers should consider the right of data protection when they develop and design their products, services and applications[10].

Article 25 GDPR establishes that, both at the time of the determination of the means for processing and at the time of the processing itself, the controller shall implement appropriate technical and organisational measures which are designed to implement data protection principles in an effective manner and to integrate the necessary safeguards into the processing[11]. The criteria expressed for DPbD are the state of the art, the cost of implementation and the nature, scope, context and purposes of the data processing[12]. In addition, the controller shall take into account the risks of varying likelihood and severity for rights and freedoms of natural persons posed by the processing[13]. Thus, the management of the data processing and the risk assessment are crucial. The data controller could demonstrate the compliance with the DPbD obligation trough an approved certification mechanism, but he or she could decide autonomously[14]. This is recognised as one of the best examples of the "accountability" approach [39].

Complying with article 25 is complex [13]. As the norm is so vague and generic, interpreting all of these criteria is a hard task both before the beginning of the data processing and during the data management cycle. For example, the state-of-the-art criterion requires to explore the most recent developments and knowledge associated with data processing [42]. Moreover, all the criteria are strictly related to the various risks of the data processing, which are extremely variable. Therefore, the appropriate technical and organisational measures are not defined and settled, but they should be both appropriate and effective. In particular, to be appropriate, the measures should address the data protection principles, the data subject rights and the other requirements of the GDPR [42]. The effectiveness may instead be measurable, but the evaluation depends on the specific data processing and it requires a professional judgement.

The European Data Protection Supervisor noted that DPbD differs from PbD [39]. DPbD is a legal obligation established by the law, whereas PbD is an ethical dimension consistent with the principles and values of the EU Charter of Fundamental Rights [39]. As argued by the EDPS, PbD has an international dimension.

---

[8] Recital 78, GDPR.
[9] Ibid.
[10] Ibid.
[11] Article 25 (1), GDPR.
[12] Ibid.
[13] Ibid.
[14] Article 25 (3), GDPR.

As the text of article 25 is vague, the legal requirement can be applied in the long term to various contexts independently from the technology progression and the context. The EU legal provisions impose an obligation to data controllers and miss the direct reference (and so the legal obligation) to the technology programmers, producers and developers. Nevertheless, as declared in recital 78 of the GDPR, "producers of the products, services and applications should be encouraged to take into account the right to data protection" in the design stage "to make sure that controllers and processors are able to fulfil their data protection obligations"[15]. The EDPS in the Opinion 5/2018 asserts that the obligation for products and technology providers is not included in the substantial provisions of the GDPR and this is a serious limitation [39]. However, it is argued that, despite such a formulation of the legal provision, the goal of article 25 is to force data controllers to pressure engineers to come up with adequate solutions [13]. Indeed, the design decisions in information systems development are neither exclusively nor predominantly taken by data controllers [43]. Therefore, the developers should consider the application of article 25 because controllers might select products and services on the basis of the adopted DPbD choices. Moreover, the GDPR imposes other constraints to joint controllers (i.e. when two or more controllers jointly determine the purposes and means of the processing) and processors (e.g. subcontractors and service providers)[16]. They cooperate and assist the data controller for the fulfilment of the DPbD obligation. In the future the EU courts will specify the DPbD obligation and will give more guidance for organisations to comply [44].

On December, 2018 the new Regulation 2018/1725 entered into force [45]. In this Regulation there are laid down two DPbD requirements in the articles 27 and 85[17]. So Union institutions, bodies, offices and agencies shall implement DPbD measures when they process personal data and operational personal data.

The third section will now focus on the health care field and will give a brief overview of the data protection requirements applicable in the context of EHRs.

3 Electronic Health Records and Data Protection Law

In general, when the personal data processed is related to the health status of the data subject, the processing is limited by special legal conditions. It is particularly sensitive and so requires special protection [3]. As previously mentioned, potential discrimination and insurances' speculations are possible and dramatic consequences for a data subject that may arise if the personal health data is misused. Since the EHRs systems are comprehensive medical documentations of the data subject, the personal data involved are mostly sensitive. Any processing of personal data should comply with the general and particular legal provisions of data protection law. This part will briefly summarise the existing privacy protection of EHRs by considering the European jurisdiction.

---

[15] Recital 78, GDPR.

[16] Articles 26 and 28 of the GDPR.

[17] Article 27 and 85, Regulation (EU) 2018/1725. For the purposes of this study, the formulations of these articles are equal to the article 25 of the GDPR.

3.1   The EU Legal Framework for EHRs

The applicable data protection legal framework for the European EHR systems is mainly the General Data Protection Regulation. The GDPR gives more importance to personal data concerning health than its predecessor, Directive 95/46/EC [46].

The GDPR states that "personal health data" should include all data pertaining to the health status of a data subject which reveal information relating to the past, current or future physical or mental health status of the data subject[18]. Recital 35 GDPR explains that personal data concerning health includes information collected in the course of the registration for, or the provision of, health care services and other information like the number, the symbol or a particular assigned to the data subject to uniquely identify him for health purposes[19]. Information derived from the examination, genetic data, biological samples, information on a disease, or disability, the medical history, the clinical treatment, or the physiological or biomedical state of the data subject, are all personal health data[20].

These kinds of information are "special categories of data". Therefore, the GDPR prohibits the processing of health sensitive data in principle [47]. However, the Regulation specifies a list of exemptions. In fact, processing health data in the EHRs is covered by certain exemptions listed in article 9 (2) of GDPR.

Firstly, there is the consent of the data subject, which must be specific, informed, given freely and explicit[21]. Most of the time the creation of EHRs is subjected to the express consent of the patient and it is not necessarily written. In 2014, a full study had shown that some Member States require the consent of the patient for the creation of an EHR and others do not [48]. Moreover, health personal data may be processed because of the vital interests of the data subject or another natural person and there is not another legal ground for the processing[22]. Then, processing sensitive data may be permitted by Member States' provisions for reasons of substantial public interest[23]. In 2007, the Article 29 Working Party argued that EHR could be considered as prominent example of public interest because it made available health personal data to health care providers on a large scale [3]. Another possible exemption occurs when the processing is necessary for the specific purposes listed in article 9 (2) (h) GDPR. For example, the data processing is allowed for the purposes of preventive or occupational medicine. In the end, the GDPR includes the exception for the processing related to the public interest in the area of public health[24].

---

[18] Article 4 (15), GDPR.
[19] Recital 35, GDPR.
[20] Ibid.
[21] Article 9 (2) (a) and Article 7, GDPR.
[22] Article 9 (2) (c), GDPR.
[23] Article 9 (2) (g), GDPR.
[24] Article 9 (2) (i), GDPR.

Generally, it is argued that in the context of EHR, even if the processing is not entirely founded on consent, the patient has the right to take a role on "when and how" his or her personal health data are used [3].

Then, the GDPR prescribes the other general rules to be complied with when data are processed in the EHR system[25]. For example, Data protection impact assessment is required in case of the processing on a large scale of special categories of data as health personal data[26].

According to article 25 GDPR, data controllers processing health personal data shall implement DPbD measures. The DPbD legal obligation has already been illustrated[27]. To ensure compliance with all relevant legal provisions regarding European data protection law, EHR systems should be designed with DPbD measures.

DPbD is currently mandatory with the GDPR, but many companies still find difficulties with the concept, both in terms of what it exactly means and how to implement it as a system quality attribute [49]. Moreover, the law imposes high administrative fines in case of infringements[28]. For these reasons, the following part will provide some operative guidelines for EHRs. Indeed, as indicated previously, in the forth section a comprehensive model for privacy management in the EHRs will be proposed.

4   A DPbD Model for Privacy Management for the EHRs

This section provides a model of a DPbD privacy management with technical and organisational measures to be implemented in the EHRs in the European legal framework. The current data protection law in EU is the foundation of the model. The purpose is to provide more guidance for data controllers and developers on how to comply with DPbD obligation.

The DPbD model for the privacy management has been organised in the following way. To demonstrate compliance with the law, each section assigns the related data protection principles to the various suggested measures. As stated above, the protection of the data protection principles is the goal to achieve[29]. The model will be divided into four groups. The order is not related to temporal factors. As a matter of fact, all the measures highlighted should be implemented in EHR continuously and reviewed often to comply with the DPbD approach.

---

[25] The information to be provided to the data subject (Articles 13-14, GDPR), the rights of the data subject to be guarantee (Articles 15-23, GDPR), the general obligations of the controller and processor (Articles 24-31, GDPR), the norms on the security of the data (Articles 32-34, GDPR) and on the data protection impact assessment, the prior consultation with the authority and the data protection officer (Articles 35-39, GDPR).

[26] Article 35, GDPR.

[27] See Sect. 2.3.

[28] Article 83, GDPR.

[29] As previously stated, the data protection principles are listed in the article 5 of the GDPR mainly.

The classification instead depends on the actors mainly involved: one part for the developer of the EHR and three parts for the data controller and data processor. The benefit of this approach is that the data controller and the developer could focus directly on their respective duties. However, the developer should participate in the other categories of measures because some of them require a technical intervention in the system. First of all, "the technical measures" section traces the measures for the EHR related to the technique and the security of the system. Secondly, "the creation of the EHR" and "the use of the EHR" sections describe the obligations and the measures to be followed when the data is collected and processed in the EHR. In the end, "the organisational and administrative measures" section will be presented.

Generally, a DPbD approach may be divided into four steps: gap analysis with the specific legal framework, risk analysis, project steering and budget planning, and implementation [44]. Firstly, to identify the appropriate DPbD measures, developers should get an overview of the flow of personal data. The first gap analysis is crucial to identify the legal requirements. From an individual viewpoint, according to a DPbD approach, the data subject should have control over the collections, the uses, the storage and the disclosures of his or her personal data in the EHR.

Secondly, the privacy risks should be evaluated and pseudonymization and anonymization should be considered above all [44]. For EHRs, which are used for providing healthcare, the anonymization of personal data is not a feasible choice[30]. The more health personal data is collected and processed, the easier it is to manage care for the data subject/patient. Nevertheless, pseudonymization and security features must be encouraged as much as possible.

Moreover, the risk analysis is mandatory according to the GDPR[31]. So, a Data Protection Impact Assessment (DPIA) should be carried out. The DPIA may be considered as a DPbD organisational measure. It is argued that the DPIA is a preliminary step of any PbD process [42]. The loss of confidentiality, integrity and availability of data concerning health is a high risk. Once the risks have been identified, the DPbD efficient and appropriate solutions should balance and take into account the state-of-the-art of the technology and the costs of implementation.

The European Union Agency for Network and Information Security (ENISA) is a pivotal centre and institution for the scientific research on privacy by design and privacy enhancing technologies[32]. The ENISA's reports provide innovative criteria and parameters on available privacy tools and initiatives to ensure PbD.

---

[30] The secondary use of data for medical research is not illustrated in this work. However, the data collected in EHR systems are often anonymized before being used for secondary scientific research purposes.

[31] Article 35, GDPR. As early stated, for EHRs the data protection impact assessment is highly recommended. The data controller of EHRs often process on a large scale personal health data.

[32] See the various publications in the field of privacy technologies and the engineering approach at https://www.enisa.europa.eu/topics/data-protection/privacy-by-design, last accessed 10th Mar 2019.

The Report "Privacy and Data Protection by Design, from policy to engineering" sets out some strategies for the implementation and defines eight PbD strategies and three data protection goals [50]. These recommendations are strictly related to the Hoepman et alia's Privacy by design Strategies [51]. These documents have been the starting point for the present study.

The Fig. 1 illustrates the model of a comprehensive privacy management for EHRs. Despite the classification, the different measures work together to fulfil the DPbD requirement.

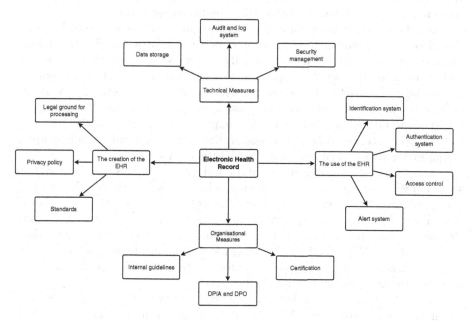

Fig. 1. DPbD Model for EHR

4.1   Technical Measures for EHR

There should be effective technical measures for an EHR. Implementing technical measures is essential and finding the related strategies is the key issue. As concerns this part, the data protection principles mainly involved are integrity, confidentiality, and accountability.

Limits should be settled to the data storage. Name and surname of the data subject/patient, birth date, home address, email address, telephone number and billing data are administrative personal data in the EHR. When different administrative data reveals information about the health status of the data subject (e.g. the typology of the medical visit or the scheduled controls) it should be considered as sensitive "data concerning health". Sensitive data are necessary for the medical treatment, but they are detrimental because of the possible discrimination. Removing the correlation between different types of health data prevents the understandability to unauthorised people. Administrative personal data could be separated from sensitive data through the software separation of databases.

As mentioned, in the EHR all personal health data are collected. Some health data are particularly sensitive (e.g. data related to an abortion or a suicide). Allowing the data subject for the exclusion of particularly sensitive data from any processing in the system is disputable. So, particularly sensitive data could be stored in separate modules with strict conditions for access.

Even if encryption is not an explicit legal requirement, this technical process should be used for storage to better protect personal information[33]. Other DPbD measures are the usage of different identifiers and pseudonymization[34]. Back-up and recovery mechanisms are important to secure the content of the system [3].

Secondly, the EHR system should provide the processes to exercise the rights of the data subjects. For example, the right to rectification implies the implementation of specific technical solutions. The request of rectification of the data subject could be introduced and processed in the EHR. A patient-friendly graphic design makes easier the exercise of right by the data subject.

Other technical measures are the audit and the log systems. An audit system should track user activity on the record. This is a key point of EHR system because it can determine ex post any responsibility. In fact, the collection of id number, date and hour, type of the operation and access motivation allows the precise identification of the user and the source of the illegal processing. The activity on the record should be tracked and any discrepancies must be reported. Moreover, logging, reporting and auditing as evidences are tactics to demonstrate the compliance with the law [51].

The international standards for developing security and privacy are designed to improve data protection. Adopting these solutions may facilitate the data controller to prove and certificate the legal compliance[35].

---

[33] In the ENISA's report "Reinforcing trust and security in the area of electronic communications and online services, sketching the notion of "state-of-the-art" for SMEs in security of personal data processing" of December 2018 it is underlined that several tools for encryption are available on the market and, as an example, it is recommended that in the context of a medical clinic "the server where patients' comprehensive electronic health records are stored should be encrypted using robust and known weakness-free encryption algorithms". https://www.enisa.europa.eu/publications/reinforcing-trust-and-security-in-the-area-of-electronic-communications-and-online-services, last accessed 10th Mar 2019.

[34] Ibid. An interesting polymorphic technique is there mentioned as a pseudonymization example in the health sector.

[35] See for example ISO/IEC 19608, ISO/IEC 15408 and ISO/IEC DIS 27552, https://www.iso.org/standard/61186.html and https://www.iso.org/standard/71670.html, last accessed 10th Mar 2019.

Moreover, security management is fundamental. The EHR system should be updated frequently and protected with intrusion controls systems [13]. In addition, implementation of firewall can better protect EHR network. The secure policy should be reviewed and revised regularly, and IT resources should be reviewed and updated on annual basis [52]. Incidents and data breaches should be recorded along with details.

Hereafter, as it will be explained in the following sections, technical measures should be implemented in EHR for the legal grounds of processing, as alert systems, and for the authentication and the identification of users.

4.2   The Creation of the EHR

For the creation of the EHR, it is necessary to find the legal ground for the data processing, create the privacy policy and provide the information to the data subject. Among the data protection principles, lawfulness, purpose limitation and storage limitation play a crucial role in this part.

The data collected by EHRs are both personal and sensitive. The personal data processed by the medical IT systems consist of contact information, social insurance number, medical examination results, pathology, diagnosis and administrative and financial information. The purpose of the data processing is the provision of healthcare services and the data subject is the patient[36]. This purpose, the collection and the storage must be limited to medical treatment[37].

In the beginning, the system should request to the user to obtain the patient consent or any possible legal grounds and to prove the lawfulness of the processing[38]. The request should occur before the use of EHR and the legal ground

---

[36] See the Italian Data Protection Authority's Guidelines on the Electronic Health Record and the Health File, published in 2009: "to safeguard data subjects, the purposes in question should accordingly only consist in prevention, diagnosis, care and rehabilitation of the given data subject and exclude any other objective - in particular planning, managing, supervising and assessing health care activities, which can actually be performed in several circumstances without using personal data. This is without prejudice to any requirements arising under criminal law". https://www.garanteprivacy.it/web/guest/home/docweb/-/docweb-display/docweb/1672821, last accessed 10th Mar 2019.

[37] As stated above, the secondary use of data for medical research is not considered in this study.

[38] See Article 9 (2) (a) (c) (g) (h) (i), GDPR. So the processing is allowed if there is/are: (a) explicit consent; (c) vital interest of the data subject or of another natural person where the data subject is physically or legally incapable of giving consent; (g) substantial public interest; (h) purposes of preventive or occupational medicine, for the assessment of the working capacity of the employee, medical diagnosis, the provision of health or social care or treatment or the management of health or social care systems and services on the basis of Union or Member State law or pursuant to contract with a health professional and subject to the conditions and safeguards referred to in paragraph 3 capacity; (i) reasons of public interest in the area of public health.

could be signalled with an icon[39]. If the legal basis is the vital interest, after the first medical treatment to save the life, the controller shall obtain the consent. For example, to collect the consent standard ISO/TS 17975:2015 provides an informational consent framework for health care organisations [53]. When the data subject withdraws the consent, the system should alert the data controller. Therefore, another legal ground should be indicated, or the system should be stopped for that patient. When the data subject is a child, the consent is given by the holder of parental responsibility over him or her. When the patient becomes an adult, it is mandatory to collect the new consent. Meanwhile, the system must be stopped for that patient. An alert system could be operative every day.

In the meantime, the data controller should create the privacy policy and should make available all the necessary information to the patient[40]. The information should be provided in a transparent and easily accessible form, using clear and plain language. The same information could be stored in the EHR. So, it should be accessible anytime in the EHR system (and signalled with an icon to be identify easily).

4.3   The Use of the EHR

As regards the use of the EHR, the data controller and the data processor should organise the identification and the authentication of the staff and the healthcare professionals. The principles mainly related to the use and the access in the EHR are fairness, confidentiality and transparency.

The subjects who have access are treating healthcare professionals, administration officers and public health system officers. The access is restricted to authorised persons. The authorisation should be given only and temporally to those are involved in the patient's treatment [3]. Moreover, the access should be limited to specific categories of health care professionals. A modular or granular access set-up is a relevant option to limit the number of individuals that can access to the EHR system. So, the data controller should prearrange the organisational chart and the register of authorised subjects should be constantly updated. E-signature or smart cards are better than username and passwords [48]. The multi-factor authentication is a recommended method to confirm identity[41]. So, after using username and password, users should need also a token to get access. Making the patient aware of the accesses improves the control over the information. Then, the EHR system should record and report all the

---

[39] Article 12 (7), GDPR includes standardised icon as possible mechanisms to provide information to the data subject.

[40] Article 13 and 14, GDPR.

[41] In the ENISA's report "Reinforcing trust and security in the area of electronic communications and online services" (See footnote n. 32 for the complete reference) it is argued that "the number of required factors for each access control system should be proportionate to the sensitivity of IT systems and related information to be accessed". The two-factor authentication is a widely adopted practice in cases of high risks as in the remote monitoring systems of patients. Therefore, there are already some experiences of multi-factor authentication in the health context.

accesses. Moreover, the data subject should have the possibility to access to personal data collected in the EHR[42].

4.4   Organisational Measures for EHR

The organisational and administrative measures are expressions of a data protection by design approach. Many data protection principles are related to organisational measures: fairness, transparency, accuracy, confidentiality and accountability.

The data controller should provide evidence that the processing is privacy-friendly. Data concerning health should be up to date and accurate. Nevertheless, someone considers appropriate that the patient has the mechanisms to control the processing and to select or exclude some categories of data from any processing [54]. As expressed previously, the purpose of the data processing is to provide healthcare. So, to safeguard patient's healthcare the whole data should be available, and the complete removal of the data in the EHR is possible only if the information is collected on paper. As specified for the storage measures[43], administrative data, when they are simple personal data, should be separated from sensitive health data. So, for booking and paying medical examinations, sensitive data could be obscured from the administrative staff[44] [54].

The data controller should give clear and documented instructions to authorised subjects. Internal guidelines on privacy should be established. They may participate to a brief course on data protection and they should be bound to specific confidentiality clauses.

In general, if it is not allowed, transferring data should be prohibited. However, the interoperability of EHRs (and so the sharing of information among Member States in EU) is in the eHealth Action Plan 2012–2020[45].

As mentioned above, a Data Protection Impact Assessment should be performed as a organisational measure to control the processing and to integrate the necessary safeguards into it. An insurance policy for the data breaches is another

---

[42] Recital 63, GDPR: "A data subject should have the right of access to personal data which have been collected concerning him or her, and to exercise that right easily and at reasonable intervals, in order to be aware of, and verify, the lawfulness of the processing. This includes the right for data subjects to have access to data concerning their health, for example the data in their medical records containing information such as diagnoses, examination results, assessments by treating physicians and any treatment or interventions provided (...)".

[43] See Sect. 4.1.

[44] In these cases the typology of the medical visit or the related information of the scheduled controls could be obscured. Some health related inferences might be made by the administrative staff. Nevertheless, the employees are usually bound to confidentiality clauses.

[45] See the website of the European Commission at https://ec.europa.eu/digital-single-market/en/interoperability-standardisation-connecting-ehealth-services, last accessed 10th Mar 2019.

measure recommended. Moreover, certification may be a good investment for the data controller[46].

Finally, the data controller may ask an opinion on a privacy expert to choose the EHR system which is designed more compliance with the law. A data protection officer shall be designated where the core activities of the data controller consist of processing on a large scale of special categories of data as health one[47]. Then, in the case of EHRs there should be the designation of the DPO, who may or may not be the same person for several data controllers[48].

5   Concluding Remarks

As personal health information is a very sensitive data for a subject, it requires strong protection.

The first purpose of the current research was to analyse the DPbD legal obligation in the European framework. This paper has explained the history and the philosophy of PbD and the legal provisions involved. In 2010, the concept of PbD became an international principle for privacy protection and nowadays some norms explicitly mandate its implementation. This is the case of the article 25 of the GDPR. So, in the European Union DPbD is an enforceable obligation that all data controller must comply with. To evaluate the approach and to understand the deeper meaning of the concept, this study has identified and compared the advantages and disadvantages of the implementation of PbD. Balancing the benefits and the challenges, PbD still remains a good solution to implement privacy principles, values and rights. Moreover, as stated by the EDPS, an effective implementation of PbD is also an opportunity to boost the respect to ethics in technology. Then, the paper has examined the data protection by design legal obligation established by the GDPR.

The second goal of this paper was to determine how DPbD can be implemented in the context of e-health for Electronic Health Records and to provide more guidance to fulfil the legal requirement. The study has shown briefly the applicable EU legal provisions for EHRs systems. After that, the paper provided a comprehensive DPbD model for the privacy management with technical and organisational measures to be implemented in the EHRs. The DPbD measures were divided into four parts: "the technical measures", "the creation of the EHR", "the use of the EHR", and "the organisational and administrative measures". Overall, in the presented model the compliance with article 25 of the GDPR is only achieved if all the measures are implemented as a whole.

Therefore, healthcare providers and controllers must choose in the market or develop by themselves a EHR system which is compliant with DPbD requirement. Producers and technology developers are forced to adopt DPbD solutions to be competitive in the market.

---

[46] As article 25 GDPR suggests, the certification process for DPbD is possible. See for more articles 42 and 43, GDPR.

[47] Article 37 (1) (c), GDPR.

[48] Article 37 (3), GDPR.

In the future the aim of the research is to investigate more detailed DPbD measures and outline the relevant technologies for implementing a model of "DPbD EHR" in the European framework. Future work could also focus on analysing if and how far a EU DPbD model could be included in other legal frameworks.

References

1. Commission of the European Communities: Communication from the Commission to the Council, the European Parliament, the European Economic and Social Committee and the Committee of the Regions, E-Health - making healthcare better for European citizens: An action plan for a European e-Health Area. COM (2004) 356 final, Brussels (2004)
2. European Commission: Communication from the Commission to the European Parliament, the Council, the European Economic and Social Commitee and the Commitee of the Regions on the Mid-Term Review on the implementation of the Digital Single Market Strategy, A Connected Digital Single Market for All. COM (2017) 228 final, Bruxelles (2017)
3. Article 29 Working Party: Working Document on the processing of personal data relating to health in electronic health records (EHR), WP 131, Brussels (2007)
4. Council of the European Union: Draft Council conclusions on Health in the Digital Society - making progress in data-driven innovation in the field of health. 14078/17, Bruxelles (2017)
5. 32nd International Conference of Data Protection and Privacy Commissioners: Resolution on privacy by design, Jerusalem, Israel, 27–29 October 2010
6. Lessig, L.: Code, Version 2.0. A Member of the Perseus Books Group/Basic Books, New York (2006)
7. Regulation (EU) 2016/679 of the European Parliament and of the Council of 27 April 2016 on the protection of natural persons with regard to the processing of personal data and on the free movement of such data, and repealing Directive 95/46/EC (General Data Protection Regulation). OJ L 119, 4.5. (2016)
8. Cavoukian, A.: Privacy by Design. Information and Privacy Commissioner, Ontario (2009)
9. Cavoukian, A.: Operationalizing privacy by design: a guide to implementing strong privacy practices. Information and Privacy Commissioner, Ontario, Canada (2012)
10. Federal Trade Commission: Protecting Consumer Privacy in an Era of Rapid Change, Recommendations for Businesses and Policymaker. FTC Report (2012). https://www.ftc.gov/reports/protecting-consumer-privacy-era-rapid-change-recommendations-businesses-policymakers. Accessed 10 Mar 2019
11. Solove, D.J., Hartzog, W.: The FTC and the new common law of privacy. Colum. L. Rev. **114**, 583 (2014)
12. Rubinstein, I.S.: Regulating privacy by design. Berkeley Tech. LJ **26**, 1409 (2011)
13. Tamò-Larrieux, A.: Designing for Privacy and its Legal Framework. LGTS, vol. 40. Springer, Cham (2018). https://doi.org/10.1007/978-3-319-98624-1
14. Lessig, L.: Code and Other Laws of Cyberspace. A Member of the Perseus Books Group. Basic Books, New York (1999)
15. Klitou, D.: Privacy-Invading Technologies and Privacy by Design, Safeguarding Privacy, Liberty and Security in the 21st Century. 25 Information Technology and Law Series. T.M.C. Asser Press, Hague (2014)

16. Mulligan, D.K., King, J.: Bridging the gap between privacy and design. U. Pa. J. Const. L. **14**, 989 (2012)
17. Bernstein, G.: When new technologies are still new: windows of opportunity for privacy protection. Vill. L. Rev. **51**, 921 (2006)
18. Schartum, D.W.: Making privacy by design operative. IJLT **24**, 151 (2016)
19. Grimmelmann, J.: Privacy as product safety. Widener LJ **19**, 793 (2010)
20. Cavoukian, A.: Privacy by design: the definitive workshop - a foreword by Ann Cavoukian. IDIS **3**, 247 (2010)
21. Kianieff, M.: The evolution of consumer privacy law: how privacy by design can benefit from insights in commercial law and standardization. CJLT **10**, 1 (2012)
22. Hustinx, P.: Privacy by design: delivering the promises. IDIS **3**, 253 (2010)
23. Hartzog, W.: Reexamining privacy value: the value of modest privacy protections in a hyper social world. Colo. Tech. LJ **12**, 333 (2014)
24. Tien, L.: Architectural regulation and the evolution of social norms. Yale J. L. Tech. **7**, 1 (2004)
25. Koops, B.J., Leenes, R.: Privacy regulation cannot be hardcoded, a critical comment on the "privacy by design" provision in data-protection law. Int. Rev. Law Comput. Tech. **28**, 1 (2013)
26. Kamara, I.: Co-regulation in EU personal data protection: the case of technical standards and the privacy by design standardisation "mandate". EJLT **8**(1) (2017)
27. Gürses, S., Troncoso, C., Diaz, C.: Engineering privacy by design. In: 4th Conference on Computers Privacy and Data Protection, vol. 317 (2011)
28. Hintze, M.: Viewing the GDPR through a de-identification lens: a tool for compliance, clarification, and consistency. IDPL **8**, 1 (2018)
29. Krebs, D.: "Privacy by design": nice-to-have or a necessary principle of data protection law? JIPITEC **4**, 2190 (2013)
30. Reidenberg, J.R.: Lex informatica: the formulation of information policy rules through technology. Tex. L. Rev. **76**, 553 (1997–1998)
31. Hijmans, H.: The European Union as Guardian of Internet Privacy. LGTS, vol. 31. Springer, Cham (2016). https://doi.org/10.1007/978-3-319-34090-6
32. Gutwirth, S., Leenes, R., De Hert, P.: Data Protection on the Move, Current Developments in ICT and privacy/data protection. 24 Law, Governance and Technology Series. Springer, Netherlands (2016)
33. Pagallo, U.: On the principle of privacy by design and its limits: technology, ethics and the rule of law. In: Gutwirth, S., Leenes, R., De Hert, P., Poullet, Y. (eds.) European Data Protection: In Good Health?. Springer, Dordrecht (2012). https://doi.org/10.1007/978-94-007-2903-2_16
34. Bair, J.L.: Electronic health records and respect for patient privacy: a prescription for compatibility. Vand. J. Ent. Tech. L. **13**, 441 (2011)
35. European Union Agency for Network and Information Security (ENISA): Privacy by design in big data, an overview of privacy enhancing technologies in the era of big data analytics (2015). https://www.enisa.europa.eu/publications/big-data-protection. Accessed 10 Mar 2019
36. Rubinstein, I.S., Good, N.: Privacy by design: a counterfactual analysis of Google and Facebook privacy incidents. Berkeley Tech. LJ **28**, 1333 (2013)
37. U.S. Department of Health, Education & Welfare: Report of the Secretary's Advisory Committee on Automated Personal Data Systems, Records Computers and the Rights of citizens, United States (1973)
38. Rotenberg, M.: Fair information practices and the architecture of privacy (what Larry doesn't get). Stan. Tech. L. Rev. **2001**, 1 (2001)

39. European Data Protection Supervisor (EDPS): Preliminary Opinion on privacy by design. Opinion 5/2018 (2018)
40. Commission Nationale de l'Informatique et des Libertés (CNIL): La forme des choix, Données personnelles, design et frictions désirables. Cahier IP 6 (2019). http://linc.cnil.fr. Accessed 10 Mar 2019
41. Article 29 Data Protection Working Party: The Future of Privacy, Joint contribution to the Consultation of the European Commission on the legal framework for the fundamental right to protection of personal data. WP 168 02356/09/EN (2009)
42. Jasmontaite, L., Kamara, I., Zanfir-Fortuna, G., Leucci, S.: Data Protection by Design and by Default. EDPL **4**, 2 (2018)
43. Bygrave, L.A.: Data Protection by design and by default: deciphering the EU's legislative requirements. Oslo L. Rev. **4**, 105 (2017)
44. Voigt, P., Von dem Bussche, A.: The EU General Data Protection Regulation (GDPR). A Practical Guide. Springer, Netherlands (2017)
45. Regulation (EU) 2018/1725 of the European Parliament and of the Council of 23 October 2018 on the protection of natural persons with regard to the processing of personal data by the Union institutions, bodies, offices and agencies and on the free movement of such data, and repealing Regulation (EC) No 45/2001 and Decision No 1247/2002/ECText with EEA relevance, PE/31/2018/REV/1. OJ L 295, 21 November 2018
46. De Hert, P., Papakonstantinou, V.: The proposed data protection Regulation replacing Directive 95/46/EC: a sound system for the protection of individuals. CLSR **28**, 130 (2012)
47. European Union Agency for Fundamental Rights: Handbook on European data protection law (2018). http://fra.europa.eu/en/publication/2018/handbook-european-data-protection-law. Accessed 10 March 2019
48. European Commission and Milieu Ltd.: eHealth: Digital health and care Project, Overview of the national laws on electronic health records in the EU Member States (2014). https://ec.europa.eu/health/ehealth/projects/nationallaws_electronichealthrecords_it. Accessed 10 Mar 2019
49. European Union Agency for Network and Information Security (ENISA): Privacy and data protection in mobile applications. A study on the app development ecosystem and the technical implementation of GDPR (2018). https://www.enisa.europa.eu/publications/privacy-and-data-protection-in-mobile-applications. Accessed 10 Mar 2019
50. Danezis, G., et al.: European Union Agency for Network and Information Security (ENISA): Privacy and Data Protection by Design, from policy to engineering (2015). https://www.enisa.europa.eu/publications/privacy-and-data-protection-by-design. Accessed 10 Mar 2019
51. Colesky, M., Hoepman, J.H., Hillen, C.: A critical analysis of privacy design strategies. In: International Workshop on Privacy Engineering - IWPE 2016, San Jose, CA, USA (2016)
52. European Union Agency for Network and Information Security (ENISA): Handbook on Security of Personal Data Processing (2018). https://www.enisa.europa.eu/publications/handbook-on-security-of-personal-data-processing. Accessed 10 Mar 2019
53. ISO/TS 17975:2015: Health informatics - Principles and data requirements for consent in the Collection, Use or Disclosure of personal health information (2015). https://www.iso.org/home.html. Accessed 10 Mar 2019
54. Carro, G., Masato, S., Parla, M.D.: La privacy nella sanità. Giuffrè, Torino (2017)

Security Analysis of Subject Access Request Procedures

How to Authenticate Data Subjects Safely When They Request for Their Data

Coline Boniface[1], Imane Fouad[2], Nataliia Bielova[2], Cédric Lauradoux[1(✉)], and Cristiana Santos[3]

[1] Univ. Grenoble Alpes, Inria, France
{coline.boniface,cedric.lauradoux}@inria.fr
[2] Université Côte d'Azur, Inria, France
{imane.fouad,nataliia.bielova}@inria.fr
[3] School of Law, University Toulouse 1 Capitole, SIRIUS Chair, Toulouse, France
cristiana.santos@ut-capitole.fr

Abstract. With the GDPR in force in the EU since May 2018, companies and administrations need to be vigilant about the personal data they process. The new regulation defines rights for data subjects and obligations for data controllers but it is unclear how subjects and controllers interact concretely. This paper tries to answer two critical questions: is it safe for a data subject to exercise the right of access of her own data? When does a data controller have enough information to authenticate a data subject? To answer these questions, we have analyzed recommendations of Data Protection Authorities and authentication practices implemented in popular websites and third-party tracking services. We observed that some data controllers use unsafe or doubtful procedures to authenticate data subjects. The most common flaw is the use of authentication based on a copy of the subject's national identity card transmitted over an insecure channel. We define how a data controller should react to a subject's request to determine the appropriate procedures to identify the subject and her data. We provide compliance guidelines on data access response procedures.

Keywords: GDPR · Data protection · Privacy · Right of access · Identity verification · Subject access request (SAR)

1 Introduction

With the GDPR in place since May 2018, the rights of the European users have been strengthened. The GDPR defines users' rights and aims at protecting their personal data. Every European Data Protection Authority (DPA) provides advices, explanations and recommendations on the use of these rights. However,

© Springer Nature Switzerland AG 2019
M. Naldi et al. (Eds.): APF 2019, LNCS 11498, pp. 182–209, 2019.
https://doi.org/10.1007/978-3-030-21752-5_12

the GDPR does not provide any prescriptive requirements on how to authenticate a data subject request. This lack of concrete description undermines the practical effect of the GDPR: it hampers the way to exercise the subject access right, to check the lawfulness of the processing and to enforce the derived legal rights therefrom (erasure, rectification, restriction, etc).

Every data subject would like to benefit from the rights specified in GDPR, but still wonders: *How do I exercise my access right? How do I prove my identity to the controller?* These questions are critical to build trust between the data subject and the controller. The data subject is concerned with threats like *impersonation* and *abusive identity check*. Impersonation is the case of a malicious party who attempts to abuse the subject access request (SAR) by impersonating a subject to a controller. Abusive identity check occurs when a data controller is too curious and verifies the identity of a subject by asking irrelevant and unnecessary information like an electricity bill or government issued documents.

Symmetrically, every data controller needs to know how to proceed when they receive an access request: *Is the request legitimate? What is necessary to identify the subject's data?* These concerns aggravate when controllers deal with indirectly-linked identifiers, such as IP addresses, or when they have no prior contact with data subjects, as in *Google Spain*[1]. Most of all, data controllers want to avoid data breaches, as it can result in legal proceedings and heavy fines. Such consequence occurs in two cases: *(i)* the data controller releases data to an illegitimate subject, or *(ii)* he releases data of a subject A to a legitimate subject B.

All these questions concern the authentication procedure between the data subject and the controller. They both share a common interest in holding a strong authentication procedure to prevent impersonation and data breaches. The subject must be careful during the authentication procedure, as for providing too much personal information could compromise her right of privacy. Additionally, the controller needs to ask the appropriate information to identify the subject's data without ambiguity. There is clearly a tension during this authentication act between the controller, who tries to get as much information as possible, and the data subject who wants to provide as little as possible. Plausibly, subject access rights can probably increase the incidence of personal records being accidentally or deliberately opened to unauthorised third parties [57].

This paper studies *the tension during the authentication between the data subject and the data controller.* We first evaluate the threats to the SAR authentication procedure and then we analyze the recommendations of 28 DPAs of European Union countries. We observe that four of them can potentially lead to abusive identity check. On the positive side, six of them are recommending to enforce the data minimization principle during authentication. This principle, on one hand, protects the right to privacy of data subjects, and on the other hand

---

[1] Google Spain SL and Google Inc. v Agencia Española de Protección de Datos (AEPD) and Mario Costeja González, Case C-131/12, https://eur-lex.europa.eu/legal-content/EN/TXT/PDF/?uri=CELEX:62012CJ0131&from=EN.

prevents data controllers to massively collect personal data that is not needed for authentication, thus preventing abusive identity check (Sect. 2).

We have then evaluated the authentication procedure when exercising the access right of the 50 most popular websites and 30 third-party tracking services (Sect. 3). Several popular websites require to systematically provide a national identity card or government-issued documents to authenticate the data subject. Among third-party tracking services, 9 of them additionally to cookies demand other personal data from the data subjects, like the identity card or the full name. We explain that such demands are not justified because additional information can not prove the ownership of the cookie.

We then provide guidelines to Data Protection Authorities, website owners and third party services on how to authenticate data subjects safely while protecting their identities, and without requesting additional unnecessary information (complying with the data minimization principle). More precisely, we explain how data controllers and data subjects must interact and how digital identifiers can be redesigned to be compliant with the GDPR (Sect. 4). Finally, we overview related work (Sect. 5) and then conclude the paper.

2   Threats to SAR Authentication and Recommendations of the DPAs

Chapter 3 of the GDPR [58] is dedicated to the rights of the data subject: right to access, object, rectification, erasure, restriction of processing, notification, portability and the right not to be subject to a decision based solely on automated processing. Some of these rights are not new and they already appeared in the Directive 95/46/EC, like the right of access. The right of access by the data subject is defined in Article 15, but Article 12 and Recital 64 of the GDPR are also important for our work, as these provisions regard the *modalities for the exercise of the rights of the data subject*. Three key elements can be extracted from this article. First, a data controller must answer each data subject request without undue delay. Second, the identity of the data subject making a request needs to be proven. Third, the data controller should also provide means for requests to be made electronically, where appropriate.

Access requests can be *direct, indirect* or *mixed*. The "normal way" for subjects to access their data is directly: the subject sends a request to the data controller and no third parties are involved. As for indirect requests, the DPA or a court can be involved only if the data controller does not respect the subject's rights, upon a complaint procedure. For certain special files, data subjects can not directly exercise their rights. The national DPA, acting as a proxy controller, has to verify the subject's identity and make the request on his behalf; then, the DPA reports its finding to the subject. Mixed access requests corresponds to situations in which some accesses are direct and other are indirect. A good example is the Schengen information system. Depending on the country, the access to this file can be direct, indirect or mixed, as defined in [27]. Our work is dedicated to direct accesses, but it also applies to the case of indirect and mixed access.

These elements are important to understand how the access right is exercised in practice, but these are still insufficient to let the subject and the data controller understand what is at stake. From now, we focus our attention on the second point: how can the data controller check the identity of the subject making a request. We first consider the issues that can occur (Sect. 2.1), and then we examine what are the recommendations of the European Data Protection Authorities (Sect. 2.2).

2.1   Threat Model

In the last decades, researchers have made a substantial advancement in the field of authentication by means of cryptographic protocols. These protocols are often run automatically by computers and they are (almost) transparent to end users. They are the straightforward solution for a data controller to authenticate a data subject. However, this is true only if the data controller has created automatic tools for the subject to extract her data. But in practice it is often the case that the access request of the subject is handled by a human (often a data privacy officer of the data controller). All the research advancement on authentication is suddenly irrelevant because a human can not execute complex cryptographic operations.

Therefore, we question what are the consequences of weak authentication procedures. The main purpose of the authentication is to establish the identity of the data subject to the data controller. This goal is explicitly stated in the GDPR, however the GDPR does not explain the major consequence of an incorrect authentication, which we devise in this analysis. In our paper, we have considered that both the data subject and the data controller can be malicious. In our definition of the threat model, we take the perspective of the data subject making the request. In our quadrant analysis, three issues can occur: *data breach, privacy invasion and denial of access.*

(i) Data Breach – A data controller discloses information of a data subject to someone else than the concerned subject. Any data controller wants to avoid this situation which can result in being fined by one of the EU DPAs. The data subject is also interested in protecting herself from such breaches and from her private data being exposed. The data can be exposed to an external adversary or to another different legitimate subject. Unauthorized disclosures are qualified as data breach, under Article 3(12) of the GDPR.

(ii) Privacy Invasion – In this situation, the data controller is perceived as malicious. He aims to exploit the authentication as a method to obtain from the data subject. This can be viewed as a sort of data breach made by the data controller himself whose goal is to access more data of the data subject. The qualification of *privacy invasion* derives from our interpretation of non-compliance to the principles of data minimization and storage limitation:

- *Minimization principle: personal data shall be adequate, relevant and limited to what is necessary in relation to the purposes for which they are processed*

(Article 5(1)(c). Recital 39 specifies further that *personal data should be processed only if the purpose of the processing could not reasonably be fulfilled by other means.* The "necessity" or "proportionality" requirement that both these provisions afford, refers both to the quantity and also to the quality of personal data. It is thus clear that the controller should not process excessive data if this entails a disproportionate interference in the data subject's rights, and hence, a privacy invasion. Ultimately, if the personal data processed by a controller does not permit him to identify a user, the data controller should not be obliged to acquire additional information in order to identify the data subject for the sole purpose of complying with SAR, in accordance to Recital 57;

- *Storage Limitation Principle: personal data shall be kept in a form which permits identification of data subjects for no longer than is necessary for the purposes for which the personal data are processed,* (Article 5(1)(e)). Aligned with this principle, recital 64 further refers that a controller should not retain personal data for the sole purpose of being able to react to potential future requests. Recital 39 invites controllers to establish time limits for erasure or for a periodic review. This will ensure that the personal data are not kept longer than necessary.

(iii) Denial of access – This situation is often mentioned in the papers [39, 43, 44] testing the access right. The data controller refuses to allow a legitimate subject to access her data. The reasons can be numerous. We focus in our work on cases, where authentication is used as a mean to refuse the access to the data.

After having identified the purposes of authentication, we propose to define the threats, *i.e.* the attacks that can be carried out by an adversary. Any successful attack results in a significant privacy issue, either for the data subject making the request, or for another data subject. Instances of these threats are: impersonation, incorrect disclosure, abusive identity check and impossibility of authentication.

(i) Impersonation (data breach) – A malicious individual is able to impersonate a legitimate data subject to the data controller. The adversary forges a valid access request and goes through the identity verification enforced by the data controller. The data controller sends to the adversary the data of a legitimate data subject. Defeating impersonation is the primary objective of any authentication protocol. The result of this attack is a data breach (e.g. blaggers pretend to be someone they are not in order to wheedle out the information they are seeking obtaining information illegally which they then sell for a specified price).

(ii) Incorrect disclosure (data breach) – A data subject makes a legitimate request to a data controller to access her data. The data controller verifies successfully her identity and sends the data back to the data subject. However, some of the sent data belongs to another data subject. This is clearly an incorrect procedure made by the data controller. This error will be sooner or later exploited by an adversary who will create an account at the data controller and

send a legitimate request to access the data of someone else. This is clearly a data breach. It is very easy to imagine an incorrect disclosure. Let us consider the case of a subject using IP address XXX.WWW.YYY.ZZZ. This address is actually shared by several subjects in Virtual Private Network (VPN). The subject asks a data controller for all the data collected and associated to XXX.WWW.YYY.ZZZ. If a controller sends data associated to WWW.XXX.YYY.ZZZ, he might commit an incorrect disclosure.

(iii) Abusive identity check (privacy invasion) – The adversary in this case is the data controller itself. The term *abusive identity check* is associated with discriminatory controls by law enforcement authorities, but we use it in a different meaning. We consider that the identity verification is abusive when the data controller asks unnecessary or irrelevant information. Let us consider a case of a subject who has registered to a service using a pseudonym. The data controller of the service has no clue on the real identity of the subject. Despite using a pseudonym, the GDPR still applies and the subject can request access to her data to the controller. The controller requires a copy of her passport to verify that the request is legitimate. We contend that this verification is abusive for two reasons:

- the information is irrelevant because getting a copy of her passport does not help the controller to check that the request is legitimate; and
- there is no reason for the data subject to reveal her real identity to the data controller through such document. The documents requested by the controller must be *proportional* or *necessary* to the controller's knowledge of the data subject. Can we state that each time a data controller asks for a copy of her passport we are dealing with abusive identity checks? No, it depends on what the data subject has already revealed to the data controller. If the data controller knows the true identity of the data subject, it is legitimate to ask for an official document. It can be the case, for instance, if the data controller is a national administration. However, as we will see in Sect. 3, some data controllers require extra information to authenticate data subjects (and thus perform abusive identity check), claiming they follow Article 12(6) of GDPR saying *"where the controller has reasonable doubts concerning the identity of the natural person making the request, the controller may request the provision of additional information necessary to confirm the identity of the data subject"* even though the identity check is already established.

(iv) Impossibility of authentication (denial of access) – Upon receiving an access request, the data controller can declare that he is not in a position to identify the data subject, due to difficulties to prove ownership of the data. He cannot satisfy the condition of Article 12 of the GDPR and will not grant access to the data to prevent a data breach. Hence, the controller shall inform the data subject accordingly, if possible (Article 11(2)), providing the reasons for his non fulfillment of a specific access request.

We excluded from our study the more generic threat of denial of service (DoS) attacks. An example of DoS attack in our settings would consist in a huge number of malicious data subjects sending access requests to the data controller at the same time of the request of the targeted subject. Being overflown by malicious requests, the data controller cannot answer the request of the targeted subject. DoS attack in this case results in a privacy issue: the data subject is deprived from her rights.

Summary: Our threat model shows that there is a *tension between privacy and security* during the authentication procedure when the data subject wants to exercise her access rights. First, a zealous data controller can ask too much information from the data subject to ensure her identity. Second, a zealous data controller can reject all the subject access requests claiming that he cannot authenticate the data subject. Finally, a negligent data controller may obtain insufficient information to prevent impersonation or incorrect disclosure.

2.2 Recommendations of the EU Data Protection Authorities

The goal of our work is to analyze the recommendations emanated by the DPAs of the members of European Union regarding authentication procedures when data subjects exercise the right to access their data. In particular, we aim to determine if DPAs provide recommendations on how a data subject can exercise her rights and if any authentication process was mentioned or suggested. In this work, we take the perspective of data subjects visiting a website of a DPA searching for recommendations to exercise their subject access requests. We acknowledge that DPA recommendations can be interpreted to be either addressed for data subjects to exercise SAR with the DPAs directly, or it can also configure a recommendation for the DPOs of the data controllers. However, since our study is data subject-centric, we analyse the issued recommendations from the perspective of the data subject who is trying to follow procedures to exercise her rights.

To achieve this goal, we adopted the following methodological steps: we have visited the webpages of French, English, Italian and Spanish speaking countries. Regarding the other countries, we have asked the assistance of colleagues who speak the language of the given country: each colleague was provided with the website of a DPA and was asked to find pages related to the exercise of access right in 30 min. We received answers from all members states. The results of our inspections can be found in Table 1.

From our analysis, we report that all DPAs explain what are subject rights. However not all the authorities explain how the data subject can exercise her rights. 17 authorities provide guidelines and explanations for the subject to access her data. Several of them provide also a template for the subject to make her request via email or post. It is noticeable that we have not found any authority providing guidelines or recommendations for data controllers on how to authenticate a data subject and to let her exercise her rights. It follows from the foregoing analysis that, to the best of our knowledge, the Bulgarian DPA does not provide any information on how to fill in a request. However, it has an interesting page [55] entitled "Who can copy your identity card" whose goal

Table 1. State of recommendations by the data protection authorities of the european union.

Country	Recom.	Authentication	Country	Recom.	Authentication
Austria [45]	✓	Customer ID or copy of the national identity card	Italy [83]	✗	Data minimization
Belgium [47]	✓	Copy of the national identity card	Latvia [63]	✓	Data minimization
Bulgaria [55]	✗	Copy of the national identity card	Lithuania	✗	
Croatia [60]	✗		Luxembourg [75]	✓	
Cyprus [56]	✗		Malta [80]	✓	
Czech Republic [101]	✗		Netherlands [48]	✓	Least privacy sensitive
Denmark [64]	✓		Poland [97]	✗	
Estonia [42]	✗		Portugal [54]	✗	
Finland [81]	✓		Romania [100]	✓	
France [53]	✓	Proportionality	Slovakia [79]	✓	
Germany [65]	✓	Copy of the national identity card + masking	Slovenia [68]	✓	Relevant Identifying data
Greece [67]	✗		Spain [40]	✓	Copy of the national identity card
Hungary [62]	✗		Sweden [78]	✓	
Ireland [61]	✓	Copy of the national identity card	UK [98]	✓	Any information used by the organisation to identify or distinguish you

is to warn the subjects that the copy of an ID card is a sensitive document. This document also states that a data controller is legitimate to ask a copy of a subject's ID to authenticate her access request.

From the websites of 28 European DPAs that we have analyzed, we found that four DPAs (Belgium, Bulgaria, Ireland and Spain) require a copy of government-issued documents to make an access request by default. Such recommendations can lead to abusive identity checks. The German authority [65] suggests to use the copy of an ID card, but it strongly recommended to blur unnecessary information.

Some recommendations made by the authorities are particularly interesting. The Austrian DPA [45] does not provide any specific recommendations, but gives a template form for a data subject to make a subject access request. In the part "Identity" field in the form [45], the Austrian DPA lets the data subject choose how she should be identified: (i) if the subject already had a contact with the data controller, then customer number would suffice, (ii) otherwise, the subject should attach an ID proving her identity. The Austrian DPA lets the subject choose whether she wants to be contacted electronically or not, but does not provide any security conditions for the data transmission.

In France, the CNIL [53] advises to apply the proportionality principle when sharing information to authenticate to the controller. The Italian DPA [83] does not provide any specific indications on how to authenticate a data subject, but requires, like the Latvian DPA [63] that the data minimization principle is respected.

The Slovenian DPA [68] suggests to provide *"birthday or other identification data on the basis of which the manager can find in your collections your personal information you request"*. The subject needs to provide only information necessary for the controller to find her data. The recommendation of the ICO in United Kingdom [98] is very similar. The subject must provide *"Any information used by the organisation to identify or distinguish you"*

Data protection authorities are the main enforcers of the GDPR. Moreover, two additional actors at the EU level are involved in the implementation of the GDPR: the European Data Protection Supervisor (EDPS) [31] and the European Data Protection Board (EDPB) [30]. The EDPS supervises the EU institutions to help them to be exemplary. The EDPB advises the European Commission on any issue related to data protection in the EU and to rule by binding decisions on disputes regarding cross-border processing activities, ensuring therefore a uniform application of the EU rules. The EDPB is also a data controller and provides a privacy notice at https://edpb.europa.eu/about-edpb/legal-notices/data-protection-notice_en. Data subjects can exercise their access rights by sending an email to EDPB-DPO@edpb.europa.eu or contacting the EDPB DPO by post in a sealed envelope. It also states that:

Your request should contain a detailed, accurate description of the data you want access to. When there are reasonable doubts regarding your identity, you might be asked to provide a copy of a document, which help us to verify your identity. It can be any document such as your ID card or passport. Should you provide any other documents, personal details such as your name and your address should be in clear in order to be able to identify you, while any other data such as a photo or any personal characteristics, may be blacked out.

3 Practical Evaluation of Websites and Third Party Trackers

When a subject visits a website, data may be collected by the website owner and by third party trackers present on the website. In our work, we consider the website owner and the third party tracker present on the website as joint data controllers. Both joint controllers could distribute their responsibilities concerning SAR, and hence, data subjects could exercise their rights of access against each of the controllers. Irrespective of the contractual provision allocation tasks between joint controllers, they are both liable for non-compliance of subject access rights (Article 26(3)).

In a practical setting, and following the cognition of Mahieu et al. [71] *"a data subject can direct a request to access to the website administrator, irrespective of the fact that the personal data is collected through the use of cookies by Facebook and the administrator has no access to data. The administrator could solve this practically by redirecting the request to Facebook. However, if Facebook would not adequately comply, the organization integrating their plugin may also be held accountable".* The CJEU decision of Wirtschaftsakademie [28] deems both these organizations as joint controllers.

In this section we investigate authentication procedures presented in privacy policies of 50 popular websites and implemented in 30 third party services that track users on popular websites.

3.1 Evaluation of Popular Websites

In this work, we have analyzed privacy policies of the 50 top Alexa websites[2]. By doing so, we obtained information about the procedure enforced by websites for a data subject to get a copy of her data. Notice that the overall effectiveness of the GDPR rights from a European resident point of view depends on how easily and safely a resident can exercise such rights. Right of access is the most basic example of GDPR rights.

Evaluation Criteria. To compare procedures set up by popular websites, we propose three criteria: *Known identifiers, requested identifiers* and *accessibility*.

Known Identifiers – This criterion corresponds to the prior knowledge of the data controller on the subject. It is the information provided by the subject when she created her account on the website. We consider two cases. First, the data controller knows the subject through an identifier like a chosen username,

---

[2] Alexa measures web traffic and provides a ranking of the websites with respect to their traffic: https://www.alexa.com/topsites, extracted in October 2018.

an email address, a cookie or mobile identifier. Second, the data controller knows the real identity of the subject. This criterion is important to verify whether the identifiers requested to authenticate the subject are proportional to the knowledge of the data controller has about her.

Requested Identifiers – During the authentication, the data controller can ask for more information on the subject to confirm her identity. For instance, he can ask for the copy of a government-issued document or a proof of residence. One important question for the requested identifier is the eligibility. According to its territorial scope, the GDPR applies to European companies handling personal data from all over the world and to companies handling data of European residents (as defined in par. 2 of Article 3 of the GDPR). European data controllers do not need to verify whether the subject is a European resident or not because they have to enforce the GDPR anyway. The case of foreign companies is different. They can decide to check the eligibility of the subject by demanding a copy of her national identity card. However, this is not sufficient because a non-EU citizen can reside in the EU and have the same GDPR rights. To check eligibility, data controllers should instead ask for a proof of residence (which may be different from citizenship), such as an electricity or a phone bill. However, this reveals more information about the data subject, such as her home address or phone number. Such collection can lead easily to an *abusive identity check attack* (see Sect. 2.1).

Accessibility – The data controller creates procedures to let the subject access her data. These procedures can be automatic (direct access): the subject logs into her account and can directly download her data. Another possibility is that the subject needs to send an email or a letter to the data protection officer. Data exchanged by emails are likely to be exposed to the knowledge of many people. Their use can lead to data breach.

Results of Our Evaluation. Table 2 shows the results of our evaluation on the three criteria defined above. We have analyzed privacy policies of the top 50 Alexa websites and for simplicity we have regrouped all the entries related to the same company in one table raw: Google (Google.com, Google.co.in, Google.co.jp, Google.com.hk, Google.com.br, Google.co.uk, Google.ru, Google.fr, Google.de, Youtube.com and Blogspot.com), Yahoo (Yahoo.com and Yahoo.co.jp) and Microsoft (Live.com, Microsoft.com, Bing.com, Microsoftonline.com, Office.com and Msn.com). After grouping, we get 27 entries in Table 2.

We have not found any websites which require or force a subject to provide her real identity at registation. The subject often provides an email address, a username or any other element of her own choice.

We have observed three behaviors in the 50 most popular websites. Some websites have created access procedures for any data subjects without checking their eligibility. Others have a special part for *"EU users only"* within their privacy policies under the section *"Additional Information for EEA users"* or

Table 2. Evaluation of the subject access right procedure of 50 popular websites.

Websites	Known identifiers		Requested identifiers			Accessibility	
	Username	Real id.	Copy of an ID	Eligibility	Other	Direct access	email
Google.com [5]	✓	✗	✗	✗	✗	✓	✗
Facebook.com [25]	✓	✗	✗	✗	✗	✓	✗
Baidu.com [3]	✓	✗	✓	✓	✓	✗	✓
Wikipedia.org [10]	–	–	–	–	–	–	–
Yahoo.com [21]	✓	✗	✗	✗	✗	✓	✗
Qq.com [11]	✓	✗	✓	✓	✗	✗	✓
Taobao.com, Tmall.com	–	–	–	–	–	–	–
Alipay.com [24]	✓	✗	✓	✓	✗	✗	✓
Twitter.com [2]	✓	✗	✗	✗	✗	✓	✗
Amazon [17]	✓	✗	✗	✗	✗	✓	✗
Instagram.com [13]	✓	✗	✗	✗	✗	✓	✗
Vk.com [14]	✓	✗	✓	✓	✗	✗	✓
Sohu.com	–	–	–	–	–	–	–
Reddit.com [4]	✓	✗	✗	✗	✗	✓	✗
Yandex.ru [19]	–	–	–	–	–	–	–
Weibo.com	–	–	–	–	–	–	–
Sina.com.cn	–	–	–	–	–	–	–
360.cn	–	–	–	–	–	–	–
Netflix [18]	✓	✗	✓	✓	✗	✗	✓
Pornhub.com [12]	✓	✗	✗	✗	✗	✗	✓
Linkedin.com [20]	✓	✗	✗	✗	✗	✓	✗
Mail.ru [7]	–	–	–	–	–	–	–
Twitch.tv [22]	✓	✗	✗	✗	✗	✓	✗
Ebay.com [15]	✓	✗	✓	✗	✓	✗	✓
Microsoft [6]	✓	✗	✗	✗	✗	✓	✗
Xvideos.com [23]	✓	✗	✓	✗	✗	✗	✓
Imdb.com [16]	✓	✗	✗	✗	✗	✓	✗

"*This section (Your Rights) applies to users that are located in the European Economic Area only*". In this case, the request form is often sent by e-mail, and by regular post for only a few websites. Finally, Amazon.com and IMDb.com have no specific procedure on their websites concerning how users can access their data.

The privacy policy of Wikipedia warrants that Wikipedia is a service only dealing with public informations posted by the users as stipulated "*If you only read Wikipedia without contributing, no more personal information is collected than is typically collected in server logs by web sites in general. If you contribute to Wikipedia, assume that it will be retained forever*". Anyone can get access to

the contributions history of any Wikipedia user and to the information given in
his profile. There is no dedicated procedure for a contributor to collect his data.

Terms of service of Mail.ru[3] does not mention EU regulations, GDPR or
subject access rights. In addition, Mail.ru doesn't take any responsibility for
not allowing to download user's data: *"2.3. All the Services Mail.Ru, including
mail service, are provided "as is". Mail.Ru does not assume any responsibility
for the delay, removal, non-delivery or impossibility to download any User data,
including User settings..."* (translated from Russian by the author).

For six Chinese websites (Taobao.com, Tmall.com, Sohu.com, Weibo.com,
Sina.com.cn and 360.cn), we examined their content with a native Chinese
speaker, but we were not able to find any information related to privacy policies.

Requesting Additional Information – The websites QQ, Baidu, Alipay, Aliex-
press, Netflix, Ebay and Xvideos ask the subject to give additional information
like national identity card or government issued documents. In these seven cases,
the subject needs to give her real identity to access her data. Most of the time,
the motivation to request these documents is eligibility. Alibaba group uses collected information to ensure the eligibility of the request: *"verifying your identity
(. . .) verifying your eligibility as an EU User of Alipay Services (including "know
your customer", anti-money laundering and counter-terrorist financing verification); processing your registration as an EU User, maintaining and managing
your registration"*. The website Xvideos does not provide any justification for
requesting a government issued document. This website is operated by WGCZ
which is located in Czech Republic. The procedure of Xvideos is clearly an abusive identity check.

Accessibility – The tech giants, such as Google and Facebook, have the best
practices regarding personal data access. When the subject authenticates herself
to the service (using `https`), the data controller grants her access to a copy of
her personal data without much effort. For example, Google uses `TakeOut`: a
tool which allows to select the subject's data for every Google service she wants
to include. `TakeOut` also sends an automated confirmation in order to detect
impersonation. Microsoft websites, Facebook, Instagram, Twitter and Linkedin
are using the same procedure which minimizes the amount of information needed
to authenticate the subject.

For seven websites, the access request was initiated using emails. The majority of these websites also asks the subject to send the copy of an ID by email.
Such practice might set this information at risk.

We also discovered two websites using a privacy proxy to manage the right
of the subjects. Pornhub uses managemydata.eu and Twitch uses onetrust.com.
OneTrust advertises on their website (https://www.onetrust.com/) to have
already 1500 customers.

---

[3] Point 2.3 of the Terms of Service, https://help.mail.ru/mail-help/UA (available only
in Russian).

3.2 Evaluation of Third Party Trackers

When a data subject visits a website, she is interacting and being observed not only by the owner of the website, but also by numerous third party services included in those websites. In the recent years, researchers found that more than 90% of Alexa top 500 websites [87] contain third party tracking content, while some sites include as much as 34 distinct third party content [70].

Such third party content is often tracking users: third party tracking is the practice by which third parties recognize users across different websites as they browse the web. One of the most common and basic technology to track users is via *third-party cookies*. Such cookies, installed by the third party content when the user visits a website, usually contain a unique identifier and allows third parties to track the user across different websites, recreate part of her browsing history and collect data about her.

To examine the effectiveness of the access right set up by the GDPR in case of third party tracking services, we crawled the top 100,000 websites according to Alexa ranking in October 2018 from a server located in France [41]. For each website, we visited the home page and other 10 webpages on the same website. Out of 100,000 Alexa top websites, we successfully crawled 84,094 websites with a total of 829,349 webpages. We have identified the top 30 third parties that set third-party identifying cookies in the user's browser. We have then analyzed the privacy policies of these 30 third party trackers, and interacted with them via email when privacy policy page analysis was not sufficient to draw conclusions. As a result, we extracted information on the authentication procedures implemented by the third party tracking services integrated in websites, and whether it is possible to exercise the subject access rights with them based on identifiers stored in the browser.

Evaluation Criteria: To evaluate the data access procedure set up by third party tracking services, we considered two main criteria *authentication* and *simplicity*.

Authentication – Authenticating the user is one of the main requirements to allow the user to access her data. By using the online identifiers–that could be either a cookie in case of web access or a mobile ID in case of mobile, third parties can uniquely identify the user. Notice that both identifiers stored in cookie or mobile ID are considered personal data according to the 29 Working Party Opinion 2/2010 on online behavioral advertising [26]. In some cases, the third parties require additional personal information, such as the name, email or even the ID document.

Simplicity – We evaluate simplicity by distinguishing how easy it is for the data subject to access her data collected by the third party trackers. Some third parties provide user-friendly access directly from the website, while for others the data subject need to suffer from long email exchanges making the data access very difficult for the data subject.

Results of Our Evaluation: Table 3 shows the results of our evaluation on the two main criteria described above. To simplify, we have grouped all the domains owned by Google (doubleclick.net, google.com, gstatic.com, youtube.com, google.fr, googlesyndication.com and 2mdn.net).

Impossible to Start Exercising SAR – Two companies, simpli.fi and casaleme-dia.com, were abusing identity check at the information extraction level. Simpli.fi refused to provide us with more information about the process unless we provide first and last name, address, phone number and email. Casalemedia.com did not explain how to exercise SAR on their website, and in order to ask a question we had to go through an online from, where we should provide additional personal data.

For four companies, teads.tv, baidu.com, innovid.com and serving-sys.com, we were not even able to start the SAR process. In their websites, teads.tv [96] and baidu.com [49] precise that data access is done upon request. We sent an email asking how we can access the third party data on December 6, 2018 and January 7, 2019 respectively but we have never received an answer as of March 18, 2019. We sent an email to innovid.com following the instruction on their website [69], but it appears that their domain isn't properly registered. Our message couldn't be delivered. The website of serving-sys.com is not accessible because of insecure connection error.

Denial of Access – Three companies answered our emails within less than one month, but their answers did not help us exercise the SAR and get the third party data. Two tech giants that set identifier cookies, Google (that covers 7 distinct third party tracking domains) and facebook.com have not given us any indication on how to access the third party data. Instead, they pointed us to their documentation and how to access the data collected directly via their services as first parties. Nr-data.net owned by New relic did not ask for the cookie identifier but only told us that the email we are using to communicate with them is not linked to any data in their dataset.

Two companies, demdex.net and everesttech.net owned by Adobe also refused to provide us with the data collected from the third party context. In our experiments, we have observed that these companies use third party cookie identifiers that allow them to identify the data subject across websites. However, when we tried to exercise SAR, these companies stated that it's not possible to confirm that any information associated with the third party cookie relates to us. On a positive side, demdex.net and everesttech.net did not ask for addition personal information, but they didn't grant us access to the third party data. According to them, their practice is in line with GDPR, they quoted:

> *This is in line with the GDPR, which recognises both that the right to obtain a copy of personal data should not adversely affect others (art.15(4)) and that rights of access do not apply where an organisation is not able effectively to identify the data subject (art.11(2)).*

Two companies, yandex.ru and openx.com refused to process our request as well. These companies claim that they act as data processors on behalf of its

Table 3. Evaluation of the subject access right procedure of top 30 third parties: "⊘" means that the request is denied by the third party, while "-" means it's not technically accessible.

Third-party domain	Authentification					Simplicity	
	Online identifier		Other data			Direct access	email
	Cookies	Mobile ID	Name and surname	email	ID card		
simpli.fi [90]	⊘	⊘	⊘	⊘	⊘	⊘	⊘
casalemedia.com [52]	⊘	⊘	⊘	⊘	⊘	⊘	⊘
teads.tv [96]	⊘	⊘	⊘	⊘	⊘	⊘	⊘
baidu.com [49]	⊘	⊘	⊘	⊘	⊘	⊘	⊘
innovid.com [69]	-	-	-	-	-	-	-
serving-sys.com	-	-	-	-	-	-	-
Google domains	⊘	⊘	⊘	⊘	⊘	⊘	⊘
facebook.com [25]	⊘	⊘	⊘	⊘	⊘	⊘	⊘
nr-data.net [76]	⊘	⊘	⊘	⊘	⊘	⊘	⊘
demdex.net	⊘	⊘	⊘	⊘	⊘	⊘	⊘
everesttech.net	⊘	⊘	⊘	⊘	⊘	⊘	⊘
yandex.ru [104]	⊘	⊘	⊘	⊘	⊘	⊘	⊘
openx.com [82]	⊘	⊘	⊘	⊘	⊘	⊘	⊘
pubmatic [84]	✓	✓	✓	✓	✓[a]	✗	✓
mathtag.com [72]	✓	✓	✓	✓	✓	✗	✓
weborama.fr [103]	✓	✓	✓	✓	✓	✗	✓
criteo.com [59]	✓	✓	✓	✓	✓	✗	✓
scorecardresearch.com [89]	✓	✓	✓	✓	✗	✗	✓
adform.com [33]	✓	✓	✓[b]	✓	✗	✗	✓
agkn.com	✓	✓	✗	✓	✗	✗	✓
smartadserver.com [91]	✓	✗	✗	✓	✗	✗	✓
adnxs.com [34]	✓	✓	✗	✗	✗	✓	✗
adsrvr.org [35]	✓	✓	✗	✗	✗	✓	✗
quantserve.com [86]	✓	✗	✗	✗	✗	✓[c]	✗
spotxchange.com [94]	✓	✓	✗	✗	✗	✓	✗

[a] Pubmatic also ask for the ID card of the witness who signs the SAR form together with the data subject.

[b] Adform declares that the provided personal data will be retained for 10 years.

[c] Quantserve provides the data subject a link that she should revisit after 30 days to fetch her data.

publisher or developer partners. Hence, the subject access requests do not apply to them and they suggest us to contact the data controllers. Notice that such interpretation is not acceptable by the recent work of Mahieu et al. [71] and the CJEU decision of Wirtschaftsakademie [28] who state that both publishers and third parties are joint data controllers (see the beginning of Sect. 3).

Abusive Identity Check – Third party domains are able to recognize the user across websites with a unique identifier, which we detected to be stored in the third party cookies. Such unique identifier is not related to the user's other personal information such as name or email. Therefore, any proof of user's name (such as the identity card) or email is not useful *to prove the ownership of the cookies.*

During our evaluation, we noticed that eight companies asked to provide not only the online identifier but other personal information as well. This practice allows third parties to link the data subject's online identifier to her personal information. Therefore, a data subject is forced to reveal even more personal data to the third party in order to practice her access right. This results in an *abusive identity check*.

Eight companies, pubmatic.com, smartadserver.com, mathtag.com, score-cardresearch.com, agkn.com, weborama.fr, adform.com and criteo.com require additional information to authenticate the user such as the full name or even the ID document. In addition to the subject's ID document, pubamtic.com asks for the name and the ID document of a witness who signs the SAR form together with the data subject. Five out of eight companies (pubmatic.com, mathtag.com, adform.com, weborama.fr and criteo.com) ask the user to fill a form, print and sign it in order to validate that she is the owner of the online identifier and of the device associated to it. Interestingly, adform.com uses this form to acknowledge the user that the company will process the additional personal data provided in the signed form (such as signature and full name) and retain it for up to 10 years! To access her data, the user has no choice except to agree and sign this form.

Direct Access Without Requesting Additional Data – Four companies, adnxs.com, adsrvr.com, quantserve.com and spotxchange.com provide direct access to third party data based on the data subject's third party cookie. To verify the identity of the user and prove the ownership of the cookie, adnxs.com and adsrvr.com add a verification step where the user confirms in an online form that she is the owner of the identifier.

4   Recommendations and Observations

After having analyzed the recommendations of the European DPAs in Sect. 2, and the practices of website owners and third party tracking services in Sect. 3, we have identified several major issues that data controllers face when they need to implement the software support tools for the subject access requests.

Moreover, the current legal framework conveyed by the GDPR in relation to the right of access only provides for an obligation of conduct, requiring indeed certain actions to assure this right (described in the modalities of the access right – as depicted in articles 12, 15 and recitals 57, 58, 59, 60, 63, 64), but without rendering any procedural undertaking or benchmark as to an effective and specific result, which could shape the practices of the companies providing a SAR [50]. Pursuant to this normative need, in this section we give recommendations to both data controllers and data subjects concerning both problems: of authentication and validation of eligibility.

4.1   Problem of Authentication

There are two ways to authenticate the data subject by the data controller: either via the real identity of the subject (through her name surname and government-issued ID) or through the digital identity (assigned identifier, cookie, IP address, etc.).

Authentication via Government-Issued ID. In case the data subject has never interacted directly with the data controller through electronic means (a typical case is the e-commerce discount cards), the data controller can rightfully ask the data subject to provide the proof of her identity, such as her ID card. In this case, there are two possible threats involved.

First, a security incident can occur on the data controller's side and the copy of the data subject's ID document can be leaked to attackers. Second, the data controller (or the attacker from the previous case) can *impersonate* the data subject to other data controllers by using her ID document to exercise the subject access requests on her behalf. Moreover, with the data subject's ID document it is possible to impersonate her at any point in the future (until the ID document expires). One obvious solution would be to blur some of the information on the data subject's ID document: this practice would protect some of her information from being leaked to attackers but it does not protect her from impersonation.

How to protect from impersonation?

The proofs provided by the data subject must satisfy the *non-transferability property* [73]: the documents provided by a data subject to a data controller, during a given authentication, cannot be reused in any other authentication. To protect the data subject's ID document, she should add a watermark which can not be removed from the copy of the document. This watermark must contain two elements:

- A *validity period* to prevent anyone from impersonating the data subject to the same data controller in the future.
- *The name of the data controller* to prevent anyone to use the copy with any other data controller.

Non-transferability can be implemented by signing the copy of the ID document with the date and the name of the data controller to prevent any further transfer.

More complex solutions based on cryptography are also available. *Affidavits* are also an interesting alternative – they rely on a trusted third party which can be used to certify that a legal identity is bounded to an identifier. However, to protect the data subject from impersonation attacks, affidavits must also satisfy the non-transferability property.

Summary: The content that DPAs provide on their websites has a strong pedagogical role both to data subjects and data controllers. DPAs should update the information they convey publicly on their websites; specifically, they should require the non-transferability property to be applied to any usage of government-issued IDs. As a result, if data subjects follow such guidelines, and no longer share their government-issued IDs in the clear, they will avoid impersonation.

Authentication via Digital Identity. In case the data subject has previously interacted with the data controller via electronic means, such as through an email or opening an account on the data controller's web portal, then these means of communication should be also used to authenticate the data subject. However, several security mechanisms must be put in place for a safe authentication of the data subject.

The communication through a web portal must at least use the secure channel https and a password. Ideally, for any online interaction, Two-Factor Authentication (2FA) is the ideal solution. 2FA requires that the user can be identified by two different factors, the most common are knowledge factors (such as password) and possession factors (such as physical or software tokens).

However, if the *data subject did not interact with the data controller via a web portal*, for example, when the data subject visited the web site where a third party (a joint controller) was tracking her, then the data subject needs to prove her identity to the controller based on her digital identifier. Examples of such identifiers are a browser cookie or an IP address.

An IP address is considered personal data according to Article 29 Working Party [8], however an IP cannot be used to uniquely identify a data subject in all cases. For example, an IP address does not allow an Internet Service Provider to distinguish data subjects who are connecting to the same wi-fi hotspot, or those using a shared computer. Hence, granting SAR within these boundary scenarios (when an IP address represents either one or many identifiable individuals) can be hard and could result in potential disclosures of other users' information.

If the data subject uses Privacy Enhancing Technologies (PETs), such as VPNs, anonymous networks like TOR[4], or cleans the browser cookies regularly, then it becomes nearly impossible to identify the data subject and hence prevents her from being able to exercise her subject access rights. Let us imagine a data subject who is visiting the website and uses TOR. Let us assume that the only

---

[4] TOR is an anonymity network, directs Internet traffic through a worldwide overlay network, and therefore the IP address of the user's device is not visible to the server that receives requests from the user, www.torproject.org.

digital identifier of the data subject visible to the data controller is the IP address observed by the data controller. However, because of the TOR network, this IP address does not belong to the data subject: it is a TOR exit point. Therefore, the data controller cannot identify the data subject by this IP address.

However, if the data subject browses the websites and is tracked by third party content present on the websites, and does not use any PETs, then third party trackers can use pseudoidentifiers (for example, stored in third party cookies) to track and recognize the data subjects. Interestingly, the IAB Europe GDPR Implementation Working Group raises the concern that pseudonymous data that is not linked to the individual's name and address cannot confirm that the data belongs to the requestor [29] and raise the subsequent question: *Should digital marketing companies that only collect pseudonymous data respond to data subject right requests?* Our answer to this question is definitely "yes", but their concern is valid: data subjects need to demonstrate and prove that the pseudoidentifiers (third party cookies, in our examples) indeed belongs to the data subject. In the following, we propose a procedure that would allow the data controllers to use pseudoidentifiers that are linked to the data subject's identity elements, like email address, yet the email address is not observable by any third party.

Without loss of generality, we consider the case of third party tracking via cookies. Cryptographic techniques can be used to bind the cookies with some identity elements, such as email, that can be checked later by the third parties. We provide a proof of concept algorithm on a cookie generation technique which is compatible with the GDPR.

In order for the data subject to be able to prove a cookie ownership, *the cookies must be generated on the client side* (in the web browser) rather than set by the server, as it is done in today's web standards. We assume that the subject has an email address denoted address, a public key K_{pub} and the corresponding private (RSA or ECC) key K_{priv}. The third party is associated with an identifier, such as third party's name or domain, denoted tp_id. The email address, K_{pub}, K_{priv} and third party identifier tp_id can be embedded in a web browser to make their usage transparent to the data subject. For a third party with identifier tp_id, we propose to compute a cookie value using the digest of a cryptographic hash function H (SHA256 or SHA3):

$$\text{cookie} = H(\text{tp\_id}, \text{address}, K_{pub}, N),$$

where N is a number (128-bit for instance).

When the data subject requests an access to her data, she provides her cookie cookie, K_{pub}, her email address address and the value N used to create the cookie. The third party tracker can recompute the cookie on his own and checks if it matches with the cookie sent by the subject. The third party can send an email to the subject at address. This email is encrypted with the data subject public key K_{pub} using software like pretty easy privacy (https://www.pep.security/). The data subject can now decrypt the message using her private key K_{priv}. Upon reception of an acknowledgement of the data subject, the third party is sure that the cookie indeed belongs to the data subject, and can now send her the data directly. An attacker that observes the communication between the data subject and the third party cannot predict or forge by himself the `cookie` of a legitimate user. The third party cannot attempt to recover by himself the value `address` and K_{pub} if the subject has not provided N. After getting her data, the data subject can renew `cookie` by changing the value N.

Currently, cookies are either set by servers (of publishers or third parties) or are programmatically set up in the browser by the JavaScript code running on a visiting webpage. Our protocol would require *to generate all the cookies at the browser side* and we believe it is possible to make it work even in a case when cookies are installed by a server: it's enough to run a client-side code that substitutes the cookies with the freshly-generated cookies that follow our algorithm. We believe it is better to have subject centric approach to create digital identifiers. There are other possibilities than our scheme like the initiative of W3C on Verifiable Claims and Distributed Identifiers [93].

Summary: As of today, we are not aware of any GDPR compliant implementation of the pseudoidentifiers that would allow data subjects to be authenticated to exercise their rights and at the same time be protected from impersonation attacks. In this section, we have proposed a scheme that allows to generate pseudoidentifiers and protect the data subjects. To protect all the components of such scheme, it has to be implemented in the trusted environment of the data subject, which is her web browser.

4.2   Problem of Validating Eligibility

Data controllers also need to validate the SAR eligibility. If a data controller is European, he should review the Subject Access Request protocol and ensure that whenever enough information is already obtained to authenticate the data subject, no additional information should be requested. This approach would prevent *abusive identity check* attack. It is harder to verify eligibility of data subjects for non-European data controllers: they need to determine whether a request is legitimate or not by identifying whether the requestor is a resident in the European Union. Therefore, eligibility checks are legitimate in this case.

We draw the attention of the data subjects that they need to be aware that eligibility checks by non-European data controllers are required and do not constitute an *abusive identity check* attack. However, it is true that it is also complicated for data subjects themselves to establish whether a certain data controller is European or not.

Additionally, eligibility checks can be done via IP address of the requestor. In this case, Privacy Enhancing Technologies (PETs) play a dual role in the validation of eligibility. On one hand, as we have described before, if the European data subject uses PETs, such as TOR network, then she will likely maintain her anonymity at the cost of not being able to exercise the rights provided by the GDPR. On the other hand, a non-European data subject can use PETs, such as

VPN, to pretend to be a EU resident to the data controller. If the data controller only relies on the IP address as a proof of eligibility, then he will allow a non EU resident to exercise her rights as well.

5 Related Work

In 1969, Miller in [74] already considered that the right to access can be abused through impersonation. He pointed the risk of sharing personal data and violating people's privacy by unthoughtfully accommodating access requests.

The most notorious case of the right to access was given by Max Schrems [92]. In 2011, he contacted Facebook to exercise his right to access. He received a 1200-page document and discovered many anomalies showing Facebook was not compliant with the European laws and created http://europe-v-facebook.org.

The AFCDP (*Association Franéaise des Correspondants aux Données Personnelles*) is a French association of the french data privacy officers. They publish every year a report [36–39] on the right to access. They benchmark between 150 and 200 companies, administrations and organizations to test how they answer to data access requests. Their work is very close to ours. They primarily focus on measuring how many data controllers respond in time. Their reports also included anomalies and observations of misbehavior concerning the access right. We extend their work to evaluate more precisely how requests are treated by the data controllers. Our evaluation criteria could be re-used in the future by AFCDP during their benchmarks.

Asghari *et al.* [43] presented a benchmark of 32 data controllers in the Netherlands at HotPETS 2017. They acknowledge in their paper the fact that all the organizations they contacted authenticate the subject making the request. However, they did not analyze the authentication process nor if secure channels were used. They also mentioned in their work an upcoming benchmark of larger scale. Our work could help to obtain more precise results.

Ausloos *et al.* [44] also conducted a benchmark of the right to access on 60 organizations. Their tests asserted some organizations requested additional information to authenticate the users and especially copy of ID card or driving license. They observe that many obstacles exist for a subject who wants to exercise her rights. They also point out the frequency with which an access request leads to an endless sequence of e-mails. Moreover, this sequence never resulted in the transfer of all the data legally allowed to be obtained. They have not taken into account security considerations as it is done in our paper.

In [77] the author points out that *"data protection law should apply to information that is used to single out people, even if no name can be tied to the information" Seeing data used to single out a person as personal data fits the rationale for data protection law: protecting fairness and fundamental rights. Data that are used to single out a person should be considered personal data"*. Although this might be enough to prevent impersonation, it could be dangerous to provide government issued documents to data controllers (unless they were required for the registration). When a data subject makes a request, she should obtain what she discloses to the data controller or what is related to her pseudonym. It is disproportional to provide governmental issued documents when the data subject has not used her real name to register on a website. Some authors [77] refer to "the visibility paradox" when dealing with the issue of disclosing additional information in order to obtain the data already disclosed.

The work of Urban *et al.* [102] is very close to ours: the authors have studied the economy of web tracking by making subject access requests to third party websites. They have observed procedures of third parties to authenticate data subjects. Our observations and conclusions in Sect. 3.2 are very similar to those of Urban *et al.*: the authors needed to sign several affidavits to access their third party data.

Grogan *et al.* [66] have analyzed how Internet users react to their right to access their data. They created a survey and distribute it to collect answers from US and Irish citizens. They observe that citizens are rather confused about their right to access and its application.

6   Conclusion

The right to access is the first and basic user right set up by the GDPR. In this paper, we have analyzed security aspects of the authentication procedures set up for subject access requests recommended by the DPAs and implemented by the website owners and third party tracking services.

While reviewing the recommendations of all the European DPAs, and the practice of the most popular websites and third party trackers, we have discovered several issues: abusive identity checks, potential data breach or denial of access. These issues are the results of incorrect procedures or a lack of means. Data controllers need to enforce the proportionality principle when they authenticate the requests to avoid abusive identity checks. The eligibility controls encountered during this work are a reminder that the relation between a data subject living in the European area and non-European data controllers is complex. Finally, webpages and third party trackers need to change their practice for the generation of identifiers to be compliant with the GDPR and avoid denial of access.

We hope that the materials provided in this paper can help to shape the design of better guidelines regarding the exercise of the users' rights and future benchmarking campaigns for the right to access.

Acknowledgments. This work is supported by the French National Research Agency in the framework of the *Investissements d'Avenir* program (ANR-15-IDEX-02) and project PrivaWEB (ANR-18-CE39-0008-01), and as well ANSWER project PIA FSN2 (P159564-2661789\DOS0060094).

References

1. Working party opinion 2/2010 on online behavioural advertising, adopted on 22 June 2010, (wp 171), p. 9. https://ec.europa.eu/justice/article-29/documentation/opinion-recommendation/files/2010/wp171en.pdf
2. 4.1 accès ou rectification de vos données à caractère personnel. https://twitter.com/fr/privacy. Accessed 28 Sept 2018
3. Access, rectification, opposition and cancellation rights. https://www.baidu.eu/privacy-policy. Accessed 28 Sept 2018
4. Accessing your reddit data. https://www.reddithelp.com/en/categories/using-reddit/your-reddit-account/accessing-your-reddit-data. Accessed 28 Sept 2018
5. Googletakeout. https://takeout.google.com/?utm_source=pp&hl=en. Accessed 28 Sept 2018
6. I want to make a request regarding personal data microsoft has about me related to my microsoft account. https://www.microsoft.com/en-us/concern/privacy. Accessed 28 Sept 2018
7. Mail.Ru terms of service. https://help.mail.ru/mail-help/UA. Accessed 1 Oct 2018
8. Opinion n° 4/200 on the concept of personal data - wp 136, p. 17. https://ec.europa.eu/justice/article-29/documentation/opinion-recommendation/files/2007/wp136en.pdf
9. Privacy policy. https://alidropship.com/privacy-policy/. Accessed 28 Sept 2018
10. Privacy policy/FAQ. https://foundation.wikimedia.org/wiki/Privacypolicy/FAQ#anonymize. Accessed 28 Sept 2018
11. QQI DS rights request form. https://dl.url.cn/myapp/bhqq/iQQ/QQiDSRIGHTSREQUESTFORM.pdf. Accessed 28 Sept 2018
12. Request a copy of my personal data. https://fr.pornhubpremium.com/terms. Accessed 28 Sept 2018
13. Vi. How can you exercise your rights provided under the GDPR? Data download. https://www.instagram.com/about/legal/terms/api/. Accessed 28 Sept 2018
14. Vk.com privacy policy. https://vk.com/privacy/eu for logged-in users. Accessed 1 Oct 2018
15. Ways you can access, control, and correct your personal information. https://www.ebay.com/help/policies/member-behaviour-policies/user-privacy-notice-privacy-policy?id=4260#section6. Accessed 28 Sept 2018
16. What choices and access do i have. https://www.imdb.com/privacy?ref=helpmshelpftrprivacy. Accessed 28 Sept 2018
17. What information can i access. https://www.amazon.co.uk/gp/help/customer/display.html?nodeId=502584. Accessed 28 Sept 2018
18. What personal information Netflix holds about you and how to request a copy. https://help.netflix.com/en/node/100624?ba=SwiftypeResultClick&q=request%20a%20copy%20of%20my%20data. Accessed 28 Sept 2018
19. Yandex.ru privacy policy. https://yandex.com/legal/privacy/. Accessed 1 Oct 2018
20. Your choices and obligations. https://www.linkedin.com/legal/privacy-policy. Accessed 28 Sept 2018
21. Your control and privacy rights. https://policies.oath.com/ie/en/oath/privacy/index.html. Accessed 28 Sept 2018
22. Your privacy choices. https://www.twitch.tv/p/legal/privacy-choices/. Accessed 28 Sept 2018

23. Your rights. https://info.xvideos.com/legal/privacy/. Accessed 28 Sept 2018
24. Your rights with respect to your personal information. https://render.alipay.com/p/f/agreementpages/alipayeuprivacypolicy.html. Accessed 28 Sept 2018
25. Yourfacebookinformation.   https://www.facebook.com/full_data_use_policy. Accessed 28 Sept 2018
26. Opinion 2/2010 on online behavioural advertising. Technical report 171 (2010)
27. The Schengen Information System A Guide For Exercising The Right of Access (2015). https://edps.europa.eu/sites/edp/files/publication/16-11-07_sis_ii_guide_of_access_en.pdf
28. Case C-210/16 Wirtschaftsakademie Schleswig-Holstein (2018). ECLI:EU:C:2018:388. http://curia.europa.eu/juris/document/document.jsf?docid=202543&doclang=EN
29. Data subject requests, working paper 04/2018 (2018). https://www.iabeurope.eu/wp-content/uploads/2018/04/20180406-IABEU-GIG-Working-Paper04_Data-Subject-Requests.pdf
30. European Data Protection Board (2018). https://edpb.europa.eu
31. European Data Protection Supervisor (2018). https://edps.europa.eu
32. Addthis - privacy policy. https://www.addthis.com/privacy/privacy-policy/
33. Adform - privacy policy. https://site.adform.com/privacy-center/website-privacy/website-privacy-policy/
34. Adnxs - appnexus data subject rights. https://www.appnexus.com/data-subject-rights-policy
35. Adsrvr. https://www.adsrvr.org/
36. AFCDP. Données personnelles - Index AFCDP du Droit d'accès. Technical report (2013, in french)
37. AFCDP. Données personnelles - Index AFCDP du Droit d'accès. Technical report (2014, in french)
38. AFCDP. Données personnelles - Index AFCDP du Droit d'accès. Technical report (2015, in french)
39. AFCDP. Données personnelles - Index AFCDP du Droit d'accès. Technical report (2017, in french)
40. Agencia de Protección de Datos. Ejerce tus derechos. https://www.aepd.es/media/formularios/formulario-derecho-de-acceso.pdf. Accessed 28 Sept 2018
41. Alexa. https://www.alexa.com/
42. Andmekaitse Inspektsioon. Andmekaitse Inspektsioon. http://www.aki.ee/. Accessed 28 Sept 2018
43. Asghari, H., Mahieu, R.L.P., Mittal, P., Greenstadt, R.: The right of access as a tool for privacy governance. In: Proceedings of Hot Topics in Privacy Enhancing Technologies (HotPETs 2017) (2017)
44. Ausloos, J., Dewitte, P.: Shattering one-way mirrors - data subject access rights in practice. Int. Data Priv. Law **8**(1), 4–28 (2018)
45. Ihre rechte als betroffener (2018). https://www.dsb.gv.at/rechte-der-betroffenen. Accessed 28 Sept 2018
46. Antrag gemäß art. 15 DSGVO auf auskunft (2018). https://www.dsb.gv.at/at.gv.bka.liferay-app/documents/22758/844171/Antrag+an+den+Verantwortlichen+Recht+auf+Auskunft+Art+15.pdf/00315f65-1ea8-438b-8f1f-766d20002702. Accessed 28 Sept 2018
47. Autorité de protection des données. Lettre Type Droit Acces Direct. https://www.autoriteprotectiondonnees.be/node/3995. Accessed 28 Sept 2018
48. Autoriteit Persoonsgegevens. Recht op inzage. https://autoriteitpersoonsgegevens.nl/nl/zelf-doen/privacyrechten/recht-op-inzage#. Accessed 28 Sept 2018

49. Baidu - privacy policy. http://usa.baidu.com/privacy/
50. Bayamlıoğlu, E.: Transparency of automated decisions in the GDPR: an attempt for systemisation (2018). https://ssrn.com/abstract=3097653
51. Borgesius, F.Z.: Singling Out People Without Knowing Their Names - Behavioural Targeting, Pseudonymous Data, and the New Data Protection Regulation (2016). https://ssrn.com/abstract=2733115
52. Casalemedia - privacy policy. http://casalemedia.com/
53. CNIL Commission Nationale de l'Informatique et des Libertés. Guide sécurité des données personnelles. https://www.cnil.fr/fr/le-droit-dacces-connaitre-les-donnees-quun-organisme-detient-sur-vous. Accessed 28 Sept 2018
54. Comissão Nacional de Protecção de Dados. Comissão Nacional de Protecção de Dados. https://www.cnpd.pt. Accessed 28 Sept 2018
55. Commission for Personal Data Protection. Who can copy your identity card. https://www.cpdp.bg/index.php?p=element&aid=423. Accessed 28 Sept 2018
56. Commissioner for Personal Data Protection. Commissioner for Personal Data Protection. http://www.dataprotection.gov.cy/. Accessed 28 Sept 2018
57. Cormack, A.: Is the subject access right now too great a threat to privacy? Eur. Data Prot. Law Rev. 2(1), 15–27 (2016)
58. Council of European Union. Council regulation (EU) no 2016/679 (2016). https://eur-lex.europa.eu/legal-content/EN/TXT/?uri=CELEX:32016R0679
59. Access right criteo. https://www.criteo.com/privacy/
60. Croatian Personal Data Protection Agency. Croatian Personal Data Protection Agency. https://azop.hr/. Accessed 28 Sept 2018
61. Data Protection Commissioner. A guide to your rights. https://www.dataprotection.ie/docs/A-guide-to-your-rights-Plain-English-Version/r/858.htm. Accessed 28 Sept 2018
62. Data Protection Commissioner of Hungary. Annual report of the Hungarian National Authority for Data Protection and Freedom of Information (NAIH) (2017). http://www.naih.hu/annual-reports.html. Accessed 28 Sept 2018
63. Data State Inspectorate. Datu subjekta tiesibas. http://www.dvi.gov.lv/lv/wp-content/uploads/DVIbroshuradatusubjektties.pdf. Accessed 28 Sept 2018
64. Datatilsynet. Guidance on the registrants' rights. https://www.datatilsynet.dk/media/6893/registreredes-rettigheder.pdf. Accessed 28 Sept 2018
65. Die Bundesbeauftragte für den Datenschutz und die Informationsfreiheit. Auskunftsrecht. https://www.bfdi.bund.de/DE/Datenschutz/Ueberblick/MeineRechte/Artikel/Auskunftsrecht.html. Accessed 28 Sept 2018
66. Grogan, S., McDonald, A.M.: Access denied! contrasting data access in the United States and Ireland. PoPETs 2016(3), 191–211 (2016)
67. Hellenic Data Protection Authority. Law 2472/1997 & Citizen's rights. http://www.dpa.gr/portal/page?_pageid=33,43290&dad=portal&schema=PORTAL. Accessed 28 Sept 2018
68. Information Commissioner. Request for acquaintance with your own personal data. https://www.ip-rs.si/fileadmin/user_upload/doc/obrazci/ZVOP/ZahtevazaseznanitevzlastnimiosebnimipodatkiObrazecSLOP.doc. Accessed 28 Sept 2018
69. Access right Innovid. https://www.innovid.com/privacy-policy/
70. Lerner, A., Simpson, A.K., Kohno, T., Roesner, F.: Internet Jones and the raiders of the lost trackers: an archaeological study of web tracking from 1996 to 2016. In: 25th USENIX Security Symposium (USENIX Security 2016). USENIX Association (2016)

71. Mahieu, R., van Hoboken, J., Asghari, H.: Responsibility for data protection in a networked world - on the question of the controller, "effective and complete protection" and its application to data access rights in Europe (2019). https://ssrn.com/abstract=3256743

72. Mathtag - privacy policy. http://www.mediamath.com/privacy-policy/#Section-11

73. Menezes, A., van Oorschot, P.C., Vanstone, S.A.: Handbook of Applied Cryptography. CRC Press, Boca Raton (1996)

74. Miller, A.R.: Personal privacy in the computer age: the challenge of a new technology in an information-oriented society. Mich. Law Rev. **67**(6), 1089–1246 (1969)

75. National Commission for Data Protection. The right of access. https://cnpd.public.lu/en/particuliers/vos-droits/droit-acces.html. Accessed 28 Sept 2018

76. New relic - privacy policy. https://www.simpli.fi/site-privacy-policy/

77. Norris, C., de Hert, P., L'Hoiry, X., Galetta, A. (eds.): The Unaccountable State of Surveillance. LGTS, vol. 34. Springer, Cham (2017). https://doi.org/10.1007/978-3-319-47573-8

78. Office for Personal Data Protection of the Slovak Republic. Dina rättigheter enligt personuppgiftslagen. https://www.datainspektionen.se/globalassets/dokument/gammalt/dina-rattigheter-enligt-personuppgiftslagen.pdf. Accessed 28 Sept 2018

79. Office for Personal Data Protection of the Slovak Republic. How to submit a petition initiating the procedure of personal data protection. https://dataprotection.gov.sk/uoou/en/content/how-submit-petition-initiating-procedure-personal-data-protection. Accessed 28 Sept 2018

80. Office of the Data Protection Commissioner. What is the Right of Access?. https://idpc.org.mt/en/Pages/faq.aspx#3. Accessed 28 Sept 2018

81. Office of the Data Protection Ombudsman. When you want to inspect your data. https://tietosuoja.fi/en/when-you-want-to-inspect-your-data. Accessed 28 Sept 2018

82. OpenX - privacy policy. https://www.openx.com/legal/privacy-policy/

83. Garante per la protezione dei dati personali. Guida all'applicazione del regolamento europeo in materia di protezione dei dati personali - diritti degli interessati (2018). https://www.garanteprivacy.it/regolamentoue/diritti-degli-interessati. Accessed 28 Sept 2018

84. Data subject rights notice, PubMatic. https://pubmatic.com/legal/eea-data-subject-rights-notice/

85. PubMatic - cookie policy. https://pubmatic.com/legal/platform-cookie-policy/

86. Quantserve - privacy policy. https://www.quantcast.com/privacy/

87. Roesner, F., Kohno, T., Wetherall, D.: Detecting and defending against third-party tracking on the web. In: Proceedings of the 9th USENIX Symposium on Networked Systems Design and Implementation, NSDI 2012, pp. 155–168 (2012)

88. Access right Rubiconproject. https://rubiconproject.com/terms-conditions/subject-access-request-policy/

89. Access right Scorecardresearch. https://www.scorecardresearch.com/privacy.aspx

90. Simpli - privacy policy. https://www.simpli.fi/site-privacy-policy/

91. Smart Ad Server - privacy policy. https://smartadserver.com/end-user-privacy-policy//

92. Solon, O.: How much data did facebook have on one man? 1.200 pages of data in 57 categories. Wired (2012). https://www.wired.co.uk/article/privacy-versus-facebook

93. Sporny, M., Longley D.: Verifiable claims data model and representations. Technical report, W3C (2017). https://www.w3.org/TR/verifiable-claims-data-model/

94. SpotXchange - privacy policy. https://www.spotx.tv/privacy-policy/
95. SpotXchange portal. https://www.spotx.tv/privacy-policy/gdpr/
96. Teads - privacy policy. https://www.teads.tv/privacy-policy/
97. The Bureau of the Inspector General for the Protection of Personal Data - GIODO. Rights of data subject. https://giodo.gov.pl/en/293. Accessed 28 Sept 2018
98. The Information Commissioner's Office. Your right of access. https://ico.org.uk/your-data-matters/your-right-of-access/. Accessed 28 Sept 2018
99. The Information Commissioner's Office. Your right to get copies of your data. https://ico.org.uk/your-data-matters/your-right-of-access/. Accessed 28 Sept 2018
100. The National Supervisory Authority for Personal Data Processing. Derptul de Acces. http://www.dataprotection.ro/servlet/ViewDocument?id=386. Accessed 28 Sept 2018
101. The Office for Personal Data Protection. The Office for Personal Data Protection. http://www.uoou.cz/. Accessed 28 Sept 2018
102. Urban, T., Tatang, D., Degeling, M., Holz, T., Pohlmann, N.: The Unwanted Sharing Economy: An Analysis of Cookie Syncing and User Transparency under GDPR. CoRR, abs/1811.08660 (2018)
103. Weborama - privacy policy. https://weborama.com/weborama-privacy-commitment/
104. Yandex.ru - privacy policy. https://yandex.com/legal/privacy/

Author Index

Printed in the United States
By Bookmasters